TEACHER'S BOOK

Jennifer Heath

D1721010

NATIONAL GEOGRAPHIC LEARNING | CENGAGE Learning·

Australia • Brazil • Japan • Korea • Mexico • Singapore • Spain • United Kingdom • United States

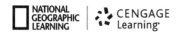

Happy Trails 1 Teacher's Book
Jennifer Heath

Publisher: Jason Mann

Director of Content Development: Sarah Bideleux

Development Editor: Dione Davids, Ivana Kohut

Media Editor: Liz Hammond

Art Director/Cover Designer: Natasa Arsenidou

Text Designer: Natasa Arsenidou

Compositor: Vasiliki Christoforidou

National Geographic Editorial Liaison:
   Leila Hishmeh

Acknowledgements

Illustrated by Panagiotis Angeletakis and Theodoros Piakis

Song Credits: Music composed by Evdoxia Banani and Vagelis Markantonis

Recorded at Motivation Sound Studios and GFS-PRO Studio

Production at GFS-PRO Studio by George Flamouridis

ISBN: 978-1-111-06233-0

National Geographic Learning
Cheriton House, North Way, Andover, Hampshire, SP10 5BE
United Kingdom

Cengage Learning is a leading provider of customized learning solutions with office locations around the globe, including Singapore, the United Kingdom, Australia, Mexico, Brazil and Japan. Locate your local office at: **international.cengage.com/region**

Cengage Learning products are represented in Canada by Nelson Education, Ltd.

Visit National Geographic Learning online at **ngl.cengage.com**

Visit our corporate website at **www.cengage.com**

Printed in the United Kingdom by CPI, Antony Rowe
Print Number: 03   Print Year: 2014

Contents

Pupil's Book Contents

Introduction to Happy Trails

Happy Trails is a two-level English course for young learners. It teaches reading, listening, speaking and writing in a carefully graded way enabling pupils to develop their English skills successfully and confidently. The course entertains young learners through fun stories, breathtaking images and fascinating facts about the world around them inspired by National Geographic content. A variety of lesson and task types are used to motivate young learners. The course also uses spectacular National Geographic photography which has been carefully chosen to appeal to young learners.

Course components

Happy Trails 1 Pupil's Book

Happy Trails 1 Pupil's Book consists of an Introduction section, twelve units, four review sections and, at the back of the book, plays, celebration lessons, character masks and stickers.

The Introduction section teaches pupils the alphabet, colours, numbers 1-10, and some simple functional language. It also introduces Trek and his reporters who are the main characters pupils will meet in the cartoon stories in the units of the pupil's book.

The twelve units are divided into four sections, each consisting of a section opener, three units and a review section. The section opener features a stunning National Geographic photograph and a map. The purpose of this photograph is to introduce pupils to the country that Trek's reporters will visit in the cartoon story presented in the following three units. Each of the following three units contains three, two-page lessons. Each lesson begins with a presentation of the new vocabulary and continues with a reading task. Lesson 1 contains an episode of the cartoon story, Lesson 2 has a short real-life reading text illustrated with a National Geographic photograph and Lesson 3 contains a reading text that pupils can relate to, for example a poster, a dialogue, an email and so on. The lessons then continue with an illustrated grammar presentation and a task before moving on to speaking, listening, and in lesson 3, writing. Each unit also contains a simple pronunciation task and a song, which allows pupils to practise vocabulary and grammar and keeps motivation high. After the three main units, there is a review section consisting of *Let's remember!* with tasks to consolidate vocabulary and grammar, and *Fun & Games* with a National Geographic photograph to talk about, a fun task, a song and a craft project or activity.

At the back of *Happy Trails 1 Pupil's Book*, there are two plays based on well-known tales for pupils to listen to, read and perform and three celebration lessons; one for Christmas, one for Easter and one for Carnival. There are also character masks of Trek and his reporters that pupils can wear to role play the episodes in the main units.

Happy Trails 1 Pupil's Book is accompanied by an audio CD that contains the episodes of the cartoon stories, narration of the Lesson 2 readings, the songs and the plays. Pupils can be asked to listen to the episodes and reading passages at home after the relevant lessons to get used to hearing English spoken by native speakers. They should use the recording of the plays to help them learn their lines. Pupils will also enjoy listening to and singing along to the songs they do in class.

Happy Trails 1 Activity Book

Happy Trails 1 Activity Book accompanies *Happy Trails 1 Pupil's Book*. Like the pupil's book, it consists of an introduction section, twelve units and four reviews. It recycles and consolidates the content of the pupil's book through easy-to-understand tasks which pupils can complete on their own. Activities include crosswords with picture clues, spell checks, word banks and picture-based tasks. At the back of the activity book, there are twelve wordsearches; one for each unit, for further practice of key vocabulary.

Pupils will be motivated by the full-colour pages, lively illustrations and photographs. The clear and simple format means that it can be used at home as well as in class.

Happy Trails 1 Teacher's Book

The Teacher's Book offers practical step-by-step instructions on how to approach the lessons and reviews, guidance on how to put on the plays and deal with the celebration lessons in the pupil's book. It also contains photocopiable DVD worksheets, templates for the craft activities, four progress tests and the keys to the progress tests and *Happy Trails 1 Activity Book*.

At the beginning of each lesson, there is a box outlining the aims of each lesson and a list of materials needed for the lesson. A *Lead-in* section provides suggestions for recapping what was learnt in the previous lesson, checking homework and preparing for the current lesson. The *New vocabulary* section explains how to teach the key vocabulary for the lesson. Detailed teaching notes follow, giving clear directions on how to approach each of the tasks, together with the answer key and the recording script where necessary. *Background information* boxes include further information on topics that come up in the pupil's book. There are also *Extension activities* to ensure pupils have ample opportunity to practise the grammar of the lesson, and *Optional activities* which promote fluency and learning.

The DVD worksheets can be photocopied for use with *Happy Trails 1 DVD* to aid comprehension of the episodes, and the photocopiable progress tests can be used to track pupils' progress.

Happy Trails 1 Teacher's Resource Pack

The teacher's resource pack is an invaluable source of material for teachers. It contains:

- The *Happy Trails* map of the world
- Four educational posters
- Alphabet flashcards
- Key vocabulary flashcards
- A CD-ROM with printable pdfs
- 12 unit tests and the 4 progress tests.

The *Happy Trails* map of the world is designed to aid pupils in understanding the location of the countries Trek's reporters visit in the cartoon stories. The educational posters are designed to provide classroom-based practice and promote communication.

The alphabet and key vocabulary flashcards are essential for teaching vocabulary. A variety of activities are structured around the flashcards.

Printable pdfs of colouring pages, handwriting pages, and extra tasks are contained on the CD-ROM. These are designed to provide teachers with material for use either in class as extra practice or with pupils who finish early, or for homework. There are also printable unit tests and progress tests that can be used throughout the course to check pupils' progress. The key to all tests is also included on the CD.

Happy Trails 1 Class Audio CDs

The class audio CDs contain the recordings of the cartoon stories, the listening tasks, the *Say it!* pronunciation tasks, the songs and the plays found in *Happy Trails 1 Pupil's Book.*

Happy Trails 1 CD-ROM

The CD-ROM is designed to recycle vocabulary and grammar from each unit of the pupil's book in an enjoyable way. There is also an introduction section that allows pupils to consolidate the alphabet, colours and numbers they learnt at the beginning of the pupil's book, and games that increase pupils' motivation for what they are learning. The CD-ROM is compatible with both PCs and Macs.

Happy Trails 1 DVD

The DVD contains animation of the cartoon stories contained in Lesson 1s in the pupil's book. The stories are brought to life and pupils will enjoy watching each story unfold as they progress through the course. There are photocopiable worksheets in *Happy Trails 1 Teacher's Book* for classroom use with the DVD that will aid pupils' comprehension.

Happy Trails 1 Interactive Whiteboard Software

Happy Trails 1 Interactive Whiteboard contains the Pupil's Book, including the audio material, the DVD and the educational posters from the teacher's resource pack. Most of the tasks found in the Pupil's Book are interactive and easy to use by both pupils and teachers alike. Justification for reading comprehension and listening tasks is available at the touch of a button, as is the key to all tasks. The DVD can be played with or without subtitles and the song lyrics change colour as they are sung to make it easier for pupils to sing along. *Happy Trails 1 Interactive Whiteboard Software* is compatible with any interactive whiteboard hardware.

Teaching Happy Trails 1

Flashcards

The course is accompanied by 26 full-colour alphabet flashcards and corresponding words from the Introduction section of the pupil's book. There are also another 56 full-colour vocabulary flashcards which have a picture on one side and the corresponding word on the other. Flashcards are essential for teaching vocabulary

since they are both visual and tangible, thus promoting pupils ability to learn and retain. Flashcards can be used to teach new words in these suggested ways:

- Hold up the flashcards one at a time. Say the word and ask pupils to repeat after you. Do this a number of times. Ask pupils to repeat together and individually.
- Stick the flashcards on the board with blu-tack. Point to one flashcard and say the word. Ask pupils to repeat after you. Repeat a number of times. Do the same with another flashcard. When pupils know all the words, ask volunteers to come to the board, to point to a flashcard and to say the word.
- Say the word and ask pupils to repeat. Then hold up the flashcard and say the word again. Ask pupils to repeat a number of times. Then hold up a flashcard without saying the word and ask pupils to call out the word.
- Hold up the flashcards one at a time. Say the word and ask pupils to repeat after you a number of times. Write one of the words on the board. Read out the word. Ask a volunteer to choose the correct flashcard and stick it under the word on the board.
- Hold up the flashcards one at a time. Say the word and ask pupils to repeat after you. Ask volunteers to come to the front of the class and give them one flashcard each. Call out a word. The pupil with the corresponding flashcard should hold it up.

New words

Young learners will remember new words if they find the learning process fun. Here are some suggested ways for teaching new words without flashcards. There are more suggestions in the lesson plans.

- Bring objects to the class (eg food items, classroom objects). Put all the objects in a bag. Pull out the objects one at a time and hold them up. Say the word and ask pupils to repeat after you. Do this a number of times. Ask pupils to repeat together and individually. Then hand out the objects to volunteers. Call out a word. The pupil with the corresponding object should hold it up.
- Cut out magazine pictures which represent the words (eg people, sports). Stick the pictures on the board. Point to one picture and say the word. Ask pupils to repeat after you. Repeat a number of times. Do the same with the other pictures. When pupils know all the words, ask volunteers to come to the board, point to any picture and say the word.
- If a word cannot be represented with an object, explain the meaning of the word in L1 (eg *cool*). Then use the word in English appropriately (eg Trek is cool.) Ask pupils to repeat after you.
- If you are comfortable with drawing, draw simple pictures on the board (eg clothes, parts of the body). Point to the picture, say the word and ask pupils to repeat. Do this a number of times. Ask pupils to repeat together and individually.
- Use actions to illustrate a word (eg action verbs). Do the action. Say the word and ask pupils to repeat. Say the word and ask volunteers to do the action.

Vocabulary strip

Pre-teach the new words before pupils open their books. The vocabulary strip can then be used to practise new words which have been learnt. This is outlined in the lesson plans.

Listen and read.

These tasks use all new vocabulary and introduce new grammar structures. Focus pupils' attention on the task by asking them to look for new words in the text, or pictures that represent any words they know. After pupils listen to the recording, ask a few simple questions in L1 to check comprehension.

Young learners enjoy reading aloud. By hearing a recording of the reading text, pupils will acquire correct pronunciation and intonation. Play the whole recording first and tell pupils to follow the text with their fingers. Then play the recording again and stop after each sentence. Encourage pupils to repeat what they hear as a class. Repeat this a few times. Then ask volunteers to read out the text.

Encourage pupils to listen to the recording of the reading tasks at home on their Pupil's Audio CD. Tell them which track to find on their CD and also inform parents about the CD so they can help them at home.

Look and learn.

There are two additional characters, Amber and Chris, who are the same age as the pupils. They illustrate the new grammar points with funny mini dialogues.

Read out the dialogue to pupils. Read it out again and ask pupils to repeat. Then explain the grammar box and make sure pupils understand everything. Then ask pupils to find examples of the grammar point in the dialogue and the example sentences.

Explain the task to pupils and then allow them enough time to complete it on their own. Go round the class helping and encouraging pupils. Then check the answers together. It's a good idea to write the answers on the board, so pupils are sure of the correct answers.

Say it!

There is one pronunciation task in each unit. These tasks deal with consonant and vowel sounds, for example *f* and *ph* and double vowels sounds. There are two parts to this task. Play the first part of the recording (Listen and say.) once asking pupils to repeat the words each time they hear them. (This part will be heard twice.) Then ask volunteers to try out the pronunciation of the example. Play the second part of the recording (Read and listen.) so they can check their pronunciation. (This part will be heard once.)

Listening tasks

There is one listening task in each unit. The CD track number is written next to the rubric in the teacher's book. Make sure pupils know what they have to do. Play the recording of the example first and then clearly explain why the answer is the one given. Then play each question one at a time, pausing between questions where necessary. Play the recording as many times as the pupils need in the first few units as this will help build their confidence. Start playing the recording twice when pupils have improved their listening skills enough.

Speaking tasks

There are two speaking tasks in each unit. The first speaking task appears in either Lesson 1 or 2 and practises key structures and vocabulary from the lesson. The second speaking task appears in Lesson 3 and introduces the language needed for the writing task which follows.

Make sure all pupils have a chance to speak. Ask volunteers to perform the speaking task first to allow shyer students to follow their example. To keep the attention of the whole class, ask pupils to perform pairwork at the front of the class while the others watch.

Writing tasks

Each unit ends with a simple, guided writing task. The tasks are designed to be fun and easy to complete so pupils' first experience of writing is positive. The task should be completed in class so the teacher can monitor pupils' progress and encourage them with help and correction.

Pupils have already used the language they need for the writing task in the speaking task. Explain the task first to make sure all pupils know what they have to do. Then allow pupils enough time to complete the task in class. Ask volunteers to hold their books up at the front of the class and then to read out their work. Make sure all pupils get the chance to show off their work.

Lead-in

At the beginning of each lesson plan there is a lead-in section where teachers can make sure pupils remember what they learnt in the previous lesson. Homework should also be checked. Suggestions on different ways of doing this are in the lesson plans. Then the words set for dictation are tested. This can be done in a number of ways to keep pupils interested. Here are some suggestions.

- Write the words to be checked on the board. Leave them there for a minute. Then rub out some of the letters and replace them with a _. Ask pupils to write the words in their notebooks. Ask volunteers to write the missing letters on the board. Then go round the class checking pupils' note books to make sure they have checked their dictation correctly.

- Stick the flashcards of the words on the board picture-side up. Read out the word and ask pupils to write them in their notebooks. Ask volunteers to write the words under the flashcards. Then go round the class checking pupils' notebooks to make sure they have checked their dictation correctly.

- Write the words to be checked on the board in a column. Leave the words there for a minute. Then rub out the first word. Say the word and asks pupils to write it down. Do the same with the other words. Then go round the class checking pupils' notebooks awarding a star for good work.

Songs

Young learners respond well to songs. They enjoy singing, and the music and rhythm help them to acquire and use new vocabulary. Songs improve their pronunciation and intonation and of course build confidence. Play the song to pupils once or twice before asking them to sing along. Then read out the song line by line, asking them to repeat. When pupils are confident with the words, play the recording and encourage them to sing along. The songs can be played to start or finish subsequent lessons. If pupils particularly like one song, they can sing it throughout the whole course. The happier young learners are the more receptive they are to learning!

Tips on teaching young learners

Teaching young learners is a challenge. Young children tend to tire easily and also tend to get over excited. Here are some suggestions on how to teach young learners and maintain a happy, organised classroom.

- Enter the classroom before pupils. Welcome them to 'your' classroom as they arrive. In this way you make it clear that the classroom is your domain and you are in charge.

- Decorate the classroom with pictures and posters of interest about English-speaking countries. Pupils' work should also be put on the wall. The National Geographic map of the world and the four educational posters should also be also put on the wall. These are included in the Teacher's Resource Pack.

- Meet pupils' parents at the beginning of the school year in order to gain their support. Talk about the course and explain what pupils are expected to do at home.

- Bring a supply of materials eg pencils, sharpeners, rubbers and coloured pencils with you. Children often forget theirs!

- Make sure all pupils can see the board. Write clearly and legibly on the board.

- Be patient. If pupils don't understand a task, explain it in a different way.

- Try not to raise your voice. If you shout, young children tend to shout in reaction. Keep boisterous children busy with small tasks like holding the chalk or collecting books.

- Allow children to be active. Ask pupils to stand up, come to the board, perform at the front, hold up their books, perform actions to songs, etc.

- Insist that pupils raise their hands to answer a question and wait for your cue. If all pupils call out together, it is noisy and you cannot monitor learning.

- Praise and reward pupils. Use stickers or draw stars in pupils' notebooks to reward written work. Use English phrases eg *Well done! Good job! That's fantastic!* to reward spoken work.

- Encourage all pupils to take part in the lesson. Give weak pupils tasks they can perform successfully, eg cleaning the board or handing out tests.

- Keep the pace of the lesson moving. If you spend too much time on a task, pupils lose concentration and become restless. Try a different task, eg sing a song, and then go back to the task if necessary.

- Mark homework and tests positively. Young learners need praise and reinforcement to build their confidence.

- Always have extra material and ideas ready for time fillers. You can find ideas in the lesson plans and extra material in the Teacher's Resource Pack.

- Make sure pupils are clear about what they have to do for homework. Allow time at the end of the lesson to explain their homework to them. It's a good idea to write the homework on the board and have pupils copy it into their notebooks.

National Geographic

Happy Trails is a new kind of course for young learners that aims to widen their horizons and introduce them to the world around them through English Language learning. With this aim in mind, *Happy Trails* presents spectacular National Geographic photography as a major element of the course. The photographs have been carefully chosen to appeal to young learners. They depict children of the same age group to whom pupils can relate.

We hope that this course will motivate teachers and parents to encourage pupils to learn more about the world around them. With proper supervision and guidance children can find a wealth of information in magazines, in documentaries and on the Internet.

Pupils and parents can visit this site to find out more about National Geographic for children: kids.nationalgeographic.com or littlekids.nationalgeographic.com

Alphabet

Aa Bb Cc Dd

> ### Aims
> - Learn the letters: *Aa Bb Cc Dd*
> - Learn the words: *ant, boy, car, dog*
> - Learn and use the functional language:
>   *Hi. My name's _____.*
>   *What's your name? My name's _____ .*

Materials

- Alphabet flashcards: *Aa Bb Cc Dd*
- Name cards: Optional for Extra activity: folded pieces of paper for pupils' English names
- Some red and blue colouring pencils

Lead-in

- Welcome pupils and introduce yourself.
- Ask pupils one at a time to stand up and say their names. Answer each time with *Hi*.
- Tell pupils that you are going to ask for their names again, but this time in English. Tell a pupil to stand up and ask him/her *What's your name?* Encourage the pupil to answer with his/her name. Do the same with all pupils.

> ### Extra activity
>
> Most pupils like to have English versions of their names. Write their names on the front of a piece of paper folded in half. Prop the papers up in front of the pupils facing you. Then read out the names one at a time and ask all pupils to repeat. Ask pupils to bring their name cards to the next lesson as this will help you remember their names.

New letters

- Hold up the *Aa* alphabet flashcard. Say *A* and ask pupils to repeat.
- Stick the *Aa* alphabet flashcard on the board. Tell pupils to watch carefully how to write *A*. Slowly write *A* under the flashcard. Ask pupils to mime the movement in the air with an imaginary pencil in their hand. Ask volunteers to come to the board and write *A* under your *A*.
- Point to the letter *a* on the *Aa* alphabet flashcard. Say *a* and ask pupils to repeat. Explain that this is the small *a* and that it goes with the capital *A*. Slowly write *a* under the flashcard. Ask pupils to mime the movement in the air with an imaginary pencil in their hand. Ask volunteers to come to the board and write *a* under your *a*.
- Repeat the procedure for the letters *Bb*.

- Write *A a B b* on the board in random order. Ask volunteers to come to the board and draw lines to join the small letters with the big letters.

New vocabulary

- Tell pupils to open their books at page 4 and to look at the picture at the top of the page.
- Hold up your book and point to the ant. Say *ant* and ask pupils to repeat. Then point to *Aa* saying *A* and then to the *ant* saying *ant*. Ask pupils to repeat after you. Do this a few times. Then do the same with boy and *Bb, boy*.

A Listen, say and write. 1:2

- Hold up your book and show pupils which task to look at. Tell them that they must listen first to the recording, then repeat what they hear. Make sure that they do not write anything at this stage.
- Play the recording. Ask pupils to repeat all together. Play the recording many times until pupils can complete the task successfully. Then ask volunteers to repeat on their own.
- Tell pupils to have a pencil ready. Remind them how they drew the letters in the air with their imaginary pencils. Explain to them that the arrows on the letters in their books show them how to write the letters correctly.
- Ask pupils to trace the grey letters *A a B* and *b*. Go round the class checking pupils' writing and helping them where necessary.
- Tell pupils to now write their own letters in the spaces provided. Explain to them that they should begin where the dot is. Go round the class checking pupils' writing and helping them where necessary.
- Ask pupils to hold up their books for everyone to see. Then ask volunteers to come to the front of the class and show their work. They can point to their letters and call them out.

B Colour A, a, B and b.

- Ask pupils to have red and blue colouring pencils ready.
- Hold up the *Aa* alphabet flashcard. Ask pupils to look at the task and to find the same letters. Tell them to colour them red. Go round the class helping pupils where necessary. When pupils have finished, hold up the *Bb* alphabet flashcard. Ask pupils to look at the task again and to find the same letters. Tell them to colour them blue. Go round the class helping pupils where necessary.
- Check answers.

C Write and find the stickers.

- Ask pupils to tell you which letter *ant* starts with. Elicit *a*. Then ask them to write *a* in the gap for the first word. Read out the word *ant* and ask pupils to repeat. Check answers.
- Ask pupils to tell you which letter *boy* starts with. Elicit *b*. Then ask them to write *b* in the gap for the second word. Read out the word *boy* and ask pupils to repeat. Check answers.

- Show pupils where to find the stickers in their books. Tell them to remove the stickers of the *ant* and the *boy* and stick them on their fingers or on the edge of their desk.
- Tell pupils to turn back to page 4. Ask them to point to where they think the *ant* sticker and the *boy* sticker should go. Make sure they all know which boxes to use and then let them stick the stickers. Go round the class helping pupils where necessary.

D Listen and say. 1:3

- Hold up your book and point to Amber. Say *Amber* and ask pupils to repeat.
- Explain to pupils that Amber will greet them and say her name. Play the recording. Tell pupils to listen and to repeat what they hear as a class. Play the recording a few times so pupils get used to repeating. Then ask volunteers to listen and repeat.

Extension activity

Ask pupils to stand in front of the class one at a time and to introduce themselves in the same way as Amber.
Hi. My name's _____ .

New letters

- Teach *Cc* and *Dd* in the same way as *Aa* and *Bb* with the alphabet flashcards.

Extension activity

Ask 4 volunteers to come to the front of the class and hand each pupil an alphabet flashcard. Ask them to hold up the letters and one at a time say the name of the letter they are holding. Then ask them to arrange themselves in a line so the letters are in the correct order. Repeat until all pupils have had a turn.

New vocabulary

- Tell pupils to open their books at page 5 and to look at the picture at the top of the page.
- Hold up your book and point to the car. Say *car* and ask pupils to repeat a few times. Explain that the letter is called *c* but its sound is often *k*. Repeat *car* again and ask pupils to repeat after you. Do this a few times. Then do the same with *dog* and *Dd, dog*.

A Listen, say and write. 1:4

- Hold up your book and show pupils which task to look at. Remind them how to do this task and then complete the task in the same way as with *Aa* and *Bb* on page 10.

B Circle C,c, D and d.

- Ask pupils to have a pencil ready.
- Hold up the *Cc* alphabet flashcard. Ask pupils to look at the task and to find the same letters. Tell them to circle them. Go round the class helping pupils where necessary. When pupils have finished, hold up the *Dd* alphabet flashcard. Ask pupils to

look at the task again and to find the same letters. Tell them to circle them. Go round the class helping pupils where necessary.

- Tell pupils to be careful not to circle *Aa* or *Bb* by mistake.
- Check answers.

C Write and colour.

- Ask pupils to tell you which letter *car* starts with. Elicit *c*. Then ask them to write *c* in the gap for the first word. Read out the word *car* and ask pupils to repeat. Check answers.
- Ask pupils to tell you which letter *dog* starts with. Elicit *d*. Then ask them to write *d* in the gap for the second word. Read out the word *dog* and ask pupils to repeat. Check answers.
- Ask pupils to colour in the pictures as they like.
- Check pupils' work. Ask volunteers to hold up their books and read out letters and words to the class.

D Listen and say. 1:5

- Hold up your book and point to Amber. Say *Amber* and ask pupils to repeat. Then point to Chris. Say *Chris* and ask pupils to repeat.
- Explain to pupils that Amber and Chris are meeting for the first time and Amber is asking Chris' name. Play the recording. Pause after each speech bubble and ask pupils to repeat what they hear as a class. Play the recording a few times so pupils get used to repeating. Then ask volunteers to listen and repeat.

Extension activity

- Ask two pupils, a boy and a girl, to stand in front of the class and role play the dialogue between Amber and Chris.
- Ask pupils to do the dialogue again but to use their own names.

Homework

- Activity Book, page 4: Time permitting, start some writing practice in class at the end of the lesson to make sure pupils are forming the letters correctly. This can be done on the board, in pupils' notebook or both.
- Dictation: *Aa Bb Cc Dd*

Alphabet

Ee Ff Gg Hh

Aims

- Learn the letters: *Ee Ff Gg Hh*
- Learn the words: *egg, frog, girl, hat*
- Practise in a chant:
  What's your name?
  My name's ___ .
  Hi.
- Learn and use the functional language:

  Hello. How are you?
  Fine, thank you.

Materials

- Alphabet flashcards: *Ee Ff Gg Hh*
- A boiled egg, a hat
- For Extra activity: alphabet flashcards *Aa Bb Cc Dd Ee Ff*

Lead-in

- Welcome pupils with *Hi* and *Hello*. Ask them to sit down and display their name cards. Revise *What's your name? My name's _____* . Ask a pupil *What's your name?* and elicit answer. Then the same pupil asks his/her neighbour the question. Continue round the class until all pupils have asked and answered.
- Write *A B C D* on the board. Point to the letters one at a time and ask pupils to call out the letter together. Then do the same with pupils one at a time.
- Write *a b c d* on the board in random order. Ask volunteers to match the capital letters with the small letters.
- Check homework. Go round the class and check pupils' work.
- Test dictation. Clean the board. Write *Aa* on the board and tell pupils to look at the letters carefully. Then rub the letters off the board and ask pupils to write them in their notebooks. Do the same with *Bb Cc* and *Dd*.
- Go round the class and check pupils' work. You could award a star or a sticker to pupils to help build their confidence.

New letters

- Teach *Ee* and *Ff* in the same way as *Aa* and *Bb* with the alphabet flashcards.

Extra activity

Write the capital letters along the top of the board: *A B C D E F*. Draw 6 fish under the capital letters and in random order write the small letters in them: *a b c d e f*. Tell pupils that the capital letters are fishing for the small letters. Ask volunteers to come to the board and join the capital letters to the small letters. Rub out the small letters and write them in different fish to play again. Make sure all pupils have a turn.

New vocabulary

- Teach *egg*. Hold up the boiled egg. Say *egg* and ask pupils to repeat. Do this a few times. Ask pupils what letter *egg* starts with and elicit *e*.
- Tell pupils to open their books at page 6 and to look at the picture at the top of the page. Ask pupils to hold up their books and point to an egg.
- Hold up your book and point to the frog. Say *frog* and ask pupils to repeat. Then point to *Ee* saying *E* and then to the egg saying *egg*. Ask pupils to repeat after you. Then point to *Ff* saying *F* and then to the frog saying *frog*. Ask pupils to repeat after you. Do this a few times.

A Listen, say and write. 🔊 1:6

- Hold up your book and show pupils which task to look at. Remind them how to do this task and then complete the task in the same way as with *Aa* and *Bb* on page 10.

B Join the dots.

- Explain the task to pupils. Show them that they must join the dots to form the letters. Remind them to form the letters in the same way the arrows showed them in the previous task. Go round the class helping pupils where necessary.
- Check answers. Then ask volunteers to come to the front and show their work to the class. They can point to their letters and call them out.

C Write and find the stickers.

- Ask pupils to tell you which letter *egg* starts with. Elicit *e*. Ask pupils to tell you which letter *frog* starts with. Elicit *f*. Then ask them to write *e* and *f* in the correct gaps for the words. Read out the words *egg* and *frog* and ask pupils to repeat. Check answers.
- Remind pupils how to do this task and then complete the task following the procedure on page 10.

D Chant. 🔊 1:7

- Hold up your book and point to the chant. Tell pupils to listen to the recording.
- Read out the chant one line at a time and ask pupils to repeat. Do this a few times until pupils know the chant well.
- Play the recording again. Encourage pupils to say the chant along with the recording.

New letters

- Teach *Gg* and *Hh* in the same way as *Aa* and *Bb* with the alphabet flashcards.

New vocabulary

- Teach *hat*. Hold up the hat. Say *hat* and ask pupils to repeat. Do this a few times. Ask pupils what letter *hat* starts with and elicit *h*.

- Tell pupils to open their books at page 7 and to look at the picture at the top of the page. Ask pupils to hold up their books and point to the hat.

- Hold up your book and point to the girl. Say *girl* and ask pupils to repeat. Then point to *Hh* saying *H* and then to the hat saying *hat*. Ask pupils to repeat after you. Then point to *Gg* saying *G* and then to the girl saying *girl*. Ask pupils to repeat after you. Do this a few times.

A Listen, say and write. 🔘1:8

- Hold up your book and show pupils which task to look at. Remind them how to do this task and then complete the task in the same way as with *Ee* and *Ff*.

- Ask pupils to hold up their books for everyone to see. Then ask volunteers to come to the front of the class and to show their work. They can point to their letters and call them out.

B Circle G, g, H and h.

- Ask pupils to have a pencil ready.

- Hold up the *Gg* and the *Hh* alphabet flashcards. Ask pupils to look at the picture and to find the same letters. Tell them to circle them. Tell pupils to be careful not to circle any of the wrong letters by mistake. Go round the class helping pupils where necessary.

- Check answers.

C Write and colour.

- Ask pupils to tell you which letter *girl* starts with. Elicit *g*. Then ask pupils to tell you which letter *hat* starts with. Elicit *h*. Tell pupils to write *g* and *h* in the correct gaps for the words. Go round the class helping where necessary. Read out the words *girl* and *hat* and ask pupils to repeat.

- Ask pupils to colour in the pictures as they like.

- Check pupils' work. Ask volunteers to hold up their books and read out the letters and the words to the class.

D Listen and say. 🔘1:9

- Hold up your book and point to Amber and Chris. Explain to pupils that Amber and Chris are on the phone. Tell them that Chris is asking how Amber is and she's telling him that she's fine.

- Say *How are you?* and ask pupils to repeat. Say *Fine, thank you.* and ask pupils to repeat. Explain the meaning to pupils. Practise the question and answer a few times.

- Play the recording. Pause after each speech bubble and ask pupils to repeat what they hear as a class. Play the recording a few times so pupils get used to repeating. Then ask volunteers to listen and repeat.

Alphabet

Ii Jj Kk Ll

Aims

- Learn the letters: *Ii Jj Kk Ll*
- Learn the words: *insect, jug, king, lemon*
- Practise the functional language:
  Hello. My name's _____ .
  What's your name?
  How are you?
  Fine thank you.
- Practise the functional language in a song:
  What's your name?
  My name's ___ .
  How are you?
  Fine, thank you.

Materials

- Alphabet flashcards: *Ii Jj Kk Ll*
- A lemon
- For Extra activities: alphabet flashcards Aa - Kk
- For Extra activity game: Twenty pieces of coloured card. On ten of the pieces write the capitals *A-L* and on the other ten the small letters *a-l*. Make sure the letters do not show through the card.

Lead-in

- Welcome pupils with *Hi* and *Hello*. Ask them to sit down and display their name cards. Revise *What's your name? My name's _____ .* Ask a pupil *What's your name?* and elicit answer. Then the same pupil asks his/her neighbour the question. Continue round the class until all pupils have asked and answered.
- Revise *How are you? Fine, thank you.* Ask all pupils *How are you?* and encourage them to repeat as a class. Then ask a pupil *How are you?* and elicit answer. Then the same pupil asks his/her neighbour the question. Continue round the class until all pupils have asked and answered.
- Write *e f g h* on the board. Point to the letters one at a time and ask pupils to call out the letter together. Then do the same with pupils one at a time.
- Write *E F G H* on the board in random order. Ask volunteers to match the capital letters with the small letters.
- Check homework. Go round the class and check pupils' work.
- Test dictation. Hold up the *Ee Ff Gg* and *Hh* alphabet flashcards one at a time and ask pupils to call out the letters. Put down the flashcards and call out the letters one at a time asking pupils to write the capital letters in their notebooks. Do the same with the small letters. Ask pupils to write the small letters next to the capitals.

- Go round the class and check pupils' work. You could award a star or a sticker to pupils to help build their confidence.

New letters

- Teach *Ii* and *Jj* in the same way as *Aa* and *Bb* with the alphabet flashcards.

Extra activity

Hand out the Aa - Jj alphabet flashcards to ten pupils. If you have fewer than ten pupils in the class, choose five pupils and give them two cards each. Ask these pupils to stand at the front of the class and to put themselves in the correct order. Then call out the letters in order. When a pupil hears his/her letter tell the pupil to hold it up in the air. Then call out the letters in random order. Make sure all pupils have a turn.

New vocabulary

- Tell pupils to open their books at page 8 and to look at the picture at the top of the page.
- Hold up your book and point to the insect. Say *insect* and ask pupils to repeat. Then point to *Ii* saying *I* and then to the insect saying *insect*. Ask pupils to repeat after you. Do this a few times. Then do the same with *jug* and *Jj, jug*.

A Listen, say and write. 1:10

- Hold up your book and show pupils which task to look at. Remind them how to do this task and then complete the task in the same way as with *Aa* and *Bb* on page 10.

B Find and circle the letters I, i, J and j.

- Hold up the *Ii* and the *Jj* alphabet card. Ask pupils to look at the picture and to find the same letters. Tell them to circle them. Tell pupils to be careful not to circle any of the wrong letters by mistake. Go round the class helping pupils where necessary.
- Check answers.

C Write and colour.

- Ask pupils to tell you which letter *insect* starts with. Elicit *i*. Then ask pupils to tell you which letter *jug* starts with. Elicit *j*. Tell pupils to write *i* and *j* in the correct gaps for the words. Go round the class helping where necessary. Read out the words *insect* and *jug* and ask pupils to repeat.
- Ask pupils to colour in the pictures as they like.
- Check pupils' work. Ask volunteers to hold up their books and read out the letters and words to the class.
- Check answers.

D Listen and say. 1:11

- Hold up your book and point to Amber and Chris. Tell pupils to listen to the recording.
- Play the recording. Pause after each speech bubble and ask pupils to repeat what they hear as a class. Then ask volunteers to listen and repeat.

Extension activity

- Ask two pupils to stand in front of the class and role play the dialogue between Amber and Chris using their own names.
- Ask four pupils to stand in front of the class and to act out meeting each other. Encourage them to use the functional language they know prompting them where necessary.

New letters

- Teach *Kk* and *Ll* in the same way as *Aa* and *Bb* with the alphabet flashcards.

Extra activity

- Stick the alphabet flashcards on the board in order: Aa - Ll. Say the letters one at a time and ask pupils to repeat.
- Say all the letters as a chant. Ask pupils to repeat the chant a few times as a class. Then ask volunteers to repeat the chant on their own.
- Tell pupils to close their eyes. Remove any two alphabet flashcards from the board. Pupils can open their eyes. Show them the letters you have removed and ask a volunteer to stick them back in the correct place.

New vocabulary

- Teach *lemon*. Hold up the lemon. Say *lemon* and ask pupils to repeat. Do this a few times. Ask pupils what letter *lemon* starts with and elicit *l*.
- Tell pupils to open their books at page 9 and to look at the picture at the top of the page. Ask pupils to find the piece of lemon in the picture.
- Hold up your book and point to the king. Say *king* and ask pupils to repeat. Then point to *Kk* saying *K* and then to the king saying *king*. Ask pupils to repeat after you. Then point to *Ll* saying *L* and then to the piece of lemon saying *lemon*. Ask pupils to repeat after you. Do this a few times.

A Listen, say and write. 1:12

- Hold up your book and show pupils which task to look at. Remind them how to do this task and then complete the task in the same way as with *Aa* and *Bb.*

B Join the dots.

- Explain the task to pupils. Show them that they must join the dots to form the letters. Remind them to form the letters in the same way the arrows showed them in the previous task. Go round the class helping pupils where necessary.
- Check answers. Then ask volunteers to come to the front of the classroom and show their work to the class. They can point to their letters and call them out.

C Write and find the stickers.

- Ask pupils to tell you which letter *king* starts with.

Elicit *k*. Ask pupils to tell you which letter *lemon* starts with. Elicit *l*. Then ask them to write *k* and *l* in the correct gaps for the words. Read out the words *king* and *lemon* and ask pupils to repeat. Check answers.

- Remind pupils how to do this task and then complete the task following the procedure on page 10.

D Sing. 1:13

- Tell pupils they are going to learn a song.
- Play the recording and tell pupils to listen and follow the words with their fingers.
- Read out the song one line at a time and ask pupils to repeat after you.
- Play the recording again. Encourage pupils to sing along. Practise many times until pupils are familiar with the words.
- Divide pupils into two groups. Group 1 should be on the left, and group 2 on the right. Explain that group 1 should sing the questions and group 2 the answers. When pupils sing their lines they should stand up and look at the other group. The groups can then swap so group 1 sings the answers and group 2 the questions. Play the recording and pupils sing along.

Extra activity

- Play an alphabet matching game with the coloured cards.
- Show pupils the coloured cards with the letters on them. Put all the cards face down on your table or the floor if there is more space. Ask pupils to gather round the cards in a circle. Ask a volunteer to pick a cards and to turn it over. Ask him/her to say the letter. Then tell him/her to choose another cards. If it is the same letter as on the other card he/she can keep them. If it is not, he/she turns the card back over again leaving them in the same place.
- The pupil to the right then has a turn, and so on until all the cards have been matched. Remind pupils to leave the cards in the same place so they can try to remember where they are.

Homework

- Pupil's Audio CD: Pupils listen to the song at home. Explain to pupils that they should listen to track 3 on the CD.
- Activity Book, page 6: Time permitting, start some writing practice in class at the end of lesson to make sure pupils are forming the letters correctly.
- Dictation: *Ii Jj Kk Ll*
- Optional extra homework: pupils learn to chant the letters they have learnt so far in the correct order. Aa - Ll.

Alphabet 🐾

Mm Nn Oo Pp

Aims

- Learn the letters: *Mm Nn Oo Pp*
- Learn the words: *monkey, nest, octopus, pencil*
- Learn and use the functional language:
  Look An insect.
  No! try again.
  A monkey.
  Yes! Well done.

Materials

- Alphabet flashcards: *Mm Nn Oo Pp*
- A pencil
- For Extension activity. One blank piece of paper for each pupil.
- Some purple and yellow colouring pencils
- Optional for Extension activity: A pair of glasses

Lead-in

- Revise the functional language pupils have learnt so far. Ask the whole class *How are you?* and elicit answer *Fine, thank you*. Then ask individual pupils *What's your name?* and elicit answer *My name's _____* . Then ask volunteers to act out mini dialogues in front of the class.
- Revise all the letters pupils have learnt so far. Write *A - L* on the board. Point to the letters one at a time and ask pupils to call out the letter together. Then do the same with pupils one at a time.
- Ask volunteers to write the small letters next to the capital letters on the board.
- Check homework. Go round the class and check pupils' work.
- Test dictation. Write *Ii Jj Kk Ll* on the board. Give pupils a moment to look at the letters. Then rub out one of each letter, either the capital or the small letter. Ask pupils to write the letters in their notebooks, filling in the missing letters too.
- Go round the class and check pupils' work. You could award a star or a sticker to pupils to help build their confidence.

New letters

- Teach *Mm* and *Nn* in the same way as *Aa* and *Bb* with the alphabet flashcards.

Extra activity

Chant the letters pupils have learnt so far, *Aa - Nn*. First say the letters in groups of four and ask pupils to repeat. Ask volunteers to write the capital letters on the board. When all the letters are on the board, point to them and encourage the class to say the chant together. You could then repeat the task with the small letters on the board.

New vocabulary

- Tell pupils to open their books at page 10 and to look at the picture at the top of the page.
- Hold up your book and point to the monkey. Say *monkey* and ask pupils to repeat. Then point to *Mm* saying *M* and then to the monkey saying *monkey*. Ask pupils to repeat after you. Do this a few times. Then do the same with the nest and *Nn, nest*.

A Listen, say and write. 💿1:14

- Hold up your book and show pupils which task to look at. Remind them how to do this task and then complete the task in the same way as with *Aa* and *Bb* on page 10.

B Match.

- Write *M* on the board. Ask a volunteer to write the small *m* next to it. Do the same with *N*. Then explain to pupils that in this task they must draw lines to join the capital letters with the correct small letters.
- Allow pupils enough time to complete the task alone. Go round the class helping pupils where necessary.
- Check answers.

C Write and colour.

- Ask pupils to tell you which letter *monkey* starts with. Elicit *m*. Then ask pupils to tell you which letter *nest* starts with. Elicit *n*. Tell pupils to write *m* and *n* in the correct gaps for the words. Go round the class helping where necessary. Read out the words *monkey* and *nest* and ask pupils to repeat.
- Ask pupils to colour in the pictures as they like.
- Check pupils' work. Ask volunteers to hold up their books and read out the letters and words to the class.

D Listen and say. 💿1:15

- Draw two simple pictures on the board: a car and an egg. Point to the car and say *Look! A car*. Ask pupils to repeat. Then point to the egg and say *Look! An egg*. Ask pupils to repeat.
- Practise *Look!* Point to your eyes and then one of the pictures. Ask pupils to repeat after you.
- Practise *A* and *An*. Say *A car.* and ask pupils to repeat. Then say *An egg.* and ask pupils to repeat. Do this a few times.
- Play the recording. Pause after speech bubble and ask pupils to repeat what they hear as a class. Play the recording a few times so pupils get used to repeating. Then ask volunteers to listen and repeat.

New letters

- Teach *Oo* and *Pp* in the same way as *Aa* and *Bb* with the alphabet flashcards.

New vocabulary

- Teach *pencil*. Hold up the pencil. Say *Look! A pencil.* and ask pupils to repeat. Do this a few times. Ask pupils what letter *pencil* starts with and elicit *p*.

- Tell pupils to open their books at page 11 and to look at the picture at the top of the page. Ask pupils to point to a pencil in the picture.

- Hold up your book and point to the octopus. Say *Look! An octopus.* and ask pupils to repeat. Then point to *Oo* saying *O* and then to the octopus saying *An octopus.* Ask pupils to repeat after you. Then point to *Pp* saying *P* and then to the pencil saying *A pencil.* Ask pupils to repeat after you. Do this a few times.

A Listen, say and write. 1:16

- Hold up your book and show pupils which task to look at. Remind them how to do this task and then complete the task in the same way as with *Mm* and *Nn*.

- Ask pupils to hold up their books for everyone to see. Then ask volunteers to come to the front of the class and show their work. They can point to their letters and call them out. They can also point to the pictures and say *Look! An octopus.* and *Look! A pencil.*

B Colour O, o P and p.

- Ask pupils to have purple and yellow colouring pencils ready.

- Hold up the *Oo* alphabet flashcard. Ask pupils to look at the pencils and to find the same letters. Tell them to colour them purple. Go round the class helping pupils where necessary. When pupils have finished, hold up the *Pp* alphabet flashcard. Ask pupils to look at the pencils and to find the same letters. Tell them to colour them yellow. Go round the class helping pupils where necessary.

- Check answers.

C Write and find the stickers.

- Ask pupils to tell you which letter *octopus* starts with. Elicit *o*. Ask pupils to tell you which letter *pencil* starts with. Elicit *p*. Then ask them to write *o* and *p* in the correct gaps for the words. Read out the words *octopus* and *pencil* and ask pupils to repeat. Check answers.

- Remind pupils how to do this task and then complete the task following the procedure on page 10.

D Chant. 1:17

- Hold up your book and point to the chant. Tell pupils to listen to the recording.

- Read out the chant one line at a time and ask pupils to repeat. Do this a few times until pupils know the chant well.

- Play the rest of the recording. (The words *monkey* and *octopus* have been omitted.) Encourage pupils to say the chant and say the words *monkey* and *octopus*.

Alphabet

Qq Rr Ss Tt

Aims

- Learn the letters: *Qq Rr Ss Tt*
- Learn the words: *quilt, robot, spider, tiger*
- Learn and use the functional language:
  Here you are.
  Wow! Thanks.
  You're welcome.

Materials

- Alphabet flashcards: *Qq Rr Ss Tt*
- An apple
- Some red and yellow colouring pencils

Lead-in

- Revise the functional language from the previous lesson. Draw a pencil on the board. Say *Look! A pencil.* and ask pupils to repeat. Then draw an egg shape on the board. Ask the class to say what they can see. *Look! An egg.* Reply *No, try again.* and draw some dots on the egg to make it look like a lemon. When you get the correct answer, tell pupils *Yes. Well done.* Continue with volunteers using these suggestions:
  boy/girl – add long hair
  boy/king – add a crown
  hat/octopus – add eyes and tentacles
- Revise all the letters pupils have learnt so far. Write *A B C D E F G H I J K L M N O P* on the board. Point to the letters one at a time and ask pupils to call out the letter together. Then do the same with pupils one at a time.
- Ask volunteers to write the small letters next to the capital letters on the board.
- Check homework. Go round the class and check pupils' work.
- Test dictation. Write *Mm Nn Oo Pp* on the board. Give pupils a moment to look at the letters. Then rub out one of each letter, either the capital or the small letter. Ask pupils to write the letters in their notebooks, filling in the missing letters too.
- Go round the class and check pupils' work. You could award a star or a sticker to pupils to help build their confidence.

New letters

- Teach *Qq* and *Rr* in the same way as *Aa* and *Bb* with the alphabet flashcards.

Extra activity

Write the small letters *a-r* on the board. Say a letter and ask a volunteer to come to the board and point to it.

New vocabulary

- Tell pupils to open their books at page 12 and to look at the picture at the top of the page.
- Hold up your book and point to the quilt. Say *Look! A quilt.* and ask pupils to repeat. Then point to *Qq* saying *Q* and then to the *quilt* saying *quilt*. Ask pupils to repeat after you. Do this a few times. Then do the same with *robot* and *Rr, robot*.

A Listen, say and write. 🔘 1:18

- Hold up your book and show pupils which task to look at. Remind them how to do this task and then complete the task in the same way as with *Aa* and *Bb* on page 10.

B Match.

- Write *Q* on the board. Ask a volunteer to write the small *q* next to it. Do the same with *R*. Then explain to pupils that in this task they must first draw lines to join the capital letters with the correct small letters and then the small letters with the capitals.
- Allow pupils enough time to complete the task alone. Go round the class helping pupils where necessary.
- Check answers.

C Write and colour.

- Ask pupils to tell you which letter *quilt* starts with. Elicit *q*. Then ask pupils to tell you which letter *robot* starts with. Elicit *r*. Tell pupils to write *q* and *r* in the correct gaps for the words. Go round the class helping where necessary. Read out the words *quilt* and *robot* and ask pupils to repeat.
- Ask pupils to colour in the pictures as they like.
- Check pupils' work. Ask volunteers to hold up their books and read out the letters and words to the class.

D Listen and say. 🔘 1:19

- Hold up the apple and say *Look! An apple.* Ask a volunteer to come to the front of the class. Give the apple to the volunteer saying *Here you are.* Ask pupils to repeat. Practise this a few times.
- Ask a new volunteer to give the apple to you and say *Here you are.* Reply *Wow! Thanks.* Ask pupils to repeat. Practise this a few times.
- Now give the apple to a new volunteer saying *Here you are.* Elicit the reply *Wow! Thanks.* Then reply *You're welcome.* Ask pupils to repeat. Ask pupils what they think this means and help them work out the meaning.
- Play the recording. Pause after speech bubble and ask pupils to repeat what they hear as a class. Play the recording a few times so pupils get used to repeating. Then ask volunteers to listen and repeat.

Extension activity

Give the apple to a pupil in the back row. Say *Here you are.* and elicit the reply *Wow! Thanks.* Reply *You're welcome.* Then tell the pupil to give the apple to the pupil in front of him/her and say *Here you are.* Help pupils with the functional language where necessary. When the apple reaches the front, pupils should start passing it to the back again.

New letters

- Teach *Ss* and *Tt* in the same way as *Aa* and *Bb* with the alphabet flashcards.

New vocabulary

- Tell pupils to open their books at page 13 and to look at the picture at the top of the page.
- Hold up your book and point to the spider. Say *Look! A spider.* and ask pupils to repeat. Then point to *Ss* saying *S* and then to the *spider* saying *spider.* Ask pupils to repeat after you. Do this a few times. Then do the same with *tiger* and *Tt, tiger.*

A Listen, say and write. 🔊 1:20

- Hold up your book and show pupils which task to look at. Remind them how to do this task and then complete the task in the same way as with *Aa* and *Bb* on page 10.
- Ask pupils to hold up their books for everyone to see. Then ask volunteers to come to the front of the class and show their work. They can point to their letters and call them out. They can also point to the pictures and say *Look! A spider.* and *Look! A tiger.*

B Colour Ss, T and t.

- Ask pupils to have red and yellow colouring pencils ready.
- Write *Qq Rr Ss Tt* on the board in random order. Ask a volunteer to come to the board and circle *Ss* and *Tt.* Ask pupils to look at the task and to tell you the colours they should use for *S* and *T.* Ask the volunteer to sit down.
- Allow pupils enough time to complete the task alone. Go round the class helping pupils where necessary.
- Check answers.

C Write and find the stickers.

- Ask pupils to tell you which letter *spider* starts with. Elicit *s.* Ask pupils to tell you which letter *tiger* starts with. Elicit *t.* Then ask them to write *s* and *t* in the correct gaps for the words. Read out the words *spider* and *tiger* and ask pupils to repeat. Check answers.
- Remind pupils how to do this task and then complete the task following the procedure on page 10.

D Chant. 🔊 1:21

- Hold up your book and point to the chant. Tell pupils to listen to the recording.
- Read out the chant one line at a time and ask pupils to repeat. Do this a few times until pupils know the chant well.
- Play the recording again. Encourage pupils to say the chant along with the recording.

Extra activity

- Revise the words pupils have learnt so far. Write the letters A–T on the board.
- Circle the letter *M* on the board. Ask pupils to look back through the introduction and to find the page where they learnt *M.* When they have found it they should raise their hand. Wait until all hands are raised. Help pupils find the page where necessary. Ask pupils what word they learnt which starts with *M.* Elicit *monkey.*
- Circle another letter and continue as with the letter *M.* Do the same until all the letters have been circled.

Homework

- Pupil's Audio CD: Pupils listen to the chant at home. Explain to pupils that they should listen to track 5 on the CD.
- Activity Book, page 8: Time permitting, some tasks can be done in class.
- Dictation: *Qq Rr Ss Tt*
- Optional extra homework: Ask pupils to write the letters *Aa–Tt* neatly in their notebooks.

Alphabet 🐾

Uu Vv Ww Xx Yy Zz

Aims

- Learn the letters: *Uu Vv Ww Xx Yy Zz*
- Learn the words: *bus, van, worm, fox, yo-yo, zebra*
- Learn and use the functional language:
  Bye.
  Goodbye.

Materials

- Alphabet flashcards: *Uu Vv Ww Xx Yy Zz*
- A yo-yo
- For Extra activity: all alphabet flashcards

Lead-in

- Revise *What's your name? My name's _____ .* Ask a pupil *What's your name?* and elicit answer. Then the same pupil asks his/her neighbour the question. Continue round the class until all pupils have asked and answered.
- Revise *How are you? Fine, thank you.* Ask all pupils *How are you?* and encourage them to repeat as a class. Then ask a pupil *How are you?* and elicit answer. Then the same pupil asks his/her neighbour the question. Continue round the class until all pupils have asked and answered.
- Revise *Here you are. Thanks. You're welcome.* Hand a pencil to a pupil and say *Here you are.* Elicit answer *Thanks.* and reply *You're welcome.* Then the same pupil gives his/her neighbour the pencil. Continue round the class until all pupils have asked and answered.
- Write *q r s t* on the board. Point to the letters one at a time and ask pupils to call out the letter together. Then do the same with pupils one at a time.
- Write *Q R S T* on the board in random order. Ask volunteers to match the capital letters with the small letters.
- Check homework. Go round the class and check pupils' work.
- Test dictation. Hold up the *Qq Rr Ss* and *Tt* alphabet flashcards one at a time and ask pupils to call out the letters. Put down the cards and call out the letters one at a time asking pupils to write the capital letters in their notebooks. Do the same with the small letters and tell pupils to write the small letters next to the capitals.
- Go round the class and check pupils' work. You could award a star or a sticker to pupils to help build their confidence.

New letters

- Teach *Uu, Vv* and *Ww* in the same way as *Aa* and *Bb* with the alphabet flashcards.

Extra activity

Hand out all the alphabet flashcards to pupils. They will have between two and three letters each. Call out the letters in alphabetical order one at a time. The pupil who has the letter should stand up and hold it up. Do the task slowly at first, then repeat it faster and faster.

New vocabulary

- Tell pupils to open their books at page 14 and to look at the picture at the top of the page.
- Hold up your book and point to the *bus.* Say *bus* and ask pupils to repeat. Then point to *Uu* saying *U* and then to the *bus* saying *bus.* Ask pupils to repeat after you. Ask them where they can hear the sound for *U* in the word *bus.* Hold up your book again and point to the *van.* Say *van* and ask pupils to repeat. Then point to *Vv* saying *V* and then to the *van* saying *van.* Ask pupils to repeat after you. Ask them where they can hear the sound for *V* in the word *van.* Then do the same with *worm* and *Ww, worm.*

A Listen, say and write. 💿 1:22

- Hold up your book and show pupils which task to look at. Remind them how to do this task and then complete the task in the same way as with *Aa* and *Bb* on page 10.

B Circle U, u, V, v, W and w.

- Stick the *Uu, Vv* and the *Ww* alphabet flashcards on the board. Ask pupils to look at the picture and to find the same letters. Tell them to circle them. Tell pupils to be careful not to circle any of the wrong letters by mistake. Go round the class helping pupils where necessary.
- Check answers.

C Write and find the stickers.

- Ask pupils to tell you which letter *van* starts with. Elicit *v.* Ask pupils to tell you which letter *worm* starts with. Elicit *w.* Ask pupils which letter is in the word *bus.* Elicit *u.* Then ask them to write *u, v* and *w* in the correct gaps for the words. Read out the words *bus, van* and *worm* and ask pupils to repeat. Check answers.
- Remind pupils how to do this task and then complete the task following the procedure on page 10.

D Listen and say. 💿 1:23

- Ask a volunteer to go outside the room and then enter the room. When the volunteer enters the room say *Hello.* Then ask the volunteer to leave again and say *Bye. Goodbye.* Repeat with another volunteer and ask pupils to repeat *Hello. Bye.* and *Goodbye.*
- Play the recording. Pause after each speech bubble and ask pupils to repeat what they hear as a class. Then ask volunteers to listen and repeat.

New letters

- Teach *Xx, Yy* and *Zz* in the same way as *Aa* and *Bb* with the alphabet flashcards.

New vocabulary

- Teach *yo-yo*. Hold up the yo-yo. Say *yo-yo* and ask pupils to repeat. Do this a few times. Ask pupils what letter *yo-yo* starts with and elicit *y*.

- Tell pupils to open their books at page 15 and to look at the picture at the top of the page. Ask pupils to find the two yo-yos in the picture.

- Hold up your book and point to the *fox*. Say *fox* and ask pupils to repeat. Then point to *Xx* saying *X* and then the *fox* saying *fox*. Ask pupils to repeat after you. Ask them where they can hear the sound for *X* in the word *fox*. Then do the same with *zebra* and *Zz, zebra* and *yo-yo* and *Yy, yo-yo*.

A Listen, say and write. 1:24

- Hold up your book and show pupils which task to look at. Remind them how to do this task and then complete the task in the same way as with *Aa* and *Bb* on page 10.

- Ask pupils to hold up their books for everyone to see. Then ask volunteers to come to the front of the class and show their work. They can point to their letters and call them out.

B Find and circle the letters X, x, Y, y, Z and z.

- Stick the *Xx, Yy* and the *Zz* alphabet flashcards on the board. Ask pupils to look at the picture and to find the same letters. Tell them to circle them. Tell pupils to be careful not to circle any of the wrong letters by mistake. Go round the class helping pupils where necessary.

- Check answers.

C Write and colour.

- Ask pupils to tell you which letter *yo-yo* starts with. Elicit *y*. Ask pupils to tell you which letter *zebra* starts with. Elicit *z*. Ask pupils which letter is in the word *fox*. Elicit *x* Tell pupils to write *x, y* and *z* in the correct gaps for the words. Go round the class helping where necessary. Read out the words *fox, yo-yo* and *zebra* and ask pupils to repeat.

- Ask pupils to colour in the pictures as they like.

- Check pupils' work. Ask volunteers to hold up their books and read out the letters and words to the class.

- Check answers.

D Sing. 1:25

- Tell pupils they are going to learn a song.

- Play the recording and tell pupils to listen and follow the words with their fingers.

- Read out the song one line at a time and ask pupils to repeat after you.

- Play the recording again. Encourage pupils to sing along. Practise many times until pupils are familiar with the words. As pupils sing they can wave.

Alphabet ✺

Alphabet

Aims

- Revise and consolidate the alphabet
- Play an alphabet board game
- Make an alphabet poster

Materials

- Dice, one for each group
- A counter for each pupil
- A large piece of coloured card for the poster
- Colouring pencils
- Optional for Extra activity: Alphabet cards

Lead-in

- Revise the alphabet with a class chant.
- Revise *Bye* and *Goodbye*. Ask a volunteer to leave the room and say *Bye* as he/she leaves. The other pupils reply *Goodbye*. Repeat until all pupils have had a turn.
- Write *U V W X Y Z* on the board. Point to the letters one at a time and ask pupils to call out the letter together. Ask pupils which words they learnt for these letters.
- Ask volunteers to write the small letters next to the capital letters.
- Check homework. Go round the class and check pupils' work.
- Test dictation. Ask a volunteer to call out the first letter *U* and tell pupils to write down the capital and the small letter. Ask another volunteer to call out the next letter *V* and continue the dictation in the same way.
- Go round the class and check pupils' work. You could award a star or a sticker to pupils to help build their confidence.

A Write.

- Write the capital letters of the alphabet on the board. Then ask volunteers to write the small letters next to the capitals. Leave the letters on the board so pupils can use them for reference.
- Ask pupils to open their books at page 16. Ask them to have a pencil ready. Tell them to look at the task and explain that they have to write the missing capital or small letters. Tell them to check the letters on the board as they do the task.
- Allow pupils enough time to complete the task alone. Go round the class helping where necessary.
- Check answers.

B Sing. ⊙1:26

- Tell pupils they are going to learn a song.
- Play the recording and tell pupils to listen and follow the letters and words with their fingers.
- Read out the song one line at a time and ask pupils to repeat after you.

- Play the recording again. Encourage pupils to sing along. Practise many times until pupils are familiar with the words.
- Divide the class into three groups. Each group sings a verse of the song. Then all groups sing the whole song together.

Extra activity

Hand out the alphabet flashcards. Pupils will have two or three cards each. Ask pupils to sing the song. When pupils hear their letters, they hold them high in the air.

C Play.

- Tell pupils they are going to play a game. Tell them to look at the game. Call out *Aa*. Ask pupils to look at the picture for *A* and to put up their hands if they remember the word that goes with *A*. Ask a volunteer to tell you *An ant*. Do the same with all the letters and pictures.
- Divide the class into small groups. Tell the groups to have one book open for the game. Explain the rules of the game to pupils.

Game 1:
A player throws the dice, then he/she moves the number of squares the dice says. If the player lands on a letter, he/she must say the name of the letter. If he/she can't remember he/she must move back one square. The player to reach the trophy first wins. They don't have to throw an exact number to reach the trophy.

Game 2:
This is the same as game 1, but this time the players must look at the pictures and say the words.

- Give each pupil one counter and each group one dice. As pupils play, go round the class helping where necessary.

D Make.

- Tell pupils they are going to make an alphabet poster for their classroom. Show pupils the picture in their books where two schoolchildren are making a poster. Explain that they must first draw the outline of the letters in pencil, and then they can colour in the letters.
- Ask pupils to gather round your desk. Ask a volunteer to draw an outline of the letters *A* and *a*. Then ask another pupil to do *B* and *b* and so on. Copy the number of letters per line from the pupil's book. When all the letters have been drawn, ask volunteers to colour them in. Make sure all pupils take part in making the poster. To keep other pupils occupied when they aren't colouring, play the songs from the Introduction and they can sing along.
- Stick the poster on the wall. It can be used to practise the letters all year.

Homework

- Pupil's Audio CD: Pupils listen to the song at home. Explain to pupils that they should listen to track 7 on the CD.
- Activity Book, page 10: Time permitting, some tasks can be done in class.
- Tell pupils to bring colouring pencils to the next lesson.

Colours

Aims

- Learn the colours: *red, blue, pink, brown, black, orange, white, purple, yellow, green*
- Consolidate new vocabulary with a game

Materials

- Colouring pencils: red, blue, pink, brown, black, orange, white, purple, yellow, green

Lead-in

- Revise the alphabet with the alphabet poster. Point to letters at random and ask pupils to call them out.
- Check homework. Go round the class and check pupils' work.

New vocabulary

- Hold up the red colouring pencil. Say *Look. A pencil.* Then say *Red. A red pencil.* And ask pupils to repeat. Repeat the colour a few times. Then do the same with *blue, pink, brown* and *black*.
- Ask five volunteers to come to the front of the class. Give them one pencil each. Say a colour and the pupil with that colour must hold it up high. All the class repeats the colour. Do the same with new volunteers. Make sure all pupils have a turn.

A Listen, read and say. 🔊 1:27

- Tell pupils to turn to page 18 in their books. Tell them they are going to learn how to read the colours.
- Play the recording and ask pupils to point to the words in their books. Play the recording again and ask pupils to repeat. Do this as a class a few times. Then ask volunteers to repeat on their own.
- Ask pupil to read the colours without the recording. First ask the pupils to read the colours in the right order. Then write the colours on the board. Point to the words in random order and ask the class to read them out. Then ask volunteers to do the same on their own.

Extension activity

- Write *red* on the board. Ask pupils to read it out. Then tell pupils to close their eyes. Rub out one letter from the word *red*. Ask pupils to open their eyes. Ask a volunteer to come to the board and write the missing letter. Do the same with *blue, pink, brown* and *black*.
- Do the task again, but this time, rub out two letters.

B Colour and write.

- Explain the task to pupils. Ask volunteers to read out the colours. Then ask them to find the five colouring pencils they need to colour in the pictures.
- Tell pupils to colour in the pictures. Go round the class helping where necessary.
- Tell pupils to have a pencil ready and then to trace the letters carefully. Go round the class and make sure they are forming the letters correctly.
- Check answers. Then ask volunteers to come to the front of the class and show their work. They can point to the words and read them out.

C Write and match.

- Tell pupils to look at the anagrams. Explain that they must find the colour word and write it on the line. When they have written down the colour they must draw a line to the correct colour paw print.
- Ask a volunteer to read the example. Then ask another volunteer to find the next colour word. Write *pink* on the board. Pupils can copy it down, and then draw a line to the correct paw print. Do the same for *brown*. Then tell pupils to try the last two colours alone. Go round the class helping where necessary.
- Check answers.

Answers

1 red (given)
2 pink
3 brown
4 blue
5 black

D Chant. 🔊 1:28

- Hold up your book and point to the chant. Tell pupils to listen to the recording.
- Read out the chant one line at a time and ask pupils to repeat. Do this a few times until pupils know the chant well.
- Play the recording again. Encourage pupils to say the chant along with the recording.

Extra activity

Ask pupils to stand in front of the class in groups of four and to say the chant. Encourage the other pupils to clap at the end.

New vocabulary

- Hold up the orange colouring pencil. Say *Look. A pencil.* Then say *Orange. An orange pencil.* And ask pupils to repeat. Repeat the colour a few times. Then do the same with *white, purple, yellow* and *green*.
- Ask five volunteers to come to the front. Give them one pencil each. Say a colour and the pupil with that colour must hold it up high. All the class repeat the colour. Do the same with new volunteers. Make sure all pupils have a turn.

E Listen, read and say. 🔊 1:29

- Tell pupils to turn to page 19 in their books. Tell them they are going to learn how to read five more colours.

- Play the recording and ask pupils to point to the words in their books. Play the recording again and ask pupils to repeat. Do this as a class a few times. Then ask volunteers to repeat on their own.

- Ask pupils to read the colours without the recording. First ask the pupils to read the colours in the right order. Then write the colours on the board. Point to the words in random order and ask the class to read them out. Then ask volunteers to do the same on their own.

Extension activity

- Write _range on the board. Ask pupils to tell you which letter is missing. Ask a volunteer to come to the board and complete the word. Do the same with _hite, _urple, _ellow and _reen.

- Do the task again, but this time, rub out the last letter.

F Colour and write.

- Explain the task to pupils. Ask volunteers to read out the colours. Then ask them to find the five colouring pencils they need to colour in the pictures.

- Tell pupils to colour in the pictures. Go round the class helping where necessary.

- Tell pupils to have a pencil ready and then to trace the letters carefully. Go round the class and make sure they are forming the letters correctly.

- Check answers. Then ask volunteers to come to the front of the class and show their work. They can point to the words and read them out.

G Listen, say and play the game. 🔊 1:30

- Teach *Guess*. Hold a rubber in your hand. Ask a volunteer to come to the front. Put both your hands behind your back, hide the rubber in one hand and then hold them out closed in front of the volunteer. Say *Guess*. The pupil chooses a hand. If he/she chooses incorrectly say *No. Try again*. When he/she chooses correctly say *Yes. Well done*. Repeat this a few times with more volunteers.

- Tell pupils they are going to play a guessing game in pairs. Ask them to look at the pictures. Hold up your book and say the colours and names of the objects. Ask pupils to repeat.
  A white hat.
  A black spider.
  A purple car.
  A black dog.
  A yellow lemon.
  A green frog.
  A white yo-yo.
  A purple van.
  A green worm.
  A red ant.
  A yellow pencil.
  A red fox.

- Play the recording. Tell pupils to look at the pictures and follow the words with their fingers.

- Play the recording again. Stop after each speech bubble and ask pupils to repeat.

- Ask two volunteers to stand at the front of the class and play the game. Tell them to bring their books with them, and to look at each other. One pupil chooses a colour and says *Guess*. The other pupil guesses. Prompt and help pupils where necessary.

- Repeat with two more volunteers. Do this a few times before allowing pupils to play in pairs at their desks. Go round the class helping where necessary.

Homework

- Pupil's Audio CD: Pupils listen to the chant at home. Explain to pupils that they should listen to track 8 on the CD.

- Activity Book, page 11: Time permitting, some tasks can be done in class.

- Dictation: *red, green*

- Extra optional homework: Pupils copy the colours neatly into their notebooks.

- Tell pupils to bring colouring pencils to the next lesson.

Numbers

Aims

- Learn the numbers: *1-10*

Materials

- Number cards: Make ten number cards. Write the figures *1-10* on one side and the words on the other side.
- Colouring pencils: red, blue, pink, brown, black, orange, white, purple, yellow, green

Lead-in

- Revise the colours with the colouring pencils. Put all the pencils on your desk. Hold them up one at a time, say the colour and ask pupils to repeat. Then ask volunteers to come to the desk, choose a pencil, hold it up and say the colour. Remove that pencil, and continue until there are no pencils left.
- Revise the alphabet with the alphabet poster. Say a letter and ask a volunteer to point to the letter on the poster.
- Check homework. Go round the class and check pupils' work.
- Test dictation. Hold up the *red pencil*, say *red* and ask pupils to write the word in their notebooks. Do the same with *green.*
- Go round the class and check pupils' work. You could award a star or a sticker to pupils to help build their confidence.

New vocabulary

- Stick the number cards on the board so the figures *1-10* show. Ask pupils if by any chance they already know the numbers in English. Say the numbers one at a time and ask pupils to repeat. Point to numbers as you say them.
- Turn the number cards around so the words show. Do the task again, but this time pointing to the words.
- Take the cards down. Using the figures, hold up the numbers one at a time at random and ask pupils to call out the number. Do the same with the words.

A Listen and say. 1:31

- Tell pupils to turn to page 20 in their books. Tell them they are going to learn how to read the numbers.
- Play the recording and ask pupils to point to the words in their books. Play the recording again and ask pupils to repeat. Do this as a class a few times. Then ask volunteers to repeat on their own.
- Ask pupils to read the numbers without the recording. First ask the pupils to read the numbers in the right order. Then hold up your book. Point to the words in random order and ask the class to read them out. Then ask volunteers to do the same on their own.

B Find and colour.

- Ask pupils to have their colouring pencils ready. Explain that they must colour the picture according to the colour code.
- Read out *1* and *blue*. Ask pupils to find their blue pencils and look for something in the picture they should colour blue: *the dolphin*. Do the same with numbers *2-5.*
- Tell pupils to finish the picture on their own. Allow them enough time to complete the task alone. Go round the class helping pupils where necessary.
- Check answers. Ask pupils to hold up there books and show each other their work. They can point to the numbers and colours and call them out.

C Chant. 1:32

- Hold up your book and point to the chant. Tell pupils to listen to the recording.
- Read out the chant one line at a time and ask pupils to repeat. Do this a few times until pupils know the chant well. Encourage pupils to clap as they count.
- Play the recording again. Encourage pupils to say the chant along with the recording. Then practise the chant without the recording.

D Count and write.

- Ask pupils to look at page 21 in their books. Explain that they must count the socks in English, and then write the figure and the word.
- Read out the example to pupils. Count the *socks*, and encourage pupils to count with you. Then ask pupils to count the *socks* underneath in the first column. Encourage them to count together. Write the answers on the board and ask them to copy them down. Do the same for the next set of *socks* too.
- Ask pupils to finish the task on their own. Allow them enough time to complete the task. Go round the class helping where necessary.
- Check answers. Write the numbers and words on the board so pupils can check their spelling.

Answers

1 5 / five (given)
2 6 / six
3 10 / ten
4 4 / four
5 2 / two
6 7 / seven

E Listen and write. 1:33

- Tell pupils they are going to listen to a recording and that they must write the number they hear in each box. Tell them to fill in the first line and then the second line.
- Play the recording for the example. Make sure pupils understand what to do.

- Play the rest of the recording pausing between numbers where necessary. Play the recording again and ask pupils to check their answers.

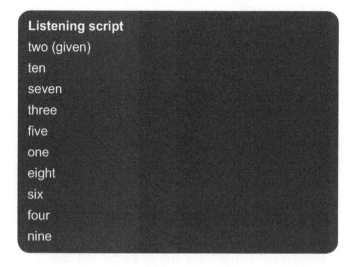

Listening script

two (given)

ten

seven

three

five

one

eight

six

four

nine

Answers

2 (given)
10
7
3
5
1
8
6
4
9

Extra Activity

- Use the socks to revise the colours. Ask a volunteer to choose some socks but not to say which ones. He/She then says which colours are on the socks and the other pupils must point to the ones he/she has chosen.

F Listen and say. 1:34

- Teach *How old are you?* Ask pupils in L1 to tell you their age. Then explain that they are going to learn how to ask each other's age in English. Say *How old are you?* and ask pupils to repeat. Practise the question a few times. Then ask a volunteer to come to the front of the class and ask *How old are you?*. Elicit an answer eg *8*. Then complete the answer *I'm 8.* and encourage all pupils to repeat.

- Play the recording. Pause after each speech bubble and ask pupils to repeat what they hear as a class. Then ask volunteers to listen and repeat.

Extension activity

- Ask two pupils to stand in front of the class and role play the dialogue between Amber and Chris, but to use their own age.

- Encourage pupils to role play a longer dialogue. First do an example with a volunteer, eg:
  Hello. What's your name?
  My name's _____ .
  How are you?
  Fine thank you.
  How old are you?
  I'm 9.
  Bye.
  Goodbye.

Homework

- Pupil's Audio CD: Pupils listen to the chant at home. Explain to pupils that they should listen to track 9 on the CD.

- Activity Book, page 12: Time permitting, some tasks can be done in class.

- Dictation: *one, two, three, four, five*

- Optional extra homework: Pupils copy the numbers neatly into their notebooks.

- Tell pupils to bring a pair of scissors, glue and two pieces of ribbon or string 30cm long to the next lesson. One A4 card can be either supplied by teacher or brought in by pupils. These materials will be used to make the character masks. Be prepared to have extra materials in the event pupils don't remember to bring these to the next lesson.

Trek & his Reporters

Aims

- Introduce the characters from the cartoon episodes: *Trek, Ty, Mia, Leo*
- Learn and use functional language: *Hi. I'm _____ .*
- Revise new vocabulary
- Revise functional language:
  Hi. / Hello.
  What's your name?
  My name's _____ .
  How are you?
  Fine, thanks.
  How old are you?
  I'm _____ .

Materials

- Materials to make the character masks: scissors (one pair for each pupil), card (one A4 piece for each pupil), glue and ribbon or string (two 30cm pieces for each pupil)
- Optional for extra activity: dice and counters for pupils to play the alphabet board game.

Lead-in

- Revise the alphabet with a class chant.
- Write *B D G H P R* on the board. Point to the letters one at a time and ask pupils to call out the letter together. Write *b d g h p r* the small letters in random order on the board and ask volunteers to match them with the capitals.
- Revise some colours. Point to an object in the classroom, eg an item of clothing or a school bag and ask pupils to say the colour.
- Check homework. Go round the class and check pupils' work.
- Test dictation. Write *1 2 3 4 5* on the board in a vertical column. Ask pupils to copy these into their notebooks and then write the words next to the figures.
- Go round the class and check pupils' work. You could award a star or a sticker to pupils to help build their confidence.

A Listen and say. 🔊 1:35

- Ask pupils to open their books at page 22. Tell pupils to look at the picture. Hold up your book and point to the characters one at a time. Say their names, Trek, Mia, Ty and Leo, and ask pupils to repeat them. Write the names on the board. Tell pupils that you are going to tell them about the characters.

Trek
He is a 9-year-old boy who loves technology things and learning about the world. He has got a laptop, a flat screen TV, a map and a globe. He has got three friends who are his reporters. They travel to different countries and make a DVD for him about their journeys and adventures. He receives the DVD in the post and then watches it on his TV. We watch the DVD with him through the book in the cartoon episodes. There is a map on Trek's wall which shows the countries the reporters visit.

Ty
He is a panda. He makes the films and takes all the pictures on the journeys. He is kind and funny and often gets into scrapes.

Mia
She is a meerkat. She records accounts of their journeys on her tape recorder. She is clever and knows many things about the places they visit.

Leo
He is a leopard. He takes down notes about their journeys. He is fun loving, likes meeting new people and is always willing to try out new things.

Character masks

- Tell pupils that they're going to make the character masks. Ask pupils to bring out the materials for the masks. Supply any materials pupils haven't got. Then tell pupils where the character masks are at the end of the book. Ask pupils to choose one character (or time permitting two characters) each and to cut out the mask carefully using the dotted lines as a guide. Go round the class helping where necessary.
- Then ask pupils to stick the mask on the A4 card using glue. Pupils then cut out the mask again carefully. Pupils can write their names on the back of the mask.
- When pupils have finished cutting out the mask on the card, help them to make a hole on each side of the mask. Show pupils how to hold up the mask to their face so that the best position for the holes can be found (about halfway down the character's face). Then tie a length of ribbon or string through each hole. Then ask pupils how to hold the mask up to their face and tie the ribbons for them.
- Pupils can wear these character masks when acting out the cartoon episodes. The masks should be handed out at the beginning of lessons with the cartoon episodes and collected at the end of that lesson. This avoids situations where pupils forget to bring these masks to class.
- The rest of the masks can be made during the year whenever new copies of these masks are needed (because of wear and tear) or alternatively each pupil can have their own set of masks which again can be kept by teachers and handed out when needed.
- Tell pupils to look at the picture. Say a character's name and ask pupils to point to the correct character.
- Play the recording. Tell pupils to look at the pictures and follow the speech bubbles with their fingers.
- Play the recording again. Pause after each speech bubble and ask pupils to repeat.
- Ask pupils to wear the character mask they have made. Then pupils can act out what the characters say on page 22. Make sure all pupils have a turn.

- Ask pupils to look at the picture and point to the four things you are going to say:
  car
  king
  ant
  spider
- Ask pupils to find any other things they know in English in the picture.
  eg
  pencil
  zebra
  monkey
  octopus
  tiger
  dog
  jug
- Revise the colours and numbers. Ask volunteers to come to the front of the class. Hold up your book, point to a colour and ask the volunteers to say what it is. Then ask pupils to count the objects eg *ants, spiders, animals, pencils, boys*.

B Match.

- Ask pupils one at a time *What's your name?* and elicit answer *My name's ____* . Then explain to pupils that they can also answer in a shorter way with *I'm ____* . Write *I'm Trek.* on the board. Ask pupils *What's your name?* again and elicit the shorter answer.
- Ask pupils to look at page 23. Explain that they must read the sentences and match them to the character who is speaking. Read out the example and ask pupils to repeat. Ask volunteers to read out the other sentences one at a time. Tell pupils to draw lines to the correct characters. Go round the class helping where necessary.
- Check answers.

> **Answers**
>
> I'm Leo. 3 (given)
> My name's Trek. 4
> I'm Ty. 2
> My name's Mia.1

C Listen and say. 🔘 1:36

- Play the recording. Tell pupils to look at the pictures and follow the speech bubbles with their fingers.
- Play the recording again. Pause after each speech bubble and ask pupils to repeat.
- Play the recording again. Then ask volunteers to read out the speech bubbles.

> **Extension activity**
>
> - Assign characters to volunteers and ask them to read out the dialogues from their books in front of the class.
> - Ask volunteer to role play dialogues in front of the class like the ones in their books, but with their own names and age. Pupils can wear the character masks.

D Colour and write.

- Ask pupils to look carefully at the pictures and to find which part of each picture isn't coloured in.
  Trek's hat
  Ty's jacket
  Leo's scarf
  Mia's bag
- Ask them to say in English which colours they need for these objects. Allow them time to colour in.
- Ask pupils to write the correct names into the boxes next to the characters. Go round the class helping where necessary.
- Ask pupils to hold up their books and show their work to the class. They can point to the characters and call out their names.

E Sing. 🔘 1:37

- Tell pupils they are going to learn the *Happy Trails* song.
- Play the recording and tell pupils to listen and follow the letters and words with their fingers.
- Read out the song one line at a time and ask pupils to repeat after you.
- Play the recording again. Encourage pupils to sing along. Practise many times until pupils are familiar with the words. Encourage pupils to clap and jump up and down when they sing *Happy Trails*! and *Party!*

> **Extra activity**
>
> Pupils can play the alphabet board game again. See page 23 for instructions.

> **Homework**
>
> - Pupil's Audio CD: Pupils listen to Trek and his Reporters and the song at home. Explain to pupils that they should listen to tracks 10 and 11 on the CD.
> - Activity Book, page 13: Time permitting, some tasks can be done in class.
> - Extra optional homework: Pupils copy the names of the characters neatly into their notebooks.

Ask pupils to look at the photo on pages 24-25 (use L1) and tell them that it's a National Geographic photo. Ask them if they have seen a National Geographic magazine. Explain that National Geographic photos are taken from all over the world, and that in the magazine we can learn about people, places, animals and nature. Ask pupils if they watch documentaries about the world, its inhabitants and amazing animals on TV.

Pupils are likely to know many African animals. Encourage them to tell you the ones they know, using the photo to start them off. At this stage use L1 for discussions, but whenever possible encourage pupils to use English for words they have learnt eg *zebra* which they will remember from the Introduction. Pupils are less likely to know where South Africa is situated. Use the map at the top of the page to show them. First show them where their own country is on the globe and then point out the area in red where the reporters are. Explain that this is Africa.

The first country the reporters visit is South Africa on the continent of Africa. On this trip, they are looking for local wildlife. In Africa there are many wild animals which can be seen in the National Parks. In episode 1 and 2, the reporters go on safari in a national park and see elephants, lions, giraffes, monkeys and an ostrich. A number of these animals are endangered and the National Parks aim to protect them and support conservation efforts. Other African animals are rhinos, leopards, cheetahs, hippos, zebras, meerkats, lizards, snakes and buffalos. In episode 3, the reporters visit Cape Town on the south coast where they see a penguin and a whale. They also see the famous flat mountain which is called Table Mountain due to its shape.

Fun facts

Here are some facts about Africa which your pupils will find interesting:

1 The elephant, lion, rhino, leopard and buffalo are known as 'The Big Five'.
2 The ostrich is the largest bird in the world, but it can't fly.
3 There are usually about 20 meerkats in a meerkat family. But some superfamilies can have 50 meerkats.
4 Baby meerkats are looked after by all the females in the family.
5 Lions have one enemy – people.
6 Lions rest and sleep for about 20 hours a day.
7 Blue whales can be 30 metres long.
8 Penguins are birds, but they can't fly. They are not usually afraid of humans.
9 African elephants are bigger than Indian elephants.
10 Giraffes are the tallest animals in the world.
11 Giraffes only sleep for 1 to 2 hours a day.
12 The little monkeys with black faces are called Vervet monkeys.
13 Vervet monkeys make different warning sounds for different dangerous animals they see.

Lesson 1   Trek's reporters in Africa

Aims

- Learn and use new vocabulary: *baby, fly, elephant, mum, photo, fantastic*
- Learn and use new grammar: *a, an*

Materials

- Flashcards: baby, elephant, fly, mum, photo
- Masks: Trek, Ty, Mia, Leo

Lead-in

- Revise and practise functional language from the Introduction. Ask volunteers questions (eg *How are you? How old are you? What's your name?*) and elicit answers. Then ask volunteers to stand at the front of the class and ask and answer questions.

- Check homework. Tell pupils to open their Activity Books at page 13. Ask volunteers to read out their answers. Write the answers on the board so pupils can check their work. Then quickly check all pupils' books.

- Revise the names of Trek and his reporters. Point to each character on page 22 and ask pupils to call out the right names. Hand out the masks to volunteers. Ask volunteers to put on the masks and to come to the front of the class. Point to each pupil and ask the class to call out the names of the characters. This can be repeated until all pupils have had a turn.

Episode outline

Africa: Episode 1

Trek's mum gives him a DVD and a photo the reporters have sent from Africa. Trek watches the reporters on safari. Mia and Ty see an elephant mum and her baby. Leo is annoyed by a fly. Then Leo sees something that scares him even more. In the next lesson, they discover it is a lion.

New vocabulary

- Teach the new words with the flashcards. See the teacher's introduction pages 7-9 for teaching suggestions.

- Tell pupils to open their books at page 26 and to look at the vocabulary box. Hold up your book and point to the first picture word. Say the word and ask pupils to repeat. Do the same with all the words. Then read out the new picture words in the vocabulary box in random order and ask pupils to point to the correct pictures.

- Read out the word *fantastic*. Explain the meaning. Then hold up your *Happy Trails* book and say enthusiastically *Fantastic!* and ask pupils to repeat. Ask volunteers to stand at the front, hold your book and say *Fantastic!*

- Read out all the words again one by one and ask pupils to repeat after you.

A Listen and read.

For teachers using the DVD

- Make sure each pupil has got a copy of the DVD Worksheet found on page 127.

- Ask pupils to work in pairs to do the *Before you watch* task to encourage discussion.

Answers
1 Trek (*the boy in the first frame*), Leo, Mia and Ty (frames 2-5)
2 Trek's mum (*the woman in the first frame holding the DVD*)
3 elephant and fly (*both in frame 3 and two elephants in frame 4*)
4 Trek is at home.
5 Trek's reporters are in Africa.

- Play the whole episode without interruption before pupils do any more tasks on the worksheet. Ask pupils to watch the DVD carefully.

While you watch

- Tell pupils to look at the *While you watch* task and tell them that they need to tick the correct column when they watch the episode for the second time. Play the whole episode again without interruption.

- Give pupils a few minutes to complete the task. If necessary play the DVD again and ask pupils to fill in any missing information.

Answers
1 Trek's mum
2 Trek
3 Mia
4 Mia
5 Ty
6 Leo
7 Mia

After you watch

- Ask volunteers to read out the story. Then assign characters to volunteers and ask them to act out the story in front of the class. Pupils can wear the character masks.

- Check pupils understand the story. Ask pupils to answer the questions in the *After you watch* section of the worksheet using L1 where necessary. Encourage pupils to use the English words for the answers.

Answers
1 A DVD and a photo
2 In Africa
3 two elephants and a fly
4 A lion

For teachers using the audio 1.38

- Tell pupils to look at the cartoon story on page 26. Say a character's name and ask pupils to point to the correct character. Do the same with *elephant* and *fly*.

- Play the recording. Tell pupils to look at the pictures and follow the speech bubbles with their fingers.
- Play the recording again. Pause after each speech bubble and ask pupils to repeat.
- Check pupils understand the story. Use L1 where necessary.

What has Trek got? (a DVD and a photo)
Where are the reporters? (Africa)
What animals do they see? (two elephants and a fly)
What do you think is behind the car? (encourage pupils to guess a lion)

- Play the recording again. Then ask volunteers to read out the story.
- Assign characters to volunteers and ask them to act out the story in front of the class. Pupils can wear the character masks.

B Look and learn.

- Read out the dialogue. Read it out again and ask pupils to repeat.
- Ask pupils to look at the grammar box. Explain that we use *an* before words that start with the letters *a e i o u*, but we use *a* before words that start with the other letters.
- Ask pupils to circle *a* and *an* in the dialogue. Ask volunteers to read out the dialogue.
- Write *a* and *an* on the board. Say a word and tell pupils to call out *a* or *an*, depending on which letter the word starts with. Write the word under *a* or *an* before saying the next word.

Words pupils have already learnt that can be used in this activity are: All the words from the Alphabet section and baby, elephant, fly, photo, and DVD.

Ask volunteers to say any other words they know that go under *a* or *an*. Write these on the board as well.

Extension activity

Revise the alphabet with the class. First ask pupils to chant the alphabet as a class. Then play the alphabet song from the Introduction (p. 16) and ask pupils to sing along. Repeat this as many times as necessary and then ask volunteers to say the alphabet on their own.

C Write a or an.

- Read out the example and ask pupils why *a* goes with *baby*.
- Explain the rest of the task to pupils. Allow them enough time to complete the task alone. Go round the class helping pupils where necessary.
- Check answers. Write them on the board if necessary.

Answers
1 a (given)   4 a
2 an   5 an
3 a   6 a

Say it! 1.39

- Write *f* and *ph* on the board. Ask pupils to say the names of letters.
- Explain that the letters *ph* make the same sound as *f* when they are together.
- Tell pupils to look at the task. Play the first part of the recording (Listen and say.) asking pupils to repeat the words *fantastic* and *elephant* each time they hear them. (*Fantastic* and *elephant* will be heard twice.)
- Ask volunteers to read out *photo* and *fly*. Play the recording and ask all pupils to repeat. (*Photo* and *fly* will be heard once.)

D Listen and tick. 1.40

- Tell pupils to look at the pictures for this task and ask them what they can see. Ask volunteers to say the words. Then ask pupils to repeat the word. Practise for a few minutes to make sure pupils know these words fairly well (as they are new words) before attempting to do the Listening task.
- Explain to pupils that for each number they will hear someone talk about only one of the pictures. Explain that they must tick the correct picture. Play the recording for the example. Make sure pupils understand what to do.
- Play the rest of the recording, pausing between questions where necessary. Play the recording again and ask pupils to check their answers.

Listening script
1 Hello Mum.
2 Look. A baby.
3 A photo. Fantastic!
4 Oh no! A fly.
5 Wow! An elephant.

Answers
1 Mum (2nd picture)
2 baby (1st picture)
3 photo (2nd picture)
4 fly (1st picture)
5 elephant (2nd picture)

E Say.

- Read out the dialogue. Read it out again and ask pupils to repeat after each speech bubble.
- Ask two volunteers to read out the dialogue either from their seats or in front of the class.
- Use the flashcards to continue the task. Hand a flashcard to a pupil. The pupil then asks another pupil how to spell the word.
- Continue the task in pairs. Ask pairs to come to the front of the class and choose a word from their books. They can use words from the lesson and the introduction.

Homework

- Pupil's Audio CD: Pupils listen to the recording of the cartoon story at home. Explain to pupils that they should listen to track 12 on the CD.

- Activity Book, pages 14-15: Time permitting, some tasks can be done in class.

- Dictation: *baby, elephant, fly, mum, photo, fantastic*

Lesson 2   My house is an igloo.

Aims

- Learn and use new vocabulary: *house, igloo, brother, sister, dad, family, cool*

- Learn and use new grammar: *to be* affirmative (*I, you, he, she, it*)

Materials

- Flashcards: baby, elephant, fly, mum, photo, brother sister, family, dad, house, igloo

Lead-in

- Revise the words from Lesson 1 with the flashcards. Ask a pupil to pick a flashcard from a pile on your desk, show it to the class and ask what the word is. Pupils can take it in turns until all words have been practised.

- Ask pupils to tell you words that go with *a* and *an*. Write them on the board.

- Check homework. Tell pupils to open their Activity Books at pages 14 and 15. Ask volunteers to read out their answers. Draw two columns on the board for *a* and *an*. Ask volunteers to write the answers from page 15 task C on the board. Then quickly check all pupils' books.

- Test dictation: *baby, elephant, fly, mum, photo, fantastic*. See the teacher's introduction pages 7-9 for teaching suggestions. Go round the class and check all pupils' dictation.

New vocabulary

- Teach the new words with the flashcards. See the teacher's introduction pages 7-9 for teaching suggestions.

- Tell pupils to open their books at page 28 and to look at the vocabulary box. Hold up your book and point to the first picture word. Say the word and ask pupils to repeat. Do the same with all the words. Then read out the new picture words in the vocabulary box in random order and ask pupils to point to the correct pictures.

- Read out the word *cool*. Explain the meaning. Then point to Trek on the front of your *Happy Trails* book and say *Trek's cool!* and ask pupils to repeat. Do the same with a pupil's name, eg *John's cool!* and ask pupils to repeat. Ask volunteers to stand at the front, and do the same with any name they like.

- Read out all the words again one by one and ask pupils to repeat after you.

A Listen and read. 🎧 1.41

- Ask a girl and a boy to stand up. Revise *girl*, and then *boy*. Ask pupils if they think the child in the photo is a boy or a girl. Ask them where they think the child is from. Tell pupils that the Inuit are people who live in the snowy North. Ask pupils what kind of house an Inuit lives in and revise *igloo*. Write *hunter* on the board, explain the meaning and ask pupils what they think the Inuit hunt.

Background Information

The Inuit people live in the Arctic regions of Canada, Greenland, Russia and Alaska. Inuit life has changed over the past century and many Inuit now live in towns and villages. However, some Inuit traditions continue.

The Inuit have been traditionally hunters and fishers. They hunted polar bears, birds and other animals like foxes. They used *kayaks* to hunt sea animals (whales, seals, walruses) and the Europeans and Americans copied this type of boat from them. On land, the Inuit used sleds with teams of *husky* dogs for transport. The traditional Inuit live in houses made of snow, called *igloos*, during the winter months. The rest of the year they live in shelters made of animal skins. Traditional clothes and boots were made from animal skins and fur. Large thick coats with big hoods, called *parkas* or *anoraks*, were worn over their clothes. Today this style of coat is worn all over the world and it is made from many other materials.

- Play the recording. Tell pupils to follow the text with their fingers.

- Play the recording again. Pause after each sentence and ask pupils to repeat.

- Play the recording again. Then ask volunteers to read out a paragraph each of the text.

B Write Yes or No.

- Read the example to pupils. Ask them to find the word *boy* in the text.

- Explain the rest of the task to pupils. Tell them to underline the words in the text which give them the answers. Allow them enough time to complete the task alone. Go round the class encouraging and helping pupils where necessary.

- Check answers. Write them on the board if necessary.

Answers
1 No (given)
2 No
3 Yes
4 Yes

C Look and learn.

- Read out the dialogue. Read it out again and ask pupils to repeat.

- Ask pupils to look at the grammar box. Read out the grammar notes and sentences. Ask pupils to repeat. Explain the meaning of the notes.

- Ask pupils to circle the person and underline the verb in the grammar sentences. Ask volunteers to read out the sentences.

- Practise the grammar. Write sentences on the board with the verb missing. Ask pupils to fill in the gaps.

I ___ fantastic.

She ___ a girl.

You ___ a boy.

Extension activity

- Write *I* on the board. Point to yourself and say *I'm cool!* Ask pupils to repeat.

- Write *You* on the board. Stand next to a pupil. Look at the pupil and say *You're cool.* Ask pupils to repeat.

- Write *He* on the board. Point to a boy and say *He's cool.* Ask pupils to repeat.

- Write *She* on the board. Point to a girl and say *She's cool.* Ask pupils to repeat.

- Write *It* on the board. Hold up the *Happy Trails* book and say *It's cool.* Ask pupils to repeat.

- Repeat the task with the long form of the verb. You could illustrate the meaning of the verb with real class situations such as: *I am fantastic.* Use the words *boy* and *girl* to refer to various pupils. Pupils can come to the front of the class and each say something about themselves or about other pupils. For example: *I am a boy/girl., You are a boy/girl., It is a pencil.*

D Write am, are or is.

- Read out the example and ask pupils why *is* is the correct answer.

- Explain the task to pupils. Check pupils remember the meanings of all the words. Allow them enough time to complete the task alone.

- Check answers. Write them on the board if necessary.

Answers
1 is (given)	4 are
2 is	5 is
3 am	6 is

E Sing. 1.42

- Tell pupils they are going to learn a song.

- Ask pupils to look at the picture and describe what they can see. Encourage them to use English for words they know. Hold up your book and point to *Mum*. Ask a volunteer to say the word. Do the same for *Dad, brother* and *sister*. Point to the boys and say *They're cool!* Encourage pupils to repeat. Count the people to revise some numbers. Ask pupils to repeat.

- Play the recording and tell pupils to listen and follow the words with their fingers.

- Read out the song one line at a time and ask pupils to repeat after you.

- Play the recording again. Encourage pupils to sing along. Practise many times until pupils are familiar with the words.

- Divide pupils into small groups. Tell them to stand up, join hands in a circle and sing the song. On the words *celebrate* and *cool* they can jump up high.

Homework

- Pupil's Audio CD: Pupils listen to the text and the song at home. Explain to pupils that they should listen to tracks 13 and 14 on the CD.

- Activity Book, pages 16-17: Time permitting, some tasks can be done in class.

- Dictation: *brother, sister, family, dad, house, igloo, cool*

Lesson 3   My family is great.

Aims

- Learn and use new vocabulary: *best friend, grandma, grandpa, great, nice*

- Learn and use new grammar: *to be* affirmative (*we, you, they*)

Materials

- Flashcards: brother, sister, family, dad, house, igloo

- 2 magazine photos to illustrate grandma and grandpa

- Optional: word cards for Extra activity. Divide two A4 pieces of card into 9 boxes. Cut out 18 cards and write one word on each card: *baby, elephant, fly, mum, photo, fantastic, brother, sister, family, dad, house, igloo, cool, best friend, grandma, grandpa, great, nice*

Lead-in

- Revise the words from Lesson 2 with the flashcards. Hold up a flashcard from a pile on your desk and show it to the class and ask what the word is. Then do the same with the words in a different order.

- Write *I, you, he, she* and *it* on the board on the left. Write *cool* on the right. Ask volunteers to write the correct verbs in the gap.

- Check homework. Tell pupils to open their Activity Books at pages 16 and 17. Ask volunteers to read out their answers. Write the questions from task D on the board. Ask volunteers to write the answers in the gaps. Then quickly check all pupils' books.

- Test dictation: *brother, sister, family, dad, house, igloo, cool.* See the teacher's introduction pages 7-9 for teaching suggestions. Go round the class and check all pupils' dictation.

- Sing the song from Lesson 2 (CD1: 42)

New vocabulary

- Teach *best friend*. Tell pupils to open their books at page 7. Ask them if they remember the names of

Amber and Chris. Ask them if they are brother and sister (no). Elicit the word *friend*. Explain that they are best friends. Write *best friend* on the board. Read it out and ask pupils to repeat. Ask two friends to come to the front of the class and tell other pupils to point to them and say: *They're best friends.*

- Teach *grandma* and *grandpa*. Hold up the magazine photo of grandpa. Say *grandpa* and ask pupils to repeat. Do the same with the magazine photo of *grandma*. Stick them on the board and label them grandma and grandpa. Read them out and ask pupils to repeat.

- Tell pupils to open their books at page 30 and to look at the vocabulary box. Hold up your book and point to the first picture word. Say the word and ask pupils to repeat. Do the same with all the words. Then read out the new picture words in the vocabulary box in random order and ask pupils to point to the correct pictures.

- Read out the words *great* and *nice*. Explain the meanings. Tell pupils you will show them a picture and ask if it is nice. Tell them to answer *Yes!* or *No!* Choose pictures from the Introduction for this task. eg Hold up page 4, point to the ant and say *Nice?* At the end of the task praise pupils by saying *Great!*

- Read out all the words again one by one and ask pupils to repeat after you.

A Read.

- Tell pupils to look at the letter and the photo. Tell pupils to read the first line of the letter. Then ask them the name of the girl who is writing the letter and how old she is.

- Tell pupils to now read the rest of the letter and to decide which person in the photo is Alex.

- Read out the letter. Stop after each sentence and ask pupils to repeat.

- Ask volunteers to read out a sentence each of the letter.

Optional activity

Put pupils into groups of two and ask them to read the letter to each other. Go round the class helping with reading and pronunciation where necessary.

B Circle

- Read the example to pupils. Ask them to find where the answer is in the letter. Ask them to underline the words.

- Explain the rest of the task to pupils. Tell them to underline the words in the letter which give them the answers. Allow them enough time to complete the task alone. Go round the class encouraging and helping pupils where necessary.

- Check answers. Write them on the board if necessary.

Answers
1 nine (given)
2 Lina
3 baby
4 friends

C Look and learn.

- Read out the dialogue and ask pupils to repeat.

- Ask pupils to look at the grammar box. Read out the grammar notes and sentences. Ask pupils to repeat. Explain the meaning of the notes.

- Ask pupils to circle the person and underline the verb in the grammar sentences. Ask volunteers to read out the sentences.

- Practise the grammar. Write these sentences on the board.
  John and I ___ nice. We ___ nice.
  Ask volunteers to write the long version in the first sentence and the short version in the second sentence.
  Do the same with these sentences.
  You and Sally ___ nice. You ___ nice.
  Dogs ___ nice. They ___ nice.
  Read out the sentences and ask pupils to repeat.

Extension activity

Ask two girls to stand at the front of the class. Tell them to point to themselves and say *We're girls*. Ask two boys to do the same for *We're boys*.
Ask one pupil to point to another pupil and say *You're cool!*
Repeat with one pupil pointing to two other pupils. Encourage pupils to think up their own sentences: eg *You're nice.*
They're fantastic boys.
We're great!

D Write We're, You're or They're.

- Read out the example and ask pupils why *We're* is the correct answer.

- Explain the task to pupils. Read out the sentences. Check pupils remember the meanings of all the words. Allow them enough time to complete the task alone.

- Check answers. If necessary write the answers on the board.

Answers
1 We're (given)
2 They're
3 You're
4 We're

E Say.

- Read out the dialogue. Read it out again and ask pupils to repeat.

- Ask two volunteers to read out the dialogue.

- Write *England* on the board and explain the meaning. Ask pupils where they are from. Write the countries the pupils say on the board. Read out the countries and ask pupils to repeat.

- Tell pupils to work in pairs. Explain that they have to change the words in orange and then act out the dialogue. Go round the class helping where necessary.

- Ask pupils to stand at the front of the class and perform their dialogues.

F Draw and write.

- Tell pupils to draw a picture of themselves in the box.
- Read out the sentences and ask pupils what they should write in the gaps.
- Tell pupils to complete the task. Help pupils with spelling where necessary.
- Ask pupils to hold up their books and to show each other their pictures. Ask volunteers to read out their work.

Homework

- Activity Book, pages 18-19: Time permitting, some tasks can be done in class.
- Dictation: *best friend, grandma, grandpa, great, nice*
- Revision for Test 1:
  Words: baby, *elephant, fly, mum, photo, fantastic, brother, sister, family, dad, house, igloo, cool, best friend, grandma, grandpa, great, nice*
  Grammar: *a, an, to be* affirmative

Revision for Test 1

- Revise the words from the flashcards and the magazine pictures. Then write the words on the board. Ask a volunteer to read out a word and come and choose the corresponding flashcard or magazine picture. Practise until all pupils remember the words well.
- Write *fantastic, cool, great* and *nice* on the board. Ask pupils to tell you the meanings. Ask volunteers to think up sentences for the words.
- Write *a* and *an* on the board. Ask pupils to tell you words that go with *a* or *an*. Ask volunteers to write the words on the board. Help with spelling where necessary.
- Write *I am* on the board. Ask pupils to tell you the short version. Write *I'm* next to *I am*. Do the same with all the persons of *to be*. Then rub out some words eg *is* from *He is*. Ask volunteers to write the missing words back on the board.

Teacher's Note

Pupils will do Test 1 in the following lesson. If you don't want to rush into Unit 2, for the rest of the lesson do these activities:

1 Pupils can read out the cartoon story from Unit 1 Lesson 1. Then ask volunteers to act out the cartoon story.
2 Pupils can read out the text from Lesson 2 and the letter from Lesson 3.
3 Repeat the *Say* task from Lesson 3.
4 Sing the song.
5 Play hangman.

Extra Activity

- Play hangman with the new words from Unit 1. NB. As pupils tend to all shout out at the same time for games, make it clear to them that to gain points in this game only one pupil from each team is allowed to speak at a time. To make this easier, the pupil speaking in each team should stand up when it is his or her turn.
- Divide the class into two teams. Hand out word cards to each team. A pupil from team 1 chooses a word and writes the first letter on the board. The remaining letters are lines. The pupil says to team 2 *Spell, please.* and a pupil from team 2 calls out a letter. Pupils take it in turns to call out letters until they find the word. If team 2 finds the word, they get 1 point.
- The game continues with team 2 choosing a word. The team with the most points at the end wins.

Lesson 1 Trek's reporters in Africa

Aims

- Learn and use new vocabulary: *camera, big, small, lion, giraffe, tall, short, funny, Let's go.*
- Learn and use new grammar: plural *s*

Materials

- A camera, magazine or Internet pictures of a lion and a giraffe
- Masks: Ty, Mia, Leo

Lead-in

- Revise the family words from Unit 1. Ask pupils to tell you the family words they remember. Ask volunteers to write them on the board.
- Revise the affirmative *to be*. Write *I'm fantastic.* on the board. Read out the sentence and ask pupils to repeat. Then write *You _____* on the board and ask a volunteer to make a sentence e.g. *You're great.* Write the sentence on the board, read it out and ask pupils to repeat. Do the same with *he, she, it, we, you* and *they*.
- Check homework. Tell pupils to open their Activity Books at pages 18 and 19. Ask volunteers to read out their answers. Ask volunteers to come to the front of the class and to read out the paragraph in task E. Then quickly check all pupils' books.
- Test dictation: *best friend, grandma, grandpa, great, nice.* See the teacher's introduction pages 7-9 for teaching suggestions. Go round the class and check all pupils' dictation.

Episode outline

Africa: Episode 2

The reporters are still on safari in Africa. They see two lions and get scared so they drive off quickly. They, then, see a giraffe and its baby, and some monkeys. Ty likes a small monkey he sees and wants to take a photo of it. But a naughty monkey behind him snatches the camera and runs off with it.

New vocabulary

- Teach *camera*. Hold up the camera and say *Look! A camera.* Ask pupils to repeat. Revise *monkey*. Write *Mm* on the board and ask pupils to remember the word they learnt with *Mm* in the introduction. Teach *giraffe* and *lion* with the pictures.
- Teach *big, small* and *tall, short.* Draw a small ball on the board and a big ball. Point to the small ball and say *small* and then to the big ball and say *big.* Ask pupils to repeat after you. Then ask pupils in L1 if a giraffe is short or tall. Teach *tall* and ask pupils to repeat. Draw a tall boy on the board and a short boy.

Point to the tall boy and say *Look! A tall boy.* Ask pupils to repeat. Then point to the short boy and teach short. Say *Look! A short boy.* And ask pupils to repeat.

- Tell pupils to open their books at page 32 and to look at the vocabulary box. Hold up your book and point to the first picture word. Say the word and ask pupils to repeat. Do the same with all the words. Then read out the new picture words in the vocabulary box in random order and ask pupils to point to the correct pictures.
- Read out the word *funny.* Explain the meaning. Then laugh and say *funny* and ask pupils to repeat. Ask volunteers to stand at the front, laugh and say *funny.* Read out the phrase *Let's go.* Explain the meaning. Ask two volunteers to stand at the front, say to them *Let's go.* and beckon them to follow you out the door. Ask more volunteers to do the same and practise *Let's go.*
- Read out all the words again one by one and ask pupils to repeat after you.

A Listen and read.

For teachers using the DVD

- Make sure each pupil has a copy of the DVD worksheet found on page 128.
- Please follow the procedure outlined in Unit 1, Lesson 1 on page 31 for teachers using the DVD.

Before you watch

Answers
1 They're in Africa.
2 There are two lions behind them.

While you watch

Answers
1 big
2 small
3 tall
4 short
5 funny

After you watch

Answers
1 two
2 big
3 two giraffes and four monkeys
4 the monkeys
5 Ty's camera

For teachers using the audio CD 1.43

- Tell pupils to look at the cartoon story on page 32. Say a character's name and ask pupils to point to the correct character. Do the same with *lion* and *giraffe.*
- Play the recording. Tell pupils to look at the pictures and follow the speech bubbles with their fingers.
- Play the recording again. Pause after each speech bubble and ask pupils to repeat.

- Check pupils understand the story. Use L1 where necessary.
  How many lions are there? (two)
  Are the lions big or small? (big)
  What animals do they see next? (two giraffes and four monkeys)
  Which animals are funny? (the monkeys)
  What does the small monkey take? (Ty's camera)
- Play the recording again. Then ask volunteers to read out the story.
- Assign characters to volunteers and ask them to act out the story in front of the class. Pupils can wear the character masks.

B Look and learn.

- Read out the dialogue. Read it out again and ask pupils to repeat.
- Ask pupils to look at the grammar box. Explain that we put an *s* on the end of a word if we have more than one. Read out the words in the grammar box and ask pupils to repeat.
- Ask pupils to circle the plural word in the dialogue. Ask volunteers to read out the dialogue.
- Ask a boy to stand at the front. Say *Look. A boy.* and ask pupils to repeat. Then ask another boy to stand next to the first boy and say *Look. Two boys.* Ask pupils to repeat. Then do the same with one girl and two girls. Ask volunteers to draw one and then two things on the board using words they remember from the introduction and describe what they draw in singular and plural eg *an egg, two eggs*. Prompt pupils where necessary.

Extension activity

Revise *a* and *an* with the class. Ask pupils to remember which letters go with *an*. Then ask volunteers to say some words they know which start with *a e i o u* and write them on the board.

C Circle.

- Read out the example and ask pupils why *lion* is the correct answer.
- Explain the rest of the task to pupils. Allow them enough time to complete the task alone. Go round the class helping pupils where necessary.
- Check answers. Write them on the board if necessary.

Answers
1 lion (given)
2 giraffes
3 camera
4 girl
5 boys

Say it! 📀1.44

- Write *s* and *sh* on the board. Ask pupils to say the names of letters.

- Explain that the letters *sh* do not make the same sound as *s* on its own. Pronounce *s* and show pupils that your tongue is right behind your front teeth. Ask pupils to practise the *s* sound with you. Then pronounce *sh* and show pupils that your tongue moves further back into your mouth. Ask pupils to practise the *sh* sound with you.
- Tell pupils to look at the task. Play the first part of the recording (Listen and say.) asking pupils to repeat the words *sister* and *short* each time they hear them (*Sister* and *short* will be heard twice.)
- Ask for volunteers to read out *six* and *she*. Play the recording and ask all pupils to repeat (*Six* and *she* will be heard once.)

D Sing. 📀1.45

- Tell pupils they are going to learn a song. Explain to pupils that the song is about people being the same and that it doesn't matter if you are tall or short, or a boy or a girl.
- Ask pupils to look at the picture and describe what they can see. Encourage them to use English for words they know. Hold up your book and point to the *Mum*. Ask a volunteer to say the word. Do the same for the *Dad, boy* and *girl*. Ask pupils to find a short person and a tall person. Ask pupils to count the boys and girls and revise the plural *s*.
- Play the recording and tell pupils to listen and follow the words with their fingers.
- Read out the song one line at a time and ask pupils to repeat after you.
- Play the recording again. Encourage pupils to sing along. Practise many times until pupils are familiar with the words.
- Ask pupils to stand up, join hands in a circle. Tell them to walk round and round as they sing the song.

Homework

- Pupil's Audio CD: Pupils listen to the text and the song at home. Explain to pupils that they should listen to tracks 15 and 16 on the CD.
- Activity Book, pages 20-21: Time permitting, some tasks can be done in class.
- Dictation: *camera, giraffe, lion, big, small, tall, short*

Lesson 2   Toys are fun.

Aims

- Learn and use new vocabulary: *ball, computer game, skateboard, toy, fun*
- Learn and use new grammar: *to be* negative

Materials

- Flashcards: ball, computer game, skateboard, toy

Lead-in

- Revise the words from Lesson 1. Ask pupils to remember the three animals (*lion, giraffe, monkey*) that the reporters saw in the last episode.

- Write *one lion* on the board. Then write *Two* _____ on the board. Ask pupils to tell you what word (lions) to write in the space. Read out the two phrases and ask pupils to repeat.

- Check homework. Tell pupils to open their Activity Books at pages 20 and 21. Ask volunteers to read out their answers. Ask volunteers to come to the front of the class and to read out the paragraph in task E. Then quickly check all pupils' books.

- Test dictation: *camera, giraffe, lion, big, small, tall, short*. See the teacher's introduction pages 7-9 for teaching suggestions. Go round the class and check all pupils' dictation.

- Sing the song from Lesson 1. (CD1.45)

New vocabulary

- Teach the new words with the flashcards. See the teacher's introduction pages 7-9 for teaching suggestions.

- Tell pupils to open their books at page 34 and to look at the vocabulary box. Hold up your book and point to the first picture word. Say the word and ask pupils to repeat. Do the same with all the words. Then read out the new picture words in the vocabulary box in random order and ask pupils to point to the correct pictures.

- Read out the word *fun*. Explain the meaning. Then point to the skateboard in the word box and say *Skateboards are fun!* and ask pupils to repeat. Do the same with the other toys and ask pupils to repeat. Ask volunteers to stand at the front of the class, and do the same with any toy they like.

- Read out all the words again one by one and ask pupils to repeat after you.

A Listen and read. 🔊1.46

- Ask pupils to remember the word they learnt for *Rr* in the introduction. Elicit *robot* and ask a volunteer to write it on the board. Ask pupils to find toys they now know in the pictures. Ask them to raise their hands, show the class the picture and say the word e.g. *Look! A _____* .

- Play the recording. Tell pupils to follow the text with their fingers.

- Play the recording again. Pause after each sentence and ask pupils to repeat.

- Play the recording again. Then ask volunteers to read out a sentence each of the text.

Extension activity

- Choose the *ball* flashcard and hold it up. Then talk about it:
  A ball is fun. Balls are good for boys and girls.

- Ask a volunteer to come to the front and choose a flashcard. Then ask the volunteer to say two things about the toy he/she has chosen. Make sure all pupils have a turn. Encourage pupils to use new vocabulary that they have learnt. Prompt pupils where necessary.

B Match.

- Read the example to pupils. Ask them to find the word *robot* and the phrase *It's a robot*.

- Explain the rest of the task to pupils. Tell them to underline the words in the text which give them the answers. Allow them enough time to complete the task alone. Go round the class encouraging and helping pupils where necessary.

- Check answers. Write them on the board if necessary.

Answers
1 picture 4 (given)
2 picture 1
3 picture 2
4 picture 3

C Look and learn.

- Read out Chris' line. Read it out again and ask pupils to repeat.

- Ask pupils to look at the grammar box. Read out the grammar notes and sentences. Ask pupils to repeat. Explain the meaning of the notes.

- Ask pupils to circle the person and underline the verb in the grammar sentences. Ask volunteers to read out the sentences.

- Practise the grammar. Write sentences on the board with the verb missing. Ask pupils to fill in the gaps.
  I ___ cool.
  He ___ a girl.
  They ___ boys.

D Write 'm not, aren't or isn't.

- Read out the example and ask pupils why *isn't* is the correct answer.

- Explain the task to pupils. Check that pupils remember the meanings of all the words. Allow them enough time to complete the task alone. Go round the class helping pupils where necessary.

- Check answers. Write them on the board if necessary.

Answers
1 isn't (given)
2 isn't
3 aren't
4 'm not
5 aren't

E Listen and number. 1.47

- Tell pupils to look at the pictures for this task. Revise *tall* and *short*. Ask pupils to point to a tall boy. Say *He's a tall boy.* and ask pupils to repeat. Then say *He isn't short.* and ask pupils to repeat. Revise *big* and *small* in the same way with the dog. Hold up your book and point to the two girls. Say *They aren't sisters.* and elicit *They're best friends.* from pupils.

- Explain to pupils that they will hear someone talk about only one of the pictures. Explain that they must write the numbers 1 to 5 under the correct pictures. Play the recording for the example. Make sure pupils understand what to do.

- Play the rest of the recording, pausing where necessary. Play the recording again and ask pupils to check their answers.

Listening script
1 He isn't short. He isn't a baby. He's ten years old.
2 She isn't ten. She's three years old. She is short.
3 He isn't my dad. He isn't tall. He's cool.
4 We aren't sisters. We're best friends. We're cool.
5 It isn't big. It isn't a tiger. It's small.

Answers
1 4th picture (given)
2 1st picture
3 3rd picture
4 5th picture
5 2nd picture

F Say.

- Tell pupils that this is a guessing game. Explain that a pupil describes one of the characters in the picture without saying the name. The other pupils then guess who it is. Read out the names of the characters and ask pupils to repeat. Then read out the example and ask pupils to repeat.

- Ask volunteers to read out the example. Then ask volunteers to make their own sentences. You could write these words on the board to help if necessary:

big	short
tall	funny
small	boy
girl	dog
monkey	

- Ask pairs to come to the front of the class and do the task.

Extension activity

Ask three volunteers to stand at the front of the class. Tell pupils you are going to describe one of them and that they must guess who it is. Use the positive and negative of *to be* eg *He is nine years old. He isn't a girl. He isn't short.* Repeat the activity until all pupils have taken part.

Homework

- Pupil's Audio CD: Pupils listen to the text at home. Explain to pupils that they should listen to track 17 on the CD.

- Activity Book, pages 22-23: Time permitting, some tasks can be done in class.

- Dictation: *ball, computer game, skateboard, toy, fun*

Lesson 3   Happy birthday!

Aims
- Learn and use new vocabulary: *birthday cake, party, present, teddy bear, happy, Happy Birthday!*
- Learn and use new grammar: *to be* interrogative

Materials
- Flashcards: ball, computer, skateboard, toy
- A teddy bear in a gift bag
- Optional for extra activity: photocopies of ten by ten square grid for pupils to make wordsearches.

Lead-in
- Revise the words from Lesson 2 with the flashcards. Stick the flashcards on the board, call out a word and ask a volunteer to come to the board and point to the correct flashcard.

- Write *I'm, you are, he is, we are, they are* on the board. Ask pupils to tell you the opposite of these verbs. Change the verbs on the board as pupils tell you. Then ask pupils to make sentences with the verbs. eg *I'm not a girl. He isn't short. We aren't sisters.* Prompt pupils where necessary.

- Check homework. Tell pupils to open their Activity Books at pages 22 and 23. Ask volunteers to read out their answers. Ask volunteers to write their answers for task C on the board. Then quickly check all pupils' books.

- Test dictation: *ball, computer game, skateboard, toy, fun.* See the teacher's introduction pages 7-9 for teaching suggestions. Go round the class and check all pupils' dictation.

New vocabulary
- Teach *birthday cake, party,* and *present.* Write *Party!* on the board. Read it out and ask pupils to repeat. Ask pupils when we have parties. When a pupil suggests birthdays, ask the class what things we have at birthdays. Elicit *present* and *birthday cake.* Draw simple pictures of these on the board, say *present* and *birthday cake* and ask pupils to repeat. Ask pupils how they feel at birthdays and elicit *happy.* Smile widely and say *I'm happy.* Ask pupils to copy you and repeat.

- Consolidate *present* and teach *teddy bear.* Hold up the gift bag for pupils to see. Ask them to tell you what this is and elicit *present.* Ask them to guess what the present might be. Encourage them to use English words they know eg *computer game, ball, car,* etc. Then slowly pull the teddy bear out of the gift bag and say *Look! A teddy bear.* Say *teddy bear* again and ask pupils to repeat.

- Tell pupils to open their books at page 36 and to look at the word box. Hold up your book and point to the first picture word. Say the word and ask pupils to repeat. Do the same with all the words. Then read out the new picture words in the vocabulary box in random order and ask pupils to point to the correct pictures.

- Read out the words *Happy Birthday*! Ask pupils when we say this to someone. Ask two volunteers to stand at the front of the class. One pupil hands the teddy bear in the gift bag to the other pupil saying *Happy Birthday!*. The other pupil can reply *Thanks.*
- Read out all the words again one by one and ask pupils to repeat after you.

A Read.

- Tell pupils to look at the photo. Ask them to tell you in English what they can see. Elicit *boy, girl* and *birthday cake*.
- Tell pupils to read the first two lines of the dialogue to find out whose birthday it is.
- Tell pupils to now read the rest of the dialogue to themselves. Allow them enough time to finish. Then ask what present Tina gave Jamie (a robot).
- Read out the dialogue. Pause after each sentence and ask pupils to repeat.
- Ask volunteers to read out a sentence each of the dialogue.

Extension activity

Pupils can perform a dialogue in pairs based on the one in their books. They can read from their books, but they must change the name and the present they are going to give. Give the pairs a few minutes to decide what present they are going to give, and then ask them to perform their dialogues in front of the class.

B Match.

- Read the example to pupils. Ask them to find that part of the dialogue and to point to it.
- Explain the rest of the task to pupils. Tell them to underline the words in the dialogue which give them the answers. Allow them enough time to complete the task alone. Go round the class encouraging and helping pupils where necessary.
- Check answers. Write them on the board if necessary.

Answers
1 Happy Birthday Jamie. Thanks. (given)
2 Is it a teddy bear? No, it isn't.
3 Thank you. You're welcome.
4 Are you happy? Yes, I am.

C Look and learn.

- Read out the dialogue and ask pupils to repeat. Ask pupils why *Chris isn't OK* (he ate a lot of birthday cake).
- Draw a question mark on the board. Tell pupils that this is the sign we put at the end of a question in English. Show pupils how to draw a question mark and tell them to copy with their fingers in the air. Then ask them to write five question marks in their notebooks. In addition ask a few volunteers to do the same on the board.

- Ask pupils to look at the grammar box. Read out the grammar notes and sentences. Ask pupils to repeat. Explain the meaning of the notes.
- Ask pupils to circle the person and underline the verb in the grammar sentences. Ask volunteers to read out the sentences.
- Further explain the grammar. Write *You are happy.* on the board. Then underneath write *Are you happy?* Ask pupils to tell you what things have changed to make the question. Help them to see that the verb goes to the beginning of the sentence and the full stop changes to a question mark.
- Practise the grammar. Write these sentences on the board and ask volunteers to change them into questions.
  He is tall.
  They are boys.
  Then use these questions to elicit answers. Ask a pupil *Are you happy?* and elicit a short answer. Do the same with *Is he tall?* and *Are they boys?* using volunteers to help.

D Match.

- Read out the example and ask pupils why *Is it a yellow quilt?* matches the answer *Yes, it is.* Help them work out that the word *it* is the key to finding the answer. Tell them the person or thing in the question must match what is in the answer. Give them some examples:
  Sally = she
  boys = they
  you = I
  I = you
  you = we
- Explain the task to pupils. Read out the sentences. Check pupils remember the meanings of all the words. Do the task as a class, making sure all pupils understand which questions match which answers.
- Check answers. Write them on the board if necessary.

Answers
1 Is it a yellow quilt? Yes, it is. (given)
2 Are zebras big? Yes, they are.
3 Am I short? No, you aren't.
4 Are you ten? Yes, we are.
5 Is Bill tall? No, he isn't.

E Say.

- Tell pupils they are going to role play mini dialogues like the one they did to practise *Happy Birthday!*
- Revise *Here you are.* and *You're welcome.* Hand a pencil to a pupil saying *Here you are.* Encourage the pupil to reply *Thanks.* and reply *You're welcome.* Ask pupils to repeat the dialogue after you.
- Read out the dialogue. Read it out again and ask pupils to repeat.
- Ask two volunteers to read out the dialogue.

- Ask pairs to stand at the front of the class and act out mini dialogues like the one in their books, changing the words in orange (the names and the present). Use the flashcards as presents. Go round the class helping where necessary.

F Draw and write.

- Tell pupils to draw a picture of a toy they have learnt in the vocabulary box.
- Explain that they should then write the word for the toy underneath their picture.
- Tell pupils to complete the task. Help pupils with spelling where necessary.
- Ask pupils to hold up their books and to show each other their pictures. Ask volunteers to read out their work.

Homework

- Activity Book, pages 24-25: Time permitting, some tasks can be done in class.
- Dictation: *birthday cake, party, present, teddy bear, happy. Happy Birthday!*
- Revision for Test 2:
  Words: *camera, giraffe, lion, big, small, tall, short, funny, Let's go. ball, computer game, skateboard, toy, fun, birthday cake, party, present, teddy bear, happy. Happy Birthday!*
  Grammar: plural *s, to be* negative and interrogative

Teacher's Note

Pupils will do Test 2 in the following lesson. If you don't want to rush into Unit 3, for the rest of the lesson do these activities:

1 Pupils can read out the cartoon story from Unit 2 Lesson 1. Then ask volunteers to act out the cartoon story.
2 Pupils can read out the text from Lesson 2 and the dialogue from Lesson 3.
3 Repeat the *Say* task from Lesson 3.
4 Sing the song.
5 Play hangman.
6 Revise the alphabet with the alphabet poster.

Optional activity

Revision for Test 2

- Revise the toy words. Write *toys* on the board and ask volunteers to call out the words they remember and then write them on the board. Ask a volunteer to read out a word and come and choose the corresponding flashcard. Practise until all pupils remember the words well.
- Write *party* on the board. Ask pupils to tell you party words they know. Write them on the board. Revise *camera* here too as a possible present. Do the same for animal words.
- Draw a small ball and big ball on the board. Revise *small* and *big*. Do the same with *short* and *tall* with stick figures.
- Revise *funny, fun, happy* and *Let's go*. Do these actions and encourage pupils to copy.
- Laugh and say *funny*.
  Smile and say *Parties are fun! I'm happy!* Choose a volunteer, open the classroom door and say *Let's go.* and leave the room.
- Write *toy* and *toys* on the board. Ask pupils to tell you the word for more than one toy and why.
- Write *I am* on the board. Ask pupils to tell you the opposite. Write *I'm not*. Do the same with all the persons for *to be*. Then rub out some words eg *isn't* from *He isn't*. Ask volunteers to write the missing words back on the board.

Extra Activity

- Pupils can make their own wordsearches with the words from Unit 2. Hand out a grid of ten squares by ten squares to each pupil. Show them how to fill in the grid with eight of the words they like from Unit 2. Tell them to use capital letters. Go round the class helping with spelling where necessary. Then tell pupils to fill in the other boxes with any letters they like.
- Pupils can swap wordsearches and then find each other's words.

3

Lesson 1   Trek's reporters in Africa

Aims

- Learn and use new vocabulary: *bird, whale, mountain, ostrich, penguin, beach*
- Learn and use new grammar: *this is, that is, that's*

Materials

- Flashcards: beach, bird, mountain, ostrich, penguin, whale
- 10 pencils
- One piece of blank paper for each pupil
- Masks: Ty, Mia, Leo

Lead-in

- Revise the party and toy words from Unit 2. Ask pupils to tell you the party words they remember. Ask volunteers to write them on the board. Then under *present* write a list of the toys. Ask volunteers to draw a picture of the toy next to each word. Read out the toys one at a time and ask pupils to raise their hands for their favourite toy on the list.

- Revise the negative and interrogative of *to be*. Ask a boy to stand up and look sad. Ask pupils *Is he happy?* and elicit answer *No, he isn't.* Say *He isn't happy.* and ask pupils to repeat. Then ask the boy *Are you happy?* and elicit answer *No, I'm not.* Say *I'm not happy.* and ask pupils to repeat. Do the same with two volunteers. Ask them to stand up and look sad. Ask pupils *Are they happy?* And elicit answer *No, they aren't.* Say *They aren't happy.* and ask pupils to repeat. Then ask the volunteers *Are you happy?* And elicit answer *No, we aren't.* Say *We aren't happy.* And ask pupils to repeat. Finally ask all pupils to look happy. Ask them *Are you happy?* and elicit answer *Yes, we are.* Then ask pupils one at a time and elicit answer *Yes, I am.*

- Revise the plural *s* and the numbers *1-10.* Hold up a pencil and say *one pencil.* Ask pupils to repeat. Then hold up two pencils and ask volunteers to say what they can see: *two pencils.* Make sure pupils remember the *s.* Do the same up to ten.

- Check homework. Tell pupils to open their Activity Books at pages 24 and 25. Ask volunteers to read out their answers. Ask pupils two at a time to come to the front of the class and to read out the questions and answers in task C. Then quickly check all pupils' books.

- Test dictation: *birthday cake, party, present, teddy bear, happy, Happy birthday!* See the teacher's introduction pages 7-9 for teaching suggestions. Go round the class and check all pupils' dictation.

Episode outline

Africa: Episode 3

The reporters are finishing their safari trip in Africa. A monkey took Ty's camera in episode 2, but an ostrich gives it back to him in episode 3. The reporters then go to the coast and see a big mountain (Table Mountain) and a penguin on the beach. Then a big whale jumps out of the sea. Here the episode ends and the reporters say goodbye to Trek. Trek liked the DVD and thinks Africa is cool.

Background information

Table Mountain is a flat-topped mountain which overlooks the city of Cape Town in South Africa. The mountain has been named Table Mountain because of a flat plateau that extends about 3 kilometres from side to side. Its highest point is 1,086m above sea level and it offers spectacular views. The mountain is part of the Table Mountain National Park which also includes the Cape of Good Hope. It is a significant tourist attraction with many visitors who use a cable car or hike to the top of Table Mountain. More than 16 million people have taken the trip to the top using the cable car since its opening in 1929.

New vocabulary

- Teach the new words with the flashcards. See the teacher's introduction pages 7-9 for teaching suggestions.

- Tell pupils to open their books at page 38 and to look at the vocabulary box. Hold up your book and point to the first picture word. Say the word and ask pupils to repeat. Do the same with all the words. Then read out the new picture words in the vocabulary box in random order and ask pupils to point to the correct pictures.

- Read out all the words again one by one and ask pupils to repeat after you.

A Listen and read.

For teachers using the DVD

- Make sure each pupil has a copy of the DVD worksheet found on page 129.

- Please follow the procedure outlined in Unit 1, Lesson 1 on page 31 for teachers using the DVD.

Before you watch

Answers
1 An ostrich gave it back to him.
2 They are on a beach.

While you watch

Answers
a	5	e	1
b	8	f	3
c	4	g	7
d	2	h	6

After you watch

For teachers using the audio CD **1.48**

- Tell pupils to look at the cartoon story. Ask pupils to look at the first frame and tell you what kind of bird they can see. Ask them *if an ostrich is big or small*. Do the same in the second frame with *penguin*.

- Play the recording. Tell pupils to look at the pictures and follow the speech bubbles with their fingers.

- Play the recording again. Pause after each speech bubble and ask pupils to repeat.

- Check pupils understand the story. Use L1 where necessary.
  What has the ostrich found? (Ty's camera)
  Is the mountain big or small? (big)
  Which three animals do they see? (an ostrich, a penguin and a whale)
  Which animals are big? (the ostrich and the whale)
  What does Trek say about Africa? (It's cool.)

- Play the recording again. Then ask volunteers to read out the story.

- Assign characters to volunteers and ask them to act out the story in front of the class. Pupils can wear the character masks.

Extra activity

- Listen again to all three episodes of the mini story. Play the recordings from Lesson 1 of Units 1, 2 and 3. Ask pupils to follow the speech bubbles with their fingers.

- Divide the class into three groups, one group for each episode. Assign roles to pupils in each group. Then ask each group to act out their episode in front of the class. Pupils can wear the character masks.

B Look and learn.

- Read out the dialogue. Read it out again and ask pupils to repeat.

- Ask pupils to look at the grammar box. Explain that we use *this* when something is close to us and *that* when something is far away. Read out the words in the grammar box and ask pupils to repeat. Explain to pupils that when we speak we can say *that's* instead of *that is*.

- Ask pupils to circle the *this* and *that* in the dialogue. Ask volunteers to read out the dialogue.

- Hold up the flashcard of the ostrich and say *This is an ostrich*. Ask pupils to repeat. Then place the flashcard at the back of the classroom, return to the front and point to the flashcard. Say *That's an ostrich*. and ask pupils to repeat. Repeat with

the *whale* flashcard. Ask volunteers to choose a flashcard and make a sentence with *This is* and a sentence with *That's* in the same way.

C Write This or That.

- Tell pupils to look at the picture for number 1 and ask them what they can see. Ask them if the ostrich is close to the boy or far away. Read out the example and ask pupils why *That* is the correct answer.

- Explain the rest of the task to pupils. Allow them enough time to complete the task alone. Go round the class helping pupils where necessary.

- Ask volunteers to read out their answers.

Say it! **1.49**

- Write *c* on the board. Ask pupils to say the name of this letter. Then ask them to remember the word they learnt for *c* in the introduction. Write *car* on the board. Ask pupils to pronounce the sound for *c* in *car*. Then write *beach* on the board and read it out. Ask pupils if the *c* in this word makes the same sound as the *c* in *car*. Circle *ch* and explain to pupils that when a *c* is with an *h* they make the sound *ch*.

- Pronounce *c* and show pupils that the sound comes from the back of your mouth. Ask pupils to practise the *c* sound with you. Then pronounce *ch* and ask pupils to practise the *ch* sound with you.

- Tell pupils to look at the task. Play the first part of the recording (Listen and say.) asking pupils to repeat the words *beach* and *camera* each time they hear them. (*Beach* and *camera* will be heard twice.)

- Ask for volunteers to read out *ostrich* and *octopus*. Play the recording and ask all pupils to repeat. (*Ostrich* and *octopus* will be heard once.)

D Listen and write. **1.50**

- Tell pupils that this task practises their spelling. Explain that they are going to listen to a boy and a girl talking about different animals and that they will hear how the animal words are spelt. They must listen carefully and fill in the missing letters in their books.

- Play the recording for the example. Make sure pupils understand what to do.

- Play the rest of the recording, pausing between questions where necessary. Play the recording again and ask pupils to check their answers.

Listening script

1
Is it a small bird?
No, it isn't. It's an ostrich.
Spell it, please.
O-S-T-R-I-C-H

2
It isn't a big bird.
Is it a penguin?
Yes, it is. Spell it, please.
P-E-N-G-U-I-N

3
Is it big?
Yes, it is. It's an elephant.
Spell it, please.
E-L-E-P-H-A-N-T

4
Is it small?
No, it isn't. It's a whale.
Spell it, please.
W-H-A-L-E

5
It's tall.
Is it a giraffe?
Yes, it is. Spell it, please.
G-I-R-A-F-F-E

Answers

1 ostrich (given)
2 penguin
3 elephant
4 whale
5 giraffe

Extension activity

- Ask a volunteer to look at the introduction pages and to choose a word. Ask another volunteer to stand at the board. The first volunteer spells the word he/she has chosen and the second volunteer writes the word on the board.

E Say.

- Read out the example and ask pupils to repeat. Ask pupils why the boy uses *this* and why the girl says *that*.

- Hand out a piece of paper to each pupil. Ask them to choose something from the introduction and to draw it on their pieces of paper. When pupils are ready, ask them one at a time to hold up their drawings and to say what they are, eg *This is a frog.*

- Ask pairs to come to the front of the class and stand apart at a small distance. Ask the first pupil to hold up his/her drawing and say *This is a _____* . Then ask the second pupil to point to the drawing and say *That is a _____* . Then the pupils swap and talk about the second pupil's drawing. Continue the task until all pupils have had a turn.

Homework

- Pupil's Audio CD: Pupils listen to the text at home. Explain to pupils that they should listen to track 18 on the CD.

- Activity Book, pages 26-27: Time permitting, some tasks can be done in class.

- Dictation: *beach, bird, mountain, ostrich, penguin, whale*

- Optional extra homework: Ask pupils to draw a picture of any of the new words they have learnt from Units 1 and 2. They should write *This is a _____* . and the correct word under the drawing. Next lesson they can practise spelling and *this* and *that* with their drawing. The drawings can be displayed on the wall.

Lesson 2   These animals are small.

Aims

- Learn and use new vocabulary: *lizard, food, hungry, animals, meerkat, snake*

- Learn and use new grammar: *these are / those are*

Materials

- Flashcards: beach, bird, mountain, ostrich, penguin, whale

- Magazine or Internet pictures of a lizard, a snake and a meerkat

- Optional for Extra activity: make 10 animal word cards with the words written clearly on one side: *elephant, dog, snake, lion, penguin, meerkat, bird, tiger, frog, giraffe*

Lead-in

- Revise the words from Lesson 1. Stick the flashcards on the board. Call out the words one at a time and ask volunteers to come to the board and point to the correct flashcard.

- Write *this* and *that* on the board. Ask a volunteer to stand next to a flashcard, touch it and say *This is a _____* . Then ask the same pupil to stand at the back of the classroom, point to the same flashcard and say *That's a _____* .

- Check homework. Tell pupils to open their Activity Books at pages 26 and 27. Ask volunteers to read out their answers. Ask volunteers to come to the front of the class and to read out the paragraph in task E. Then quickly check all pupils' books.

- Test dictation: *beach, bird, mountain, ostrich, penguin, whale* with the flashcards. See the teacher's introduction pages 7-9 for teaching suggestions. Go round the class and check all pupils' dictation.

New vocabulary

- Teach the animal words. Write *animals* on the board and read it out. Explain the meaning to pupils and then ask them to tell you any animals they know in English. Then tell them they are going to learn three new animals. Hold up the lizard picture, say *This is a lizard*. Repeat *lizard* and ask pupils to repeat. Do the same with *snake* and *meerkat*. Explain that a meerkat is a tiny animal that lives in Africa. Ask pupils which character from the mini stories is a meerkat (Mia).

- Teach *food* and *hungry*. Say *I'm hungry*. rub your tummy and then pretend to eat something. Then say *This food is yummy*. Rub your tummy again, say *hungry* and ask pupils to repeat. Then pretend to eat, say *food* and ask pupils to repeat.

- Tell pupils to open their books at page 40 and to look at the vocabulary box. Hold up your book and point to the first picture word. Say the word and ask pupils to repeat. Do the same with all the words. Then read out the new picture words in the vocabulary box in random order and ask pupils to point to the correct pictures.

- Read out all the words again one by one and ask pupils to repeat after you.

Background information

The meerkat or suricate is a small mammal that lives in all parts of the Kalahari Desert in Botswana and South Africa. Meerkats live in large underground burrows with many entrances which they leave only during the day. They are very social animals.
There are usually about 20 meerkats in a meerkat family. But some superfamilies can have 50 meerkats. Baby meerkats are looked after by all the females in the family.
Meerkats weigh an average 731 grams and have got a body length of 25 to 35 cm and a long tail which they use to balance when standing upright. Their fur is usually grey, tan or brown with a silver tint. They have got short parallel stripes across their backs and the patterns of the stripes are unique to each meerkat.
Meerkats search for food in groups with one meerkat on guard watching for predators. Their diet consists of scorpions, beetles, spiders, worms, small mammals, small snakes, birds, eggs and roots.

A Listen and read. 1.51

- Ask pupils to look at the photograph and count the meerkats. Revise the words *brother, sister* and *family*. Write *family* on the board and ask pupils to tell you the family words they know. Write them on the board, and then circle *brother* and *sister*. Ask pupils to find the words *family, brother* and *sister* in the text.

- Play the recording. Tell pupils to follow the text with their fingers.

- Play the recording again. Pause after each sentence and ask pupils to repeat.

- Play the recording again. Then ask volunteers to read out a sentence each of the text.

B Write Yes or No.

- Read the example to pupils. Ask them to find the words in the first two sentences that gives them the answer *Yes*.

- Explain the rest of the task to pupils. Tell them to underline the words in the text which give them the answers. Allow them enough time to complete the task alone. Go round the class encouraging and helping pupils where necessary.

- Check answers. Write them on the board if necessary.

Answers
1 Yes (given)
2 Yes
3 Yes
4 No

Extension activity

- Pupils can make sentences about different animals they have learnt. First ask them to name some animals they have learnt so far.
  eg

dog	*monkey*	*giraffe*
frog	*lion*	*octopus*
elephant	*tiger*	*snake*

  Write the animals on the board. Then make a sentence about the first animal. Eg *Dogs are small*. and *Dogs are big*. Then ask a volunteer to make a sentence about the next animal. Continue around the class until all pupils have had a turn. Prompt pupils where necessary.

C Look and learn.

- Read out the dialogue. Read it out again and ask pupils to repeat. Write *this* and *that* on the board and ask pupils to remember which word we use for something close to us and which word for something far away. Explain to pupils that when we have more than one thing, we use *these* for things close to us and *those* for things far away. Write *these* under *this* and *those* are under *that*. Then ask pupils to look at the dialogue and find which word we use instead of *is* (are).

- Ask pupils to look at the grammar box. Read out the grammar notes and sentences. Ask pupils to repeat. Explain the meaning of the notes.

- Ask pupils to circle *these* and *those* and underline *are* in the grammar sentences. Ask volunteers to read out the sentences.

- Practise the grammar. Stick the animal flashcards on the board. Stand next to them and say *These are animals*. Then walk to the back of the classroom, point to the flashcards and say *Those are animals*. Ask pupils to repeat each time. Then ask volunteers to do the same.

D Circle.

- Read out the example and ask pupils why *These* is the correct answer.

- Explain the task to pupils. Check pupils remember the meanings of all the words. Allow them enough time to complete the task alone. Go round the class helping pupils where necessary.

- Check answers. Write them on the board if necessary.

Extension activity

- Practise *these* and *those* with the words *boys* and *girls*. Ask two girls to stand next to you and say *These girls are nice.* Then move away from the girls and say *Those girls are nice.* Ask volunteers to do the same with words they know:
  eg *These/Those boys are tall.*
  These/Those girls are best friends.
  These/Those boys are funny.

E Sing. 1.52

- Tell pupils they are going to learn a song. Explain to pupils that the song is about animals.

- Ask pupils to look at the picture and describe what they can see. Teach *hiss*, *roar* and *wobble*. Say *hiss* and move your arm like a snake. Ask pupils to copy and repeat. Then say *roar* loudly and pretend to be a lion. Ask pupils to copy and repeat. Then say *wobble* and walk like a penguin. Ask pupils to copy and repeat.

- Play the recording and tell pupils to listen and follow the words with their fingers.

- Read out the song one line at a time and ask pupils to repeat after you.

- Play the recording again. Encourage pupils to sing along. Practise many times until pupils are familiar with the words.

- Ask pupils to do the animal actions as they sing the song.

Homework

- Pupil's Audio CD: Pupils listen to the text and the song at home. Explain to pupils that they should listen to tracks 19 and 20 on the CD.

- Activity Book, pages 28-29: Time permitting, some tasks can be done in class.

- Dictation: *animals, food, hungry, lizard, meerkat, snake*

Extra activity

- Write *Are you a _____?* on the board. Then act out that you are a lion. Ask volunteers one at a time to ask you the question on the board and guess what animal you are. Answer *No, I'm not.* until a volunteer finds the animal and then answer *Yes, I am.*

- Ask a volunteer to come to the front of the class. Show him/her an animal word from the word cards you have, but make sure the other pupils can't see the word. Then ask the volunteer to act out the animal. Pupils can ask the question *Are you a _____?* one at a time and the pupil answers accordingly. Continue until all pupils have had a turn.

Lesson 3   What's this?

Aims

- Learn and use new vocabulary: *dolphin, flower, rabbit, shark, tree*

- Learn and use new grammar: *What's this? What's that? It's a _____ . / What are these? What are those? They're _____ .*

Materials

- Magazine or Internet pictures of a dolphin, a shark and a rabbit

- For Extra activity: one blank piece of paper for each pupil.

Lead-in

- Revise the words from Lesson 2. Stick the Internet and magazine pictures of a *snake, lizard* and *meerkat* on the board. Write the words in random order on the board and ask pupils to match the words to the pictures. Then revise *food* and *hungry*. Rub your tummy, say *I'm hungry.* and ask pupils to repeat. Pretend to eat something, say *Yummy food.* and ask pupils to repeat.

- Revise *these* and *those*. Write *these* and *those* on the board. Ask two girls to stand at the front of the class. Ask pupils at the back of the classroom to point to the girls and say which word they should use since the girls are far away. Elicit *those.* Say *Those are girls.* and ask pupils to repeat. Then ask a pupil to stand next to the girls and ask which word he/she should use now. Elicit *these.* Say *These are girls.* and ask pupils to repeat.

- Check homework. Tell pupils to open their Activity Books at pages 28 and 29. Ask volunteers to read out their answers. Then sing the song from Lesson 2.

- Test dictation: *animals, food, hungry, lizard, meerkat, snake.* See the teacher's introduction pages 7-9 for teaching suggestions. Go round the class and check all pupils' dictation.

New vocabulary

- Teach *dolphin, shark* and *rabbit* with the pictures. Hold up the dolphin picture and say *Look. A dolphin.* Ask pupils to repeat. Do the same with *shark* and *rabbit.* Write *Big* and *Small* on the board. Ask pupils which animal is small and write *rabbit* under *Small.*

Ask volunteers to write *shark* and *dolphin* under *Big*. Spell the words for the volunteers. Remind pupils that *ph* makes a sound like *f* and ask them to remember any words they know with *ph* (photo, elephant).

- Draw a tree on the board and say *It's a tree*. Ask pupils to repeat. Then draw a flower on the board and do the same. You can revise some colours here by asking pupils what colour a tree is and what colours flowers can be.

- Tell pupils to open their books at page 42 and to look at the vocabulary box. Hold up your book and point to the first picture word. Say the word and ask pupils to repeat. Do the same with all the words. Then read out the new picture words in the vocabulary box in random order and ask pupils to point to the correct pictures.

- Read out all the words again one by one and ask pupils to repeat after you.

- Hold up your book, point to the first picture and say *What's this?* Ask pupils to repeat the question. Then give the answer *It's a dolphin*. Write *What* on the board and ask pupils if they remember another question they know which starts with this word. Elicit *What's your name?* Help pupils work out the meaning of *What*.

A Read and answer.

- Tell pupils to look at the photo of the boy and read out what he says. Ask pupils if they like quizzes. Explain to pupils that they are going to read one question at a time to themselves and choose what they think is the correct answer.

- Tell pupils to read the first question and to choose an answer. Check answers. Read out the question and ask pupils to repeat. Do the same with the answers.

- Allow pupils enough time to read each question and to choose an answer. Continue with one question at a time and then ask pupils to see how many answers they got right. Read out *What's your score?* and ask pupils to write it in the space provided. Ask pupils what their score is and encourage them to say the number in English.

- Read out the questions and answers again. Stop after each sentence and ask pupils to repeat.

- Ask volunteers to read out a sentence each of the quiz.

Answers
1 b
2 b
3 b
4 b
5 a
6 b

B Circle.

- Ask pupils to look at the picture and ask *What's that?* Elicit *It's a shark*. Do the same with all the pictures. Then explain to pupils that they should read the sentences with the pictures very carefully and circle the correct word to match the picture and the meaning of the sentence.

- Read the example to pupils and ask them to tell you why *dolphin* is circled. Make sure they read the sentence carefully and remember the meaning of *isn't*.

- Explain the rest of the task to pupils. Allow them enough time to complete the task alone. Go round the class helping pupils where necessary.

- Check answers. Write them on the board if necessary.

Answers
1 dolphin (given)
2 giraffe
3 bird
4 tree

C Look and learn.

- Read out the dialogue and ask pupils to repeat.

- Ask pupils to look at the grammar box. Read out the grammar notes and sentences. Ask pupils to repeat. Explain the meaning of the notes.

- Ask pupils to circle the question and underline the answer in the dialogue. Ask volunteers to read out the dialogue.

- Practise the grammar. Hold up the picture of the dolphin and ask *What's this?* Ask a volunteer for the answer and then ask the whole class to repeat the answer *It's a dolphin*. Then stick the picture on the board and move away. Ask *What's that?* Elicit the answer *It's a dolphin*. Now stick the rabbit next to the dolphin and ask pupils to count how many animals there are. Ask them which words to use when they have more than one thing and elicit *these* and *those*. Ask them also what to use in the answer instead of *It's*. Elicit *They're* and the plural *s*. Stand next to the pictures and ask *What are these?* And elicit the answer *They're animals*. Move away from the pictures and say *What are those?* Elicit the answer *They're animals*.

Extension activity

- Ask a volunteer to draw one animal on the board which they have learnt in English. Tell the volunteer to ask *What's this?* and ask for answers from the other pupils. When they find the answer, ask another volunteer to draw two toys (two the same) on the board. Then ask the volunteer to ask *What are these?* and ask for answers from the other pupils. Repeat the task until all pupils have had a turn. Pupils can draw toys, animals, party objects and people.

- Do the task again, but when the volunteer has finished drawing he/she should stand at the back of the room and ask *What's that?/What are those?*. The other pupils should answer accordingly.

D Write.

- Ask pupils to look at the first picture and to tell you if the nests are close or far away (close). Read out the example and ask pupils why *these* complete the question. Then ask them why *They're* is used in the answer. Help them work out that the we use *these* for two or more things which are close, and the answer has to be *They're* because again we are talking about two or more things.

- Explain the task to pupils. Ask pupils to say what they can see in the pictures and if they are close or far away. Allow them enough time to complete the task alone. Go round the class helping where necessary.

- Check answers.

E Say.

- Read out the dialogue to pupils and ask them to repeat.

- Ask a volunteer to draw one animal, which they have learnt in English, on the board. Tell the volunteer to ask *What's this?* and ask for answers from the other pupils. When they find the answer, ask another volunteer to draw two things (two the same) on the board. Then ask the volunteer to ask *What are these?* And ask for answers from the other pupils. Repeat the task until all pupils have had a turn. Pupils can draw toys, animals, nature objects, party objects and people.

- Do the task again, but when the volunteer has finished drawing he/she should stand at the back of the classroom and use *that* or *those*.

F Draw and write.

- Tell pupils to draw a picture of any two things (the same things) they have learnt in the lesson today. Allow them enough time to complete their drawings.

- Ask a volunteer to read out the question. Tell pupils to write the answer for their own pictures on the line. Write *They're* on the board for help. Go round the class helping with spelling if necessary. Remind pupils to use the plural *s*.

- Ask pupils to hold up their books and to show each other their pictures. Ask volunteers to read out their work.

Homework

- Activity Book, pages 30-31: Time permitting, some tasks can be done in class.

- Dictation: *dolphin, rabbit, flower, shark, tree*

- Revision for Test 3:
  Words: *beach, bird, mountain, ostrich, penguin, whale, animals, food, hungry, lizard, meerkat, snake, dolphin, rabbit, flower, shark, tree*
  Grammar: *this is / that is, that's*
  these are / those are
  What's this / that? It's a _____ .
  What are these / those? They're _____ .

Teacher's Note

Pupils will do Test 3 in the following lesson. After every three units there is a review which can be done in the same lesson as the test.

Optional activity

Revision for Test 3

- Revise the animal words. Ask pupils to remember all the animals they learnt in this unit: *bird, ostrich, penguin, whale, animals, lizard, meerkat, snake, dolphin, rabbit, shark.* Ask volunteers to write the words on the board. Read out the words and ask pupils to repeat until all pupils remember the words well.

- Do the same for the nature words: *beach, mountain, flower, tree.*

- Write *food* and *hungry* on the board. Ask volunteers to do actions for *I'm hungry.* and for *Yummy food.*

- Write *this, that, these* and *those* on the board. Hold up one pencil and ask which word you should use. Elicit *this.* Say *This is a pencil.* and ask pupils to repeat. Then place the pencil on the table, walk to the back of the classroom and ask pupils which word you should now use. Elicit *that.* Say *That is a pencil.* and ask pupils to repeat. Do the same with three pencils, first holding them in your hand and then pointing to them from the back of the classroom.

- Write *What* on the board. Hold up one pencil and ask *What's this?* Ask volunteers for the answer. Hold up three pencils and ask *What are these?* Ask volunteers for the answer. Do the same for *What's that?* and *What are those?* But this time ask a pupil to hold up the pencil(s) while you stand at the back of the classroom.

Extra activity

- Hand out blank pieces of paper and ask pupils to draw a picture with four of the things they have learnt so far which they particularly like. As pupils draw, go round the class asking *What's this? What are those?* etc., and encourage pupils to answer in English.

- When pupils have finished their pictures ask them to show their pictures to the class. Encourage them to describe what they have drawn e.g. *This is a frog. / These are cars.*

Let's remember!

Aims

- Revise vocabulary from Units 1-3
- Revise grammar from Units 1-3

Materials

- Flashcards:
  Unit 1: *baby, elephant, fly, mum, photo / brother sister, family, dad, house, igloo*
  Unit 2: *ball, computer game, skateboard, toy*
  Unit 3: *beach, bird, mountain, ostrich, penguin, whale*

Revision

- Revise the words from the flashcards. Hold up a flashcard and ask pupils to call out the word. Stick the flashcard on the board. When all the flashcards are on the board, ask volunteers to come to the board, point to a flashcard of their choice and say the word. Repeat, but when a flashcard has been pointed to, remove it from the board.

- Ask pupils to remember all the animals they have learnt in Units 1-3. They can search the vocabulary boxes at the beginning of each lesson to help them remember. Write the animals on the board, asking pupils to spell the words. Do the same for *family* words and *toys*.

- Revise the *affirmative* and *negative* of *to be*. Write *I'm fantastic.* and *I'm not hungry.* on the board and ask volunteers to read out the sentences. Then write *You _____ fantastic.* and *You _____ hungry.* on the board and ask volunteers to complete the sentences. Do the same with all persons.

- Revise the *interrogative* of *to be*. Ask pupils *Are you fantastic?* and elicit answer *Yes, we are.* Revise all persons. Here are some suggested questions:
  Is he a girl?
  Are they boys?
  Am I tall?
  Are you short?
  Is it funny?

- Revise *this, that, these* and *those*. Hold up a pencil and say *This is a pencil.* Ask pupils to repeat. Then hold up two pencils and say *These are pencils.* Ask pupils to repeat. Then do the same for *that* and *those* from a distance. Next revise *What's this?*, etc with the pencil(s).

Lead-in

- Check homework. Tell pupils to open their Activity Books at pages 30 and 31. Ask volunteers, to read out their answers. Ask volunteers, two at a time, to come to the front of the class and to read out the questions and answer in task E. Then quickly check all pupils' books.

- Test dictation: *dolphin, rabbit, flower, shark, tree.* See the teacher's introduction pages 7-9 for teaching suggestions. Go round the class and check all pupils' dictation.

A Find and stick.

- Ask pupils to open their books at page 44 and to look at task A. Ask volunteers to read out the words. Then read out the words again and ask pupils to repeat as a class.

- Show pupils where to find the stickers in their books. Tell them to remove the stickers one at a time and to stick them in the correct boxes. Allow pupils enough time to stick all the stickers. Go round the class helping pupils where necessary.

- Check answers. Ask volunteers to hold up their books and read out the words.

B Write.

- Tell pupils to look at the crossword. Ask volunteers to tell you the words for each picture. Write the words on the board in capitals asking pupils to spell them.

- Tell pupils to complete the crossword on their own using capitals. Allow them enough time to complete the task alone. Go round the class helping pupils where necessary.

- Check answers.

Answers
1 FLOWER (given)
2 PRESENT
3 IGLOO
4 BABY
5 SKATEBOARD
6 DOLPHIN

Extra activity

- Revise the capital letters of the alphabet. Write the small letters of the alphabet on the board. Ask volunteers to write the capital letters next to the small letters.

- Chant the alphabet together as a class. Then point to different letters in random order and ask volunteers to call them out.

C Circle.

- Read out the example and ask pupils why *tall* is the correct answer. Read out all the sentences and make sure that pupils remember the meanings of all the words.

- Explain the rest of the task to pupils. Allow them enough time to complete the task alone. Go round the class helping pupils where necessary.

- Check answers. Ask volunteers to read out their answers.

Answers

1 tall (given)
2 brothers
3 big
4 cake
5 best friend
6 robot

D Write.

- Read out the example and ask pupils why *is* is the correct answer. Read out all the sentences and make sure that pupils remember the meanings of all the words.

- Explain the rest of the task to pupils. Tell them to cross through a word in the box when they have used it. Allow them enough time to complete the task alone. Go round the class helping pupils where necessary.

- Check answers. Ask volunteers to read out their answers.

Answers

1 is (given)
2 am
3 isn't
4 are
5 is
6 aren't

E Circle.

- Read out the example and ask pupils why *a* is the correct answer. Read out all the sentences and make sure that pupils remember the meanings of all the words.

- Explain the rest of the task to pupils. Allow them enough time to complete the task alone. Go round the class helping pupils where necessary.

- Check answers. Ask volunteers to read out their answers.

Answers

1 a (given)
2 It's
3 girls
4 these
5 an
6 teddy bears

Extension activity

- Ask pupils to remember when we use *a* and when we use *an*. Elicit the vowels and write them on the board *a e i o u*. Ask pupils to say words that begin with these letters.

- Write *She's a girl.* on the board. Read it out. Then write *They're _____ .* and ask a volunteer to finish the sentence. Elicit *girls* and ask pupils which letter we add to a word to show there is more than one. You can practise the plural with the following words from the classroom:
  boy, boys
  pencil, pencils

F Look and match.

- Tell pupils to look at the picture. Hold up your book, point to number 1. Say *one* and ask pupils what they can see. Elicit *a mountain*. Do the same with 2-6.

- Read out the example and ask pupils to repeat. Ask pupils why *It's a mountain.* is the correct answer.

- Explain the rest of the task to pupils. Tell them to look at the pictures and to think carefully about the words in the question which will help them find the answers eg whether we are talking about one or many things. Allow them enough time to complete the task alone. Go round the class helping pupils where necessary.

- Check answers. Ask volunteers to read out their answers.

Answers

1 It's a mountain. (given)
2 No, I'm not.
3 No, it isn't.
4 They're dolphins.
5 Yes, it is.
6 Yes, they are.

Extra activity

Poster: Animals

This poster can be used to consolidate and revise vocabulary and grammar from Units 1-3 in a fun and interesting way. Pupils can also play a game with the poster. Follow the procedure outlined on the back of the poster.

Homework

- Pupil's Audio CD: Pupils listen to the songs at home. Explain to pupils that they should listen to tracks 14, 16 and 20 on the CD.

- Activity Book, pages 32-33: Time permitting, some tasks can be done in class.

- Revision for Progress Test 1. Pupils should revise all the vocabulary and grammar from Units 1-3.

Teacher's Note

Pupils will do Progress Test 1 in the following lesson. After the test you can do the lesson *Fun & Games.*

Fun & Games

Aims

- Consolidate new vocabulary with fun activities
- Consolidate new grammar with fun activities
- Make a family tree

Materials

- One photocopy of the family tree cutout for each pupil (page 139)
- Scissors, brown and green colouring pencils, black markers, glue
- One A4 blank piece of paper for each pupil
- Optional for extra activity: 12 quiz cards. Write one question on each card, so they can be shuffled to play again. See extra activity for questions.

Lead-in

- Tell pupils that today's lesson is all about fun and games. Ask them to open their books at page 46. Ask them what they can see (*a birthday party*).
- Read out the paragraph and ask pupils to follow the words with their fingers. Read it out again one sentence at a time and ask pupils to repeat. Check comprehension with these questions. Encourage pupils to use English for the words they have learnt.

  Whose party is it? (Jenny's)

  How old is Jenny? (seven)

  What do we say for someone's birthday? (Happy birthday)

- Consolidate vocabulary pupils have learnt using the picture. Here are some suggestions:
  Count the presents.
  Count the hats.
  What colour is the birthday cake?
  What colours are the balloons?
  Count the boys.
  Count the girls.
  How old are the boys/girls? Guess.
  Are they happy?
  Are they hungry?
  Who comes to your birthday parties? (consolidate best friend, family words)
  What presents do you like? (consolidate toys)

Quiz time!

- Tell pupils to look at the small picture. Read out the question and both answers and make sure pupils understand the meaning. Ask pupils to choose the correct answer (a). Ask a volunteer to read out the question and answer.

A Match.

- Tell pupils to look at the pictures on the left. Ask them to say who the people are:
  1 *Grandpa*
  2 *Mum*
  3 *a baby*
  Then tell pupils to look at the pictures on the right and to say what they are: *a flower, a teddy bear and a cake.*
- Ask pupils *What is great for Grandpa?*. Tell them to join the dots and follow the trail to find which picture they lead to. Do the same with *What is great for Mum?* and *What is great for a baby?*
- Ask volunteers for the answers. Encourage them to use complete sentences and Grandpa write them on the board.
  A cake is great for Grandpa.
  A flower is great for Mum.
  A teddy bear is great for a baby.
  Read out the answers and ask pupils to repeat.
- Check answers.

B Sing. 1:53

- Tell pupils they are going to learn a song. Explain to pupils that the song is about families and people everywhere. Teach *children* and *people*. Ask two boys to stand up and say *They're boys*. Then ask two girls to stand up and say *They're girls*. Then ask all four pupils to stand together at the front of the class and say *They're children*. Ask pupils to repeat. Explain the meaning of *children* if necessary. Then ask *Are dads children?* And elicit *No, they aren't*. Say *Mums and dads are people*. and ask pupils to repeat. Explain the meaning of *people* if necessary.
- Ask pupils to look at the song and find the family words they know. Then ask them to find the words *children* and *people* in the song.
- Play the recording and tell pupils to listen and follow the words with their fingers.
- Read out the song one line at a time and ask pupils to repeat after you.
- Play the recording again. Encourage pupils to sing along. Practise many times until pupils are familiar with the words.
- Pupils can join hands in a circle and sing the song again.

C Make.

- Tell pupils they are going to make a family tree. Tell pupils to look at the pictures in task C and explain each stage to them.
  1 Colour in the tree brown and the leaves green.
  2 Cut out the tree and the leaves.
  3 Write the family words on the leaves. It can be their own family or an imaginary family. eg *two grandmas, two sisters, mum and baby.*
  4 Stick the tree on the piece of paper, and then stick the leaves on the end of the branches.
  5 The family tree is ready.

- Ask pupils to have a green and a brown colouring pencil ready. Hand out the photocopies of the family tree cutouts and ask pupils to colour it in.

- When all pupils are ready, ask pupils to put their colouring pencils away. Then hand out the scissors. Ask pupils to cut out their trees and leaves. Go round the class helping pupils where necessary. Collect the scissors.

- Write the family names pupils have learnt on the board: *Dad, Mum, Grandma, Grandpa, brother, sister, baby.* Ask pupils to write the words of their choice on the leaves with a black marker.

- Ask pupils to put their black markers away. Then hand out a piece of paper for each pupil and glue. Show them where to stick the tree in the middle of the paper. When they have all stuck the tree, they can stick on the leaves. Go round the class helping pupils where necessary. Collect the glue.

- Ask pupils to hold up their family trees and read out the family words they have stuck on. The family trees can be displayed on the classroom wall. Remember to write the pupils' names on the back of their work so it can be returned to them.

Homework

- Pupil's Audio CD: Pupils listen to the song at home. Explain to pupils that they should listen to track 21 on the CD.

- Optional extra homework: Pupils write the colours in their notebooks.

Extra activity

- Do a class quiz using the quiz cards. Divide the class into two teams, Team A and Team B. Draw a line down the middle of the board. Write A on the left and B on the right.

- Explain to pupils that they are going to do a quiz. Each pupil in the team has a number. Starting with number 1, a pupil from Team A must answer a question or follow an instruction correctly to get a point. Then pupil 1 from Team B must answer a question. Then pupil 2 must answer a question from Team A and so on. If a pupil answers a question when it isn't his or her turn, the team loses a point.

- Here are the questions for the cards:

  1 *What's your name?*
  2 *How are you?*
  3 *How old are you?*
  4 *Are you a girl?*
  5 *Are you a boy?*
  6 *What's this?* (hold up a pencil)
  7 *Say the next letter* (use L1 for question if necessary) *a b c d ?* (stop at any letter)
  8 *What colour is this?* (choose a colour in the classroom)
  9 *Count to ten.*
  10 *Are giraffes tall?*
  11 *Are elephants small?*
  12 *Are you happy?*

- The team with the most points wins. Shuffle the cards and play again.

Ask pupils to look at the National Geographic photo on pages 48-49 (use L1) and tell them that it is a photo of the Great Barrier Reef, which is situated in Australia. It is the world's largest reef and it is also one of the seven wonders of the natural world. Pupils are unlikely to know a lot about the coral reefs in Australia. Encourage them to describe in L1 what they can see in the photo. Then explain that there are many beautiful fish and sea creatures that live around the coral reefs. Tell them that the water is shallow and warm in this part of the ocean. Ask pupils if they have seen any documentaries about coral reefs and the ocean, as they are quite likely to have seen one. Pupils might know where Australia is situated. Ask volunteers to find Australia on the classroom map. Then point to the map at the top of the page to show them. First show them where their own country is on the globe and then point out the area in red where the reporters are. Explain that this is Australia.

The second country the reporters visit is Australia. In episode 1, they visit a junior school in Sydney next to the famous Bondi Beach. They meet a class of junior school pupils and their teacher, Mr Davis. They are shown around their classroom. In episode 2, they join the pupils on a school outing to a modern zoo where animals are in open spaces rather than cages. At the zoo, they see some well-known Australian animals: a tree frog, a kangaroo and a koala bear. In Australia, there are many animals which are unique to the continent. A number of them are marsupials like the kangaroo and the koala. In episode 3, the reporters visit the Great Barrier Reef and dive down to see the corals and fish.

Fun facts

Here are some facts about Australia which your pupils will find interesting:

1   Kangaroos carry their babies in a pouch.
2   Australia is the largest island in the world.
3   The middle of Australia is a desert. But in the North, there are rainforests.
4   It has got more then 700 different kinds of reptiles.
5   The Eucalyptus tree comes from Australia.
6   Australian snakes are the most poisonous in the world.
7   Many Europeans have relatives in Australia.
8   In Australia, people speak English.
9   Most Australian school children wear school uniforms.
10 Hugh Jackman, who plays Wolverine, is Australian.
11 Football is often called footy in Australia.
12 Many families spend Christmas day on the beach, because it's summer time. Santa Claus comes to some beaches in a boat and hands out presents to the children.

4

Lesson 1   Trek's reporters in Australia

Aims

- Learn and use new vocabulary: *drawing, helicopter, pupil, school, numbers 11-20*
- Learn and use new grammar: *there's, there is, there are*

Materials

- Flashcards: *drawing, helicopter, pupil, school*
- Number cards: *1-20*

  Cut out 20 pieces of card. Write the digits on one side and the word on the other side.
- Masks: Trek, Mia, Ty, Leo

Lead-in

- Revise the numbers *1-10*. Chant them together as a class. Hand out the number cards *1-10*. Call out the numbers in random order. The pupil with the number you say should hold the number card up.
- Check homework. Tell pupils to open their Activity Books at pages 32 and 33. Ask volunteers to read out their answers. Then quickly check all pupils' books.

Episode outline

Australia: Episode 1

Trek shows his dad the DVD the reporters have sent from Australia. The reporters arrive in Sydney by helicopter. They land in the playground of a junior school next to Bondi Beach. They are met by eleven pupils and their teacher Mr Davis. They are shown round the classroom where Leo admires the children's drawings on the classroom wall. He and Trek's dad count them – there are twenty drawings.

New vocabulary

- Teach the new words with the flashcards. See the teacher's introduction pages 7-9 for teaching suggestions.
- Teach the numbers *11-20* with the number cards. Hold up the cards one at a time so pupils can see the digit, say the number and ask pupils to repeat. Then chant the numbers from *1-20* as a class.
- Tell pupils to open their books at page 50 and to look at the vocabulary box. Hold up your book and point to the first picture word. Say the word and ask pupils to repeat. Do the same with all the words. Then read out the new picture words in the vocabulary box in random order and ask pupils to point to the correct pictures.
- Repeat the numbers *11-20* and ask pupils to count with you.
- Read out all the words again one by one and ask pupils to repeat after you.

A Listen and read.

For teachers using the DVD

- Make sure each pupil has got a copy of the DVD Worksheet found on page 130.
- Please follow the procedure outlined in Unit 1, Lesson 1 on page 31 for teachers using the DVD.

Before you watch

Answers
1 a
2 b
3 b

While you watch

Answers
a 2
b 4
c 5
d 1
e 6
f 3

After you watch

Answers
1 by helicopter
2 eleven (11)
3 Mr Davis
4 twenty (20)

For teachers using the audio CD 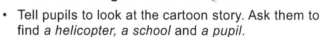 2.1

- Tell pupils to look at the cartoon story. Ask them to find *a helicopter, a school* and *a pupil*.
- Play the recording. Tell pupils to look at the pictures and follow the speech bubbles with their fingers.
- Play the recording again. Pause after each speech bubble and ask pupils to repeat.
- Check pupils understand the story. Use L1 where necessary.
  How do the reporters get to the school? (by helicopter)
  How many pupils are there? (eleven)
  What is the teacher's name? (Mr Davis)
  How many drawings are there? (twenty)
- Play the recording again. Then ask volunteers to read out the story.
- Assign characters to volunteers and ask them to act out the story in front of the class. Pupils can wear the character masks.

B Look and learn.

- Read out the dialogue. Read it out again and ask pupils to repeat.

- Ask pupils to look at the grammar box. Explain the meaning of *there is* and *there are*. Tell pupils that we can shorten *there is* to *there's*. Practise the grammar point. Hold up a pencil and say *There's a pencil*. Ask pupils to repeat. Then hold up two pencils and say *There are two pencils*. Ask pupils to repeat. Then ask volunteers to make sentences with the following prompts:
  one girl/boy
  two girls/boys
  5 drawings
  5 pupils
  school
- Ask pupils to underline *there's* and *there are* in the dialogue. Ask volunteers to read out the dialogue.

C Write There's or There are.

- Read out the example and ask pupils why *There's* is the correct answer.
- Explain the rest of the task to pupils. Tell them to think carefully about how many things we are talking about in each sentence. Read out the sentences and make sure pupils remember the meaning of all the words. Allow pupils enough time to complete the task alone. Go round the class helping pupils where necessary.
- Check answers. Write them on the board if necessary.

Answers
1 There's (given)
2 There are
3 There are
4 There's
5 There's

Say it! 2.2

- Write *helicopter* on the board. Read it out and ask pupils to repeat. Ask pupils if they can hear the letter *r* at the end of the word. Explain that in English the letter *r* at the end of a word is usually silent. Practise the *er* sound.
- Tell pupils to look at the task. Play the first part of the recording (Listen and say.) asking pupils to repeat the words *helicopter* and *flower* each time they hear them. (*Helicopter* and *flower* will be heard twice.)
- Ask for volunteers to read out *spider, tiger, brother* and *sister*. Play the recording and ask all pupils to repeat (*Spider, tiger, brother* and *sister* will be heard once.).

D Listen and circle. 2.3

- Tell pupils to look at the numbers for this task. Read out all the numbers and ask pupils to repeat. Practise for a few minutes to make sure pupils know the numbers fairly well before attempting to do the Listening task.
- Explain to pupils they will hear a boy and a girl counting objects they can see. Explain that they must circle the correct number of objects they say. Play the recording and pause it after the example. Make sure pupils understand what to do.

- Play the recording pausing between each question where necessary. Play the recording again and ask pupils to check their answers.

Listening script

1

How many pencils?
Mmm … one, two, three, four, five, six, seven, eight, nine, ten, eleven, twelve, thirteen, fourteen, fifteen pencils.

2
How many photos?
There are twelve photos.

3
How many bikes?
One, two, three, four, five, six. There are six bikes.

4
How many computer games?
Mmm … there are eight computer games.

5
How many schools?
There are seventeen schools.

Answers
1 15 (given)
2 12
3 6
4 8
5 17

E Say.

- Ask pupils to look at the picture and to tell you what it is (a child's bedroom). Read out the dialogue. Read it out again and ask pupils to repeat after each speech bubble.
- Ask two volunteers to read out the dialogue either from their seats or in front of the class.
- Ask volunteers to choose objects they know in English in the picture and count how many there are. Ask *How many _____?* and elicit answer. Reply *Well done*.
- Continue the task in pairs. Ask pairs to come to the front of the class. One pupil asks a question, choosing an object and the other pair counts and answers.
  cars: 5
  robots: 11
  skateboards: 2
  balls: 14
  pencils: 20
  yo-yos: 3
  drawings: 10
  teddy bears: 7

Extension activity

- The same Speaking task can be done with objects in the classroom. For example ask these questions and encourage volunteers to count and answer.
  How many pupils?   *How many pencils?*
  How many boys?   *How many hats?*
  How many girls?   *How many drawings?*

Lesson 2   Emma is at school.

Aims

- Learn and use new vocabulary: *notebook, pen, board, book, computer, lesson*

- Learn and use new grammar: *There isn't, there aren't, Is there ...?, Are there ...?, Yes, there is/are. No, there isn't/aren't.*

Materials

- Number cards: *1-20*

- A book, a notebook and a pen

- A magazine picture of a computer

- Optional for Extra activity: one piece of paper for each pupil

Lead-in

- Revise the words from Lesson 1 with the flashcards. Ask a pupil to pick a flashcard from a pile on your desk and show it to the class and ask what the word is. All pupils can take it in turns until all words have been practised.

- Revise the numbers *1-20* with the number cards. First chant the numbers as a class. Then hold up the word for a number and ask a volunteer to write the number in digits on the board. Continue with all the numbers. Make sure all pupils have a turn.

- Revise *there is* and *there are*. Draw a ball on the board and say *Look! There's a ball.* Ask pupils to repeat. Then draw three more balls on the board. Ask volunteers to make a sentence for four balls. Elicit *Look! There are four balls.* Practise more with *pencil/pencils*.

- Check homework. Tell pupils to open their Activity Books at pages 34 and 35. Ask volunteers to read out their answers. Write the numbers *11-20* on the board in digits in a column. Ask volunteers to write the words next to the digits. Then quickly check all pupils' books.

- Test dictation: *drawing, helicopter, pupil, school*. See the teacher's introduction pages 7-9 for teaching suggestions. Go round the class and check all pupils' dictation.

New vocabulary

- Teach *board, computer, pen, book* and *notebook* with the objects and the magazine picture. Point to the pen and say. *Look. A pen.* Ask pupils to repeat. Do the same with the other words. Then point to the objects one at a time asking *What's this?* and ask volunteers to answer.

- Teach *lesson*. Write *This is an English lesson.* on the board. Explain the meaning of *lesson* to pupils. Read out the sentence from the board and ask pupils to repeat.

- Tell pupils to open their books at page 52 and to look at the vocabulary box. Hold up your book and point to the first picture word. Say the word and ask pupils to repeat. Do the same with all the words. Then read out the new picture words in the vocabulary box in random order and ask pupils to point to the correct pictures.

- Read out all the words again one by one and ask pupils to repeat after you.

A Listen and read. 🔘 2.4

- Tell pupils that they are going to read about a girl from Alaska. Show pupils on the map where Alaska is.

Background Information
Alaska

Alaska is the largest state of the USA. According to a recent study 85% of people over five speak only English at home. There are 22 native languages and 5.2% of the population speaks one of these. Most people nowadays live in modern homes, drive cars, watch television and shop in modern shops. Although some of Alaska's smaller towns have got one-room school houses, most classrooms throughout the state are very similar to schools in the USA and are equipped with computers and modern learning tools. Subjects taught are English, geography, history, science, arts, maths, technology, etc.

- Ask pupils where they think the girl is (at school). Ask them to read the first sentence and to find out her name.

- Play the recording. Tell pupils to follow the text with their fingers.

- Play the recording again. Pause after each sentence and ask pupils to repeat.

- Play the recording again. Then ask volunteers to read out a sentence each of the text.

B Write.

- Read the example to pupils. Ask them to find the word *pupil* in the text.

- Explain the rest of the task to pupils. Tell them to underline the words in the text which give them the answers. Allow them enough time to complete the task alone. Go round the class encouraging and helping pupils where necessary.

- Check answers. Write them on the board if necessary.

Answers
1 pupil (given)
2 lesson
3 books
4 computers
5 board

Extension activity

- Ask a volunteer to stand at the front of the class. Ask *What's your name?* and elicit answer. Then using the first paragraph of the reading text, make some sentences about the volunteer. eg *This is John. He's from Greece. He's a pupil. John is at school. This is a lesson.*

- Ask pupils to do the same in pairs. Ask pairs to stand at the front and to talk about each other. They can use the book to help them. Remind them to remember to use *He* and *She* correctly. Prompt pupils where necessary.

C Look and learn.

- Read out the dialogue. Read it out again and ask pupils to repeat.

- Ask pupils to look at the grammar box. Read out the grammar notes and sentences. Ask pupils to repeat. Explain the meaning of the notes.

- Ask pupils to circle the question and underline the answer in the dialogue. Ask volunteers to read out the dialogue.

- Practise *There isn't* and *There aren't any*. Write singular words on the board of animals which aren't in your classroom. eg *frog, tiger, elephant.* Ask pupils to look around and see if they can find these animals. Say *There isn't a frog.* and ask pupils to repeat. Then ask volunteers to make sentences for the other animals and any ideas of their own. Repeat the exercise, but use plural words for toys eg *skateboards, robots, teddy bears.* Say *There aren't any skateboards.* and ask pupils to repeat. Make sure pupils remember to include the word *any* in their own sentences.

- Practise the questions and short answers. Write *Yes, there is.* and *No, there isn't.* on the board. Ask pupils questions about the classroom and tell them to choose an answer from the board.
  eg *Is there a giraffe?*
  Is there a board?
  Repeat with the plural. Write *Yes, there are.* and *No, there aren't.* on the board for pupils to choose from.
  Are there any pens?
  Are there any grandmas?

D Circle.

- Read out the example and ask pupils why *There isn't* is the correct answer.

- Explain the task to pupils. Tell them to think carefully about how many things are being talked about. Read out the sentences. Check pupils remember the meanings of all the words. Allow them enough time to complete the task alone. Go round the class helping pupils where necessary.

- Check answers.

Answers
1 There isn't (given)
2 aren't
3 There aren't
4 There are
5 Is there

E Sing. 2.5

- Tell pupils they are going to learn a song. Ask pupils if they like going to school and what they like most about school.

- Ask pupils to look at the picture. Hold up your book, point to the boy and say. *Look. This is a boy.* Then point to the school and say. *Look. That is a school.* Ask pupils *Is the boy happy?* and elicit answer *Yes, he is.*

- Play the recording and tell pupils to listen and follow the words with their fingers.

- Read out the song one line at a time and ask pupils to repeat after you.

- Play the recording again. Encourage pupils to sing along. Practise many times until pupils are familiar with the words.

- Pupils can carry their school bags and pretend they are walking to school as they sing the song. They can clap as they sing *Hooray*.

Homework

- Pupil's Audio CD: Pupils listen to the text and the song at home. Explain to pupils that they should listen to tracks 23 and 24 on the CD.

- Activity Book, pages 36-37: Time permitting, some tasks can be done in class.

- Dictation: *board, book, computer, lesson, notebook, pen*

Teacher's note

It is a good idea to invite parents into the classroom to see their children's work displayed on the wall. This boosts pupils' confidence and is also a great motivator.

Extra activity

- Tell pupils they are going to make something to display on the wall.

- Hand out one piece of paper to each pupil. Ask pupils to draw a picture of their best friend at the top. Then underneath they should copy the first paragraph of the reading text but with some changes. They should change the name, the country and if necessary, *she* to *he*. Go round the class helping with spelling where necessary.

- Ask pupils to show their work to the class and read out what they have written. Stick their work on the classroom wall.

Lesson 3   This is my classroom.

Aims

- Learn and use new vocabulary: *rubber, ruler, desk, chair, apple, classroom, teacher*

- Learn and use new grammar: *a, an, the*

Materials

- A pen, a notebook, a book and a magazine picture of a computer
- An apple, a rubber and a ruler

Lead-in

- Revise the words from Lesson 2 with the objects and pictures. Point to an object and ask *What's this?* Elicit answers from volunteers.
- Revise *Are there any ...?* Ask *Are there any boys in the school?* Ask volunteers for the answer. Ask *Are there any elephants in the school?* Ask volunteers for the answer.
- Check homework. Tell pupils to open their Activity Books at pages 36 and 37. Ask volunteers to read out their answers. Write the questions from task D on the board. Ask volunteers to write the answers in the gaps. Then quickly check all pupils' books.
- Sing the song from Lesson 2
- Test dictation: *board, book, computer, lesson, notebook, pen.* See the teacher's introduction pages 7-9 for teaching suggestions. Go round the class and check all pupils' dictation.

New vocabulary

- Teach *apple, chair, classroom, desk, rubber, ruler, teacher* with the objects and by pointing to yourself. Point to the chair and say. *Look. A chair.* Ask pupils to repeat. Do the same with the other words. Then point to the objects one at a time asking *What's this?* And ask volunteers to answer.
- Tell pupils to open their books at page 54 and to look at the vocabulary box. Hold up your book and point to the first picture word. Say the word and ask pupils to repeat. Do the same with all the words. Then read out the new picture words in the vocabulary box in random order and ask pupils to point to the correct pictures.
- Read out all the words again one by one and ask pupils to repeat after you.

A Read.

- Tell pupils to look at the boy and his drawing. Tell pupils to read the first two lines of the text. Then ask them what the boy's drawing shows. (a classroom)
- Tell pupils to now read all the text and to tick the objects on the drawing as they read about them.
- Read out the text. Pause after each sentence and ask pupils to repeat.
- Ask volunteers to read out a sentence each of the text.

B Circle

- Read the example to pupils. Ask them to find where the answer is in the letter.
- Explain the rest of the task to pupils. Tell them to underline the words in the text which give them the answers. Allow them enough time to complete the task alone. Go round the class encouraging and helping pupils where necessary.

- Check answers. Write them on the board if necessary.

> **Answers**
> 1 desk (given)
> 2 eight
> 3 big
> 4 red

C Look and learn.

- Read out the dialogue and ask pupils to repeat.
- Ask pupils to look at the grammar box. Read out the grammar notes and sentences. Ask pupils to repeat. Explain the meaning of the notes. Tell them that when we talk about something for the first time we use *a* or *an*. But if we then continue talking about it we use *the*.
- Ask pupils to circle *a* and *an* and underline *the* in the dialogue and the grammar sentences. Ask volunteers to read out the sentences.
- Practise the grammar. Write these sentences on the board.
  Look. It's _____ car. _____ car is red.
  Look. It's _____ ant. _____ is brown.
  Ask volunteers to write the answers in the gaps. Remind pupils when to use *a* and when to use *an*.

D Write a, an or the.

- Read out the example and ask pupils why *a* is the answer.
- Explain the task to pupils. Read out the sentences. Check pupils remember the meanings of all the words. Allow them enough time to complete the task alone. Go round the class helping pupils where necessary.
- Check answers. Write them on the board if necessary.

> **Answers**
> 1 a (given)
> 2 The
> 3 an
> 4 a
> 5 The
> 6 An

E Say.

- Read out the example. Read it out again and ask pupils to repeat.
- Ask volunteers to read out the example.
- Ask volunteers to change the words in orange and to make their own sentences with *a*, *an* and *the*. They can choose something in the classroom to make two sentences. eg *It's a board. The board is white.*

F Draw and write.

- Tell pupils to draw a picture of a classroom object they like in the box.
- Read out the beginning of the sentences and ask pupils what they should write in the gaps.
- Tell pupils to complete the task. Help pupils with spelling where necessary.

- Ask pupils to hold up their books and to show each other their pictures. Ask volunteers to read out their work.

Homework

- Activity Book, pages 38-39: Time permitting, some tasks can be done in class.
- Dictation: *apple, chair, classroom, desk, rubber, ruler, teacher*
- Optional extra homework: Pupils can draw an imaginary classroom and write three to four sentences about it. Their work can be displayed on the classroom wall.
- Revision for Test 4:
  Words: *drawing, helicopter, pupil, school, numbers 11-20, board, book, computer, lesson, notebook, pen, apple, chair, classroom, desk, rubber, ruler, teacher*
  Grammar: *there is, there's, there are, there isn't, there aren't, Is there ...? Are there ...? Yes, there is/are. No, there isn't/aren't., a, an, the*

Teacher's Note

Pupils will do Test 4 in the following lesson. If you don't want to rush into Unit 5, for the rest of the lesson do these activities:
1 Pupils can read out the cartoon story from Unit 4 Lesson 1. Then ask volunteers to act out the cartoon story.
2 Pupils can read out the texts from Lessons 2 and 3.
3 Repeat the *Say* task from Lesson 3.
4 Sing the song.
5 Revise classroom vocabulary and numbers 1-20. Ask pupils in pairs to draw a classroom with many objects in it (not more than 20 of the same thing). They can then perform a Speaking task like the one in Lesson 1, where another pair looks at their drawing and counts the objects.

Optional activity

Revision for Test 4

- Revise the words from the flashcards. Then write the words on the board. Ask a volunteer to read out a word and come and choose the corresponding flashcard. Practise until all pupils remember the words well.
- Revise the classroom objects. Point to the object and ask *What's this?* Ask volunteers to answer and write the words on the board.
- Write *a, an* and *the* on the board. Ask pupils to tell you words that go with *a* or *an*. Ask volunteers to write the words on the board. Then ask pupils when we use the word *the*. Ask volunteers to think up two sentences and write them on the board.
- Write *There is a frog in the classroom.* on the board. Ask pupils if this is true. Ask them to correct the sentence and elicit *There isn't a frog in the classroom.* Change *is* to *isn't*. Do the same with the plural eg *There are trees in the classroom.* Then ask questions with *Is there* and *Are there any?* and elicit answers.

  eg *Is there a teacher/king/book/pencil/dog in the classroom?*

  Are there any boys/insects/animals/pens/apples in the classroom?

Lesson 1   Trek's reporters in Australia

Aims

- Learn and use new vocabulary: *eye, nose, ear, kangaroo, koala, tail, long, Let's see ...*
- Learn and use new grammar: *have got affirmative (I, you, he, she, it)*

Materials

- Magazine or Internet pictures of a kangaroo and a koala
- Masks: Mia, Ty, Leo

Lead-in

- Revise the classroom words from Unit 4. Ask pupils to tell you the classroom words they remember and to point to the objects. Ask volunteers to write them on the board.
- Revise Affirmative *a, an* and *the*. Write *It's a pen. _____ pen is red.* on the board. Ask pupils to say the missing word. Practise with other objects and prompt pupils to make two sentences for each object.
- Check homework. Tell pupils to open their Activity Books at pages 38 and 39. Ask volunteers to read out their answers. Then quickly check all pupils' books.
- Test dictation: *apple, chair, classroom, desk, rubber, ruler, teacher*. See the teacher's introduction pages 7-9 for teaching suggestions. Go round the class and check all pupils' dictation.

Episode outline

Australia: Episode 2

The reporters go on a school trip with the junior school pupils to an animal sanctuary. They see Australian animals: a tree frog with red eyes, a koala with a large black nose and a kangaroo with a long tail.

New vocabulary

- Teach *kangaroo* and *koala*. Hold up the picture of the kangaroo and say *Look! A kangaroo.* Ask pupils to repeat. Do the same with *koala*. Write both words on the board and ask pupils to call out the letters to spell them. Teach *long* and *tail*. Point to the tail on the kangaroo and say *It is a tail*. Ask pupils to repeat. Then ask *Is it a short tail?* Elicit *No, it isn't.* Say *It's a long tail.* Repeat *long tail* and write it on the board. Read it out and ask pupils to repeat.
- Teach *eye, nose* and *ear.* Ask pupils to look at your face. Point to your eye and say *eye*. Ask pupils to copy you and repeat the word. Do the same with *ear* and *nose*. Repeat a few times.
- Tell pupils to open their books at page 56 and to look at the vocabulary box. Hold up your book and point to the first picture word. Say the word and ask pupils to repeat. Do the same with all the words. Then read out

the new picture words in the vocabulary box in random order and ask pupils to point to the correct pictures.

- Read out the phrase *Let's see ...* Explain the meaning. Then say *Let's see the kangaroo.* and then hold up the picture of a kangaroo. Repeat with *Let's see the koala.* Ask volunteers to come to the front and to choose either the kangaroo or the koala and make a sentence with *Let's see.*
- Read out all the words again one by one and ask pupils to repeat after you.

A Listen and read.

For teachers using the DVD

- Make sure each pupil has got a copy of the DVD Worksheet found on page 131.
- Please follow the procedure outlined in Unit 1, Lesson 1 on page 31 for teachers using the DVD.

Before you watch

Answers
1 Mr Davis and his pupils
2 the tree frog
3 the koala and the kangaroo

While you watch

Answers
1 see
2 red
3 big
4 tail
5 ears

After you watch

Answers
1 animals
2 the tree frog
3 green
4 a big black nose
5 big ears and a long tail

For teachers using the audio CD   2.6

- Tell pupils to look at the cartoon story. Ask them to point to the teacher. Ask them if they remember his name (Mr Davis). Then ask pupils to count the pupils in the first picture (11).
- Play the recording. Tell pupils to look at the pictures and follow the speech bubbles with their fingers.
- Play the recording again. Pause after each speech bubble and ask pupils to repeat.
- Check pupils understand the story. Use L1 where necessary.
  What are the pupils going to see? (animals)
  Which animal has got red eyes? (the tree frog)
  What colour eyes has the pupil got? (green)
  What has the koala got? (a big black nose)
  What has the kangaroo got? (big ears and a long tail)

- Play the recording again. Then ask volunteers to read out the story.
- Assign characters to volunteers and ask them to enact the story in front of the class. Pupils can wear the character masks.

B Look and learn.

- Read out Amber's speech bubble. Read it out again and ask pupils to repeat. Explain the meaning of *He's got.*
- Ask pupils to look at the grammar box. Tell pupils that we use *have got* for things we own, eg *toys*, and for things about our appearance, eg *green eyes*. Read out the words in the grammar box and ask pupils to repeat.
- Ask pupils to circle the verbs in the grammar sentences. Ask volunteers to read them out.
- Practise *have got*. Say these sentences and ask pupils to repeat.
  I've got two eyes.
  You've got a red pen.
  He's got a big nose.
  She's got a skateboard.
  It's got a long tail.
  Remind pupils we use *it* for animals.

Extension activity

- Ask pupils to make their own sentences for *I've got* and *He's got*. Allow them some time to think in pairs and then ask them to stand up and say their sentences.
- Ask pupils to repeat their sentences, but this time use the full version of the verb: *I have got* and *He has got.*

C Write have got or has got.

- Read out the example and ask pupils why *has got* is the correct answer. Tell them to think what word we can use instead of *A kangaroo* and elicit *It*. Explain that we don't always have a word like *he* or *you* to help us.
- Explain the rest of the task to pupils. Allow them enough time to complete the task alone. Go round the class helping pupils where necessary.
- Check answers. Write them on the board if necessary.

Answers
1 has got (given)
2 has got
3 have got
4 has got
5 have got

Say it! 2.7

- Write *e* on the board. Ask pupils to say the name of this letter. Then add another *e* to write *ee* on the board. Tell pupils that two *ee* make a different sound from one. Make the sound for *ee* and ask pupils to smile and practise the sound with you.
- Tell pupils to look at the task. Play the first part of the

recording (Listen and say.) asking pupils to repeat the words *tree* and *green* each time they hear them. (*Tree* and *green* will be heard twice.)

- Ask for volunteers to read out the sentence (*Let's see the three trees.*). Play the recording and ask all pupils to repeat. (*Let's see the three trees.* will be heard once.)

D Chant. 2.8

- Tell pupils they are going to learn a chant. Explain to pupils that the chant is called *The kangaroo hop.* Ask pupils to practise hopping up and down like a kangaroo.
- Ask pupils to look at the picture and describe what they can see. Encourage them to use English for words they know.
- Play the recording and tell pupils to listen and follow the words with their fingers.
- Read out the chant one line at a time and ask pupils to repeat after you.
- Play the recording again. Encourage pupils to chant along. Practise many times until pupils are familiar with the words.
- Pupils can hop around like kangaroos as they chant.

Homework

- Pupil's Audio CD: Pupils listen to the cartoon story and the chant at home. Explain to pupils that they should listen to tracks 25 and 26 on the CD.
- Activity Book, pages 40-41: Time permitting, some tasks can be done in class.
- Dictation: *eye, nose, ear, kangaroo, koala, tail, long*

Extra activity

- Play a game where pupils mime different animals. First ask pupils to remember all the animals they have learnt so far and write them on the board. These are the animals pupils have learnt so far: *ant, dog, frog, insect, monkey, octopus, spider, tiger, worm, fox, zebra, fly, elephant, lion, giraffe, bird, whale, ostrich, penguin, meerkat, snake, dolphin, rabbit, shark, kangaroo, koala*
- Say *Guess. What animal is this?* And then mime an animal yourself. eg elephant. Encourage pupils to give full sentences for answers. (*It's an elephant.*)
- Ask volunteers to mime animals while the other pupils try to guess what they are. Make sure all pupils have a turn.

Lesson 2   This is fun.

Aims

- Learn and use new vocabulary: *hair, arm, finger, leg, toe, sad, wet*
- Learn and use new grammar: *have got* affirmative (*we, you, they*)

Materials

- A glass of water
- Optional for Extra activity: one photocopy of a simple stick man for each pupil.

Draw an outline of a stick man without facial features, finger or toes. Make enough photocopies for the whole class.

Lead-in

- Revise *eye*, *nose* and *ear*. Draw a circle on the board. Say *ear* and ask a volunteer to draw an ear in the circle. Do the same with *eye* and *nose*. Then ask other volunteers to label the parts.
- Practise *he's got* and *she's got*. Write *He's got* and *She's got* on the board. Ask pupils to remember which word we use for boys and which for girls. Point to a boy with brown eyes and say *He's got brown eyes*. Ask volunteers to make sentences for other pupils.
- Check homework. Tell pupils to open their Activity Books at pages 40 and 41. Ask volunteers to read out their answers. Ask volunteers to come to the front of the class and to read out their answers for task C. Then quickly check all pupils' books.
- Test dictation: *eye, nose, ear, kangaroo, koala, tail, long*. See the teacher's introduction pages 7-9 for teaching suggestions. Go round the class and check all pupils' dictation.
- Do the chant from Lesson 1 (CD2: 8).

New vocabulary

- Teach *hair, arm, finger, leg* and *toe*. Draw a stick body on the face on the board. Then draw an arm and say *It's an arm*. Ask pupils to repeat. Do the same with the other body parts as you draw them. Then ask volunteers to label the picture and spell out the words for them.
- Teach *sad* and *wet*. First smile, look happy and revise *I'm happy*. Then look sad and say *I'm sad*. Ask pupils to repeat. Then hold up a pencil and tell pupils to watch. Make the pencil wet with the water in the glass. Say *The pencil is wet*. Then dry the pencil and say *The pencil isn't wet*. Ask pupils to repeat after you. Explain meaning in L1 to pupils if necessary.
- Tell pupils to open their books at page 58 and to look at the vocabulary box. Hold up your book and point to the first picture word. Say the word and ask pupils to repeat. Do the same with all the words. Then read out the new picture words in the vocabulary box in random order and ask pupils to point to the correct pictures.
- Read out all the words again one by one and ask pupils to repeat after you.

A Listen and read. 2.9

- Tell pupils that they are going to read about children having fun. Ask pupils to look at the picture and describe what they can see. Encourage pupils to use English for the words they know. eg *girls, children, fingers, toes, wet, happy*.
- Play the recording. Tell pupils to follow the text with their fingers.

- Play the recording again. Pause after each sentence and ask pupils to repeat.
- Play the recording again. Then ask volunteers to read out a sentence each of the text.

B Write Yes or No.

- Read the example to pupils. Ask them to underline the sentence in the text which gives them the answer.
- Explain the rest of the task to pupils. Tell them to underline the words in the text which give them the answers. Allow them enough time to complete the task alone. Go round the class encouraging and helping pupils where necessary.
- Check answers. Write them on the board if necessary.

Answers
1 No (given)
2 Yes
3 Yes
4 No

C Look and learn.

- Read out the speech bubble. Read it out again and ask pupils to repeat.
- Ask pupils to look at the grammar box. Read out the grammar notes and sentences. Ask pupils to repeat. Explain the meaning of the notes.
- Ask pupils to circle the person and verb in the grammar sentence. Ask volunteers to read out the sentence.
- Practise the grammar. Write sentences on the board with the verb missing. Ask pupils to make up funny sentences like Amber and Chris. Ask two pupils to stand together at the front of the class and choose a colour. Tell them to mime that they are putting on wigs. Then help them make a sentence with *We've got*. eg *We've got pink hair*. Ask a volunteer to change the sentence to *You've got*, and then another to *They've got*. Repeat until all pupils have had a turn.

D Write.

- Read out the example and explain to pupils that the *have got* part of the sentences is missing and that they have to write the complete sentence. Read out the example and ask pupils to repeat.
- Read out the second question. Ask volunteers to suggest answers using the short form. Say the correct answer and ask pupils to repeat. Then ask pupils to write the answer in their books. Write the answer on the board if necessary. For questions 3 and 4 explain to pupils that they must now use the full form of the verb. Ask volunteers for the answers one at a time. Write them on the board if necessary.

E Listen and write. 2.10

- Tell pupils to look at the table. Read out the names and explain to pupils that they will hear Jane describe herself, her brother Greg and her friends Eric and Ann. They must write the word they hear in the correct place in the table. Show them that the words they need are in the box. Read out the words and check pupils remember the meanings.

- Play the recording for the example. Make sure pupils understand what to do.

- Play the rest of the recording, pausing between questions to allow pupils enough time to write down the answers. Play the recording again and ask pupils to check their answers.

Listening script
Hi! I'm Jane. I've got brown eyes. I've got red hair. My brother, Greg, has got blue eyes. He's got short hair. Eric and Ann are my friends. They've got green eyes. They've got long hair.

Answers
Jane: brown eyes (given), red hair
Greg: blue eyes, short hair
Eric and Ann: green eyes, long hair

F Say.

- Tell pupils that now they will describe themselves. Read out the example one sentence at a time and ask pupils to repeat after you. Then describe yourself. Ask pupils for ideas and for words that will help and write them on the board. eg *short, tall, green, blue, brown, short, long.*

- Ask volunteers to stand at the front and describe themselves. Encourage other pupils to clap and say *Well done.*

Extension activity

- Ask pairs to stand at the front. This time they describe each other. Remind them to use *He's got* for a boy and *She's got* for a girl.

Homework

- Pupil's Audio CD: Pupils listen to the text at home. Explain to pupils that they should listen to track 27 on the CD.

- Activity Book, pages 42-43: Time permitting, some tasks can be done in class.

- Dictation: *hair, arm finger, leg, toe, sad, wet*

- Optional extra homework: pupils can draw a picture of themselves and write three sentences about it underneath. They can use the Speaking task for help. Their work can be displayed on the wall.

Extra activity

- Ask pupils to call out the words for the parts of the body they have learnt. Write them on the board: *eye, ear, nose, leg, arm, finger, toe, hair*

- Show pupils the stick man picture. Explain to pupils that they will have one stick man each and that they must draw his face and hair, fingers and toes. Hand out the pictures and allow pupils enough time to draw the body parts.

- Tell pupils to label their pictures with the words. Go round the class helping where necessary. Encourage pupils to hold up their pictures and to describe them eg *He's got black eyes / big ears / ten fingers.* etc.

Lesson 3   My cat is fat.

Aims

- Learn and use new vocabulary: *cat, fish, parrot, pet, fat, thin*

- Learn and use new grammar: *have got* negative

Materials

- Magazine or Internet pictures of a cat, a fish and a parrot

- Optional for Extra activity: grid of squares for wordsearch. See Unit 2, p.42.

Lead-in

- Revise the words from Lesson 2. Ask pupils to point to the parts of the body you call out: *hair, leg, arm, fingers, toes.*

- Revise *They've got* with two volunteers. Ask them to stand at the front of the classroom. Describe one thing about them eg *They've got brown hair.* Then ask volunteers to make more sentences.

- Check homework. Tell pupils to open their Activity Books at pages 42 and 43. Ask volunteers to read out their answers. Ask volunteers to read out their paragraphs for task E. Then quickly check all pupils' books.

- Test dictation: *hair, arm finger, leg, toe, sad, wet.* See the teacher's introduction pages 7-9 for teaching suggestions. Go round the class and check all pupils' dictation.

New vocabulary

- Teach *cat, fish* and *parrot* with the pictures and ask *What's this?* as a number of pupils may already know the word. Then say *It's a cat/fish/parrot.* and ask pupils to repeat. Teach *pet*. Stick the pictures on the board and ask pupils if these animals can live with people. Explain that animals that live with people are called pets. Say *pet* and ask pupils to repeat.

- Teach *fat* and *thin*. Explain that if a pet eats too much it will get fat, and if it doesn't eat enough it will get thin. Teach *fat* and *thin* and explain the meanings. Say *A fat cat.* and *A thin cat.* Ask volunteers to draw fat and thin cats on the board.

- Tell pupils to open their books at page 60 and to look at the word box. Hold up your book and point to the first picture word. Say the word and ask pupils to repeat. Do the same with all the words. Then read out the new picture words in the vocabulary box in random order and ask pupils to point to the correct pictures.

- Read out all the words again one by one and ask pupils to repeat after you.

A Read.

- Tell pupils to look at the photos. Ask them to tell you in English what they can see. Elicit *boys, girls, cat, fish* and *parrot*.

- Tell pupils to read number 1 to find out the children's names. Then ask them to read number 2 and find out who is fat and who is thin. For number 3 ask pupils to find out what these brothers haven't got. For number 4 ask pupils to find out what her fish hasn't got.

- Read out the paragraphs. Stop after each sentence and ask pupils to repeat.

- Ask volunteers to read out a sentence each of the paragraphs.

B Match.

- Read the example to pupils. Ask them to find that part of the text and to point to it.

- Explain the rest of the task to pupils. Tell them to underline the words in the text which give them the answers. Allow them enough time to complete the task alone. Go round the class encouraging and helping pupils where necessary.

- Check answers. Write them on the board if necessary.

> **Answers**
> 1 I haven't got a brother. (given)
> 2 I'm thin.
> 3 We haven't got a pet.
> 4 I've got a fish and a parrot.

C Look and learn.

- Read out the speech bubble and ask pupils to repeat.

- Ask pupils to look at the grammar box. Read out the grammar notes and sentences. Ask pupils to repeat. Explain the meaning of the notes.

- Ask pupils to circle the person and underline the verb in the grammar sentences. Ask volunteers to read out the sentences.

- Practise the grammar. Write these words on the board:
  brother
  sister
  cat
  dog
  car
  skateboard
  Ask pupils to look at the words and think about what they haven't got. Say *I haven't got a skateboard.* Ask volunteers to make their own sentences with *I haven't got*. Repeat the task, but this time pupils talk about their friend. eg *She/He hasn't got a brother.*

D Circle.

- Read out the example and ask pupils why *haven't got* is the correct answer. Tell them to check the grammar notes to remember where to use *have* and where to use *has*.

- Explain the task to pupils. Read out the sentences. Check pupils remember the meanings of all the words. Allow pupils enough time to complete the task. Go round the class helping pupils where necessary.

- Check answers. Write them on the board if necessary.

> **Answers**
> 1 haven't got (given)
> 2 has
> 3 have
> 4 hasn't got
> 5 have

E Say.

- Ask pupils who have got a pet to raise their hands. Ask the pupils who don't have a pet to think of their favourite animal for a pet. Ask pupils to tell you their pets and favourite pets and write any new words on the board.

- Explain to pupils that the girl in the picture has drawn her pet and she is telling her friend about it. Read out the speech bubble. Read it out again and ask pupils to repeat.

- Ask volunteers to read out the speech bubble.

- Tell pupils they are going to draw and describe their pet or favourite pet too. Tell them to draw their pet in the box in task F, but not to write anything yet. Go round the class helping where necessary.

- Ask pupils one at a time to hold up their picture and describe their drawing.

- Explain that they should change the words in orange. Prompt where necessary.

F Draw and write.

- Tell pupils that they can now write about their drawing. Read out the sentences and ask pupils for suggestions for the gaps.

- Tell pupils to complete the task. Help pupils with spelling where necessary.
- Ask volunteers to read out their work.

Homework

- Activity Book, pages 44-45: Time permitting, some tasks can be done in class.
- Dictation: *cat, fish, parrot, pet, fat, thin*
- Revision for Test 5:
  Words: *eye, nose, ear, kangaroo, koala, tail, long, Let's see …, hair, arm, finger, leg, toe, sad, wet, cat, fish, parrot, pet, fat, thin*
  Grammar: *have got* affirmative and negative

Teacher's Note

Pupils will do Test 5 in the following lesson. If you don't want to rush into Unit 6, for the rest of the lesson do these activities:
1 Pupils can read out the cartoon story from Unit 5 Lesson 1. Then ask volunteers to act out the cartoon story.
2 Pupils can read out the texts from Lesson 2 and Lesson 3.
3 Repeat the *Say* task from Lesson 2.
4 Do the chant.
5 Make another wordsearch.

Optional activity

Revision for Test 5

- Revise the parts of the body words. Ask a volunteer to draw a stick man on the board. Ask pupils to call out one at a time body parts for the volunteer to draw. Repeat until pupils remember the words well.

- Write animals on the board. Ask pupils to remember the animals they learnt in this unit. Ask volunteers to spell the words out.

- Revise the adjectives and *tail*. Write *sad, long, wet, fat* and *thin* on the board. Remind pupils of the meanings and then ask pupils to mime what you say.
  You've got a long tail.
  You're a fat cat.
  You're sad.
  You're a thin snake.

- Revise *I've got* and *I haven't got*. Describe two things about yourself. eg *I've got long hair. I haven't got a dog.* Ask volunteers to make two sentences each.

- Repeat the task for *You've got* and *You haven't got*. Ask pairs to talk about each other. Then repeat the task for *He's got* and *He hasn't got* where volunteers describe a boy in the class and the pupils have to guess which boy it is. Repeat task with a girl using *She's got* and *She hasn't got*.

- Write *I, you, he, she, it, we, you, they* on the board. Ask volunteers to help you fill in the verbs for *have got* affirmative and negative. Pupils can copy this into their notebooks.

Extra Activity

- Pupils can make their own wordsearches with the words from Unit 5. Hand out a grid of ten squares by ten squares to each pupil the same as the one in Unit 2. Show them how to fill in the grid with eight of the words they like from Unit 5. Tell them to use capital letters. Go round the class helping with spelling where necessary. Then tell pupils to fill in the other boxes with any letters they like.

- Pupils can swap wordsearches and then find each other's words.

Lesson 1 Trek's reporters in Australia

Aims

- Learn and use new vocabulary: *mask, flippers, mobile phone, bag, map, beautiful, Come on!*
- Learn and use new grammar: *have got* interrogative

Materials

- Flashcards: bag, flippers, map, mask, mobile phone
- Masks: Trek, Mia, Ty, Leo

Lead-in

- Revise the parts of the body from Unit 5. Say a word and ask pupils to point to the correct part of the body. Draw a stick man on the board. Ask a volunteer to spell out a word while another volunteer writes it on the board and labels the stick man.

- Revise the affirmative and negative of *have got*. Say *I've got two eyes.* and ask pupils to repeat. Ask volunteers to make affirmative sentences with these prompts:
I / fingers
you / nose
he / ears
they / cat
Say *I haven't got three ears.* and ask pupils to repeat. Ask volunteers to make negative sentences with the same prompts.

- Check homework. Tell pupils to open their Activity Books at pages 44 and 45. Ask volunteers to read out their answers. Ask volunteers to come to the front of the class and to show their pictures in task E to the rest of the class. Then quickly check all pupils' books.

- Test dictation: *cat, fish, parrot, pet, fat, thin.* See the teacher's introduction pages 7-9 for teaching suggestions. Go round the class and check all pupils' dictation.

Episode outline

Australia: Episode 3

The reporters are finishing their trip to Australia. The say goodbye to the pupils and then fly in their helicopter to the ocean. They go diving at the Great Barrier Reef and see fish and an octopus. At the end of the diving trip, the teacher Mr Davis telephones them to say goodbye. Here the mini story ends and the reporters say goodbye to Trek. Trek liked the DVD and thinks Australia is great.

New vocabulary

- Teach the new words with the flashcards. See the teacher's introduction pages 7-9 for teaching suggestions.

- Tell pupils to open their books at page 62 and to look at the vocabulary box. Hold up your book and point to the first picture word. Say the word and ask pupils to repeat. Do the same with all the words. Then read out the new picture words in the vocabulary box in random order and ask pupils to point to the correct pictures.

- Read out the word *beautiful.* Explain the meaning. Ask the girls in the class to stand up. Say *The girls are beautiful.* and ask pupils to repeat. Read out the phrase *Come on!* Explain the meaning. Ask two pupils to stand next to you. Say *Come on!* and tell them to follow you around the room. Ask volunteers to do the same.

- Read out all the words again one by one and ask pupils to repeat after you.

A Listen and read.

For teachers using the DVD

- Make sure each pupil has got a copy of the DVD Worksheet found on page 132.
- Please follow the procedure outlined in Unit 1, Lesson 1 on page 31 for teachers using the DVD.

Before you watch

Answers
1 the pupils
2 masks and flippers
3 Yes

While you watch

Answers
1 Mia
2 Leo
3 Ty
4 Ty
5 Leo
6 Trek

After you watch

Answers
1 Ty
2 in the bag
3 beautiful
4 an octopus
5 Mr Davis

For teachers using the audio CD 2.11

- Tell pupils to look at the cartoon story. Ask pupils to look at the story and find things which they think are beautiful. Encourage them to use English for the words they have learnt.

- Play the recording. Tell pupils to look at the pictures and follow the speech bubbles with their fingers.

- Play the recording again. Pause after each speech bubble and ask pupils to repeat.
- Check that pupils understand the story. Use L1 where necessary.
  Who has got the map? (Ty)
  Where are the masks? (in the bag)
  What are the fish like? (beautiful)
  What surprises Ty? (an octopus)
  Who telephones Leo? (Mr Davis)
- Play the recording again. Then ask volunteers to read out the story.
- Assign characters to volunteers and ask them to act out the story in front of the class. Pupils can use the character masks.

Extra activity

- Listen again to all three episodes of the mini story. Play the recordings from Lesson 1 of Units 1, 2 and 3. Ask pupils to follow the speech bubbles with their fingers.
- Divide the class into three groups, one group for each episode. Assign roles to pupils in each group. Then ask each group to act out their episode in front of the class. Pupils can wear the character masks.

B Look and learn.

- Read out the dialogue. Read it out again and ask pupils to repeat.
- Ask pupils to look at the grammar box. Read out the grammar notes and sentences. Ask pupils to repeat. Explain the meaning of the notes.
- Ask pupils to circle the person and underline the verb in the grammar sentences. Ask volunteers to read out the sentences.
- Practise the grammar. Ask volunteers questions and elicit answers.
  eg *Have you got a cat?*
  Has your mum/dad/grandma got a car?
  Have they got brown eyes?
  Then ask pairs to stand at the front of the classroom and ask each other their own questions. Prompt pupils where necessary.

C Write.

- Read out the question for number 1 and ask pupils to read out the answer. Ask them why *haven't.* is the correct answer.
- Explain the rest of the task to pupils. Check pupils remember the meanings of all the words. Allow them enough time to complete the task alone. Go round the class helping pupils where necessary.
- Check answers. Then ask pairs to read out the questions and answers.

Answers
1 haven't (given)
2 have
3 has
4 haven't
5 has

D Listen and write J (Jane) or P (Paul). 2.12

- Tell pupils that they are going to listen to a man, Paul, and a woman, Jane, talking about different things they have got in their bags. Explain that they must listen carefully to see who has got what. If Jane has got something they write *J* in the box and for Paul they write *P* in the box.
- Play the recording for the example. Make sure pupils understand what to do. Remind pupils of the meanings of the words.
- Play the rest of the recording, pausing between questions where necessary. Play the recording again and ask pupils to check their answers.

Listening script
1
Come on, Paul.
OK, Jane.
Have you got the map?
Yes, I have. The map is in my bag.

2
Have you got the flippers, Jane?
The flippers? Yes. I have.
Good.

3
Have you got the masks?
No, I haven't, Jane. You've got the masks. Look!
Oh yes. I've got the masks.

4
And the camera … Have you got it, Paul?
Yes, I've got the camera.
Cool!

5
Come on. Let's go.
Oh no! I haven't got a mobile phone.
It's OK, Paul. I've got a mobile phone. It's in my bag.

Answers
1 P (given)
2 J
3 J
4 P
5 J

F Say.

- Read out the dialogue and ask pupils to repeat. Tell pupils that the boy and girl are asking each other about things they have got at home.
- Stick the flashcards on the board. Point to the flippers and ask a volunteer *Have you got flippers?* and elicit answer. Then ask the volunteer to ask the pupil next to him a question using one of the flashcards. Continue around the class until all pupils have had a turn.
- Ask pairs to come to the front of the class and ask each other questions. They can use the words from this lesson and words they have learnt so far.

Extension activity

- Ask pupils to put a pencil on their desks. Ask a volunteer *Have you got a pencil?* Elicit answer *Yes, I have.* Then ask the volunteer to hand you the pencil. Ask pupils to remember what we say when we hand something to someone and elicit *Here you are.* Write the mini dialogue on the board.
  Have you got a pencil?
  Yes, I have. Here you are.
  Thanks.
  You're welcome.
  Read out the dialogue and ask pupils to repeat.

- Ask volunteers to perform the mini dialogue in front of the class. First leave the dialogue on the board for help. Then clean the board and ask pupils to repeat the task.

Homework

- Pupil's Audio CD: Pupils listen to the cartoon story at home. Explain to pupils that they should listen to track 28 on the CD.

- Activity Book, pages 46-47: Time permitting, some tasks can be done in class.

- Dictation: *bag, flippers, map, mask, mobile phone*

Lesson 2   Fiona is a dancer.

Aims

- Learn and use new vocabulary: *jacket, shirt, shoes, skirt, socks, clothes, dancer*

- Learn and use new grammar: possessive *'s*

Materials

- Flashcards: bag, flippers, map, mask, mobile phone

- Items of clothing: jacket, shirt, shoes, skirt, socks

- A CD with music

- Optional for song: crepe paper and scissors

Lead-in

- Revise the words from Lesson 1. Stick the flashcards on the board. Call out the words one at a time and ask volunteers to come to the board and point to the correct flashcard.

- Ask pupils questions with *Have you got?* (a pet, a mask, a skateboard) and elicit answers.

- Check homework. Tell pupils to open their Activity Books at pages 46 and 47. Ask volunteers to read out their answers. Ask pairs to come to the front of the class and to read out the questions and answers in task E. Then quickly check all pupils' books.

- Test dictation: *bag, flippers, map, mask, mobile phone*. See the teacher's introduction pages 7-9 for teaching suggestions. Go round the class and check all pupils' dictation.

New vocabulary

- Teach the clothes words. Put all the items of clothing on your desk and say *Look. Clothes.* Hold up the skirt and say *This is a skirt.* Ask pupils to repeat. Write *skirt* on the board. Do the same with the other items. Then read out the words from the board one at a time and ask volunteers to come to the front of the class and hold up the correct item of clothing.

- Teach *dancer.* In L1 ask pupils if they can dance. Play the CD with music and tell pupils to dance along to the music. Turn off the CD and say *Well done. You're dancers.* Repeat *dancer* and ask pupils to repeat after you.

- Tell pupils to open their books at page 64 and to look at the vocabulary box. Hold up your book and point to the first picture word. Say the word and ask pupils to repeat. Do the same with all the words. Then read out the new picture words in the vocabulary box in random order and ask pupils to point to the correct pictures.

- Read out all the words again one by one and ask pupils to repeat after you.

A Listen and read. 🔘 CD2: 13

- Tell pupils that they are going to read about a dancer. Ask pupils to look at the photo and to guess where the girl is from. Read out the first sentence. Show pupils on the map where Scotland is.

Background Information
Scottish highland dance

Scottish Highland dancing is a traditional Scottish form of folk dance. The girl in the picture is dancing the Sword Dance which is a solo dance. Traditionally this was danced before a battle. Nowadays this and other Scottish dances are performed in competitions and athletic events in many countries. They are considered a difficult form of dancing requiring strength, stamina and perfect timing to the music.

- Play the recording. Tell pupils to follow the text with their fingers.

- Play the recording again. Pause after each sentence and ask pupils to repeat.

- Play the recording again. Then ask volunteers to read out a sentence each of the text.

B Circle.

- Read the example to pupils. Ask them to find the sentence in the second paragraph which gives them the answer.

- Explain the rest of the task to pupils. Tell them to underline the sentences in the text which give them the answers. Allow them enough time to complete the task alone. Go round the class encouraging and helping pupils where necessary.

- Check answers. Write them on the board if necessary.

Answers
1 red (given)
2 long
3 jacket
4 has got

C Look and learn.

- Read out the speech bubble. Read it out again and ask pupils to repeat. Explain to pupils that 's shows that something belongs to someone. Ask pupils to circle the 's in the speech bubble.
- Ask pupils to look at the grammar box. Read out the grammar notes and sentences. Ask pupils to repeat. Ask pupils to circle the 's in the sentences.
- Practise the grammar. Say for example *John's pencil is red.* Ask pupils to repeat. Tell pupils to look at their friends' pencils and ask volunteers to make sentences of their own.

D Write.

- Ask a pupil to give you a pencil. Hold up the pencil and say, for example, *It's John's pencil.* Ask pupils to repeat. Write the sentence on the board. Ask pupils to look at the sentence and find the 's which shows that the pencil belongs to John. Ask pupils to remember what the 's in *It's* is short for and elicit *It is*.
- Read out the example and ask pupils to repeat. Ask them to circle the 's in the answer which means something belongs to someone.
- Explain the task to pupils. Check pupils remember the meanings of all the words. Tell them not to use *the* with names. Allow them enough time to complete the task alone. Go round the class helping pupils where necessary.
- Check answers. Write them on the board if necessary.

Answers
1 It's the dog's toy. (given)
2 It's Bert's shirt.
3 It's Mum's hat.
4 It's Izzy's jacket.

E Sing. 2.14

- Tell pupils they are going to learn a song. Explain to pupils that the song is about clothes.
- Ask pupils to look at the picture and tell you which items of clothing they can see. Ask pupils to count the *socks, hats,* and *shoes.*
- Play the recording and tell pupils to listen and follow the words with their fingers.
- Read out the song one line at a time and ask pupils to repeat after you.
- Play the recording again. Encourage pupils to sing along. Practise many times until pupils are familiar with the words.

Optional activity

- Pupils can make crazy hats to wear for the song. Cut out a square of crepe paper for each pupil, which is bigger than his/her head. Show pupils how to roll and scrunch up each corner of the square to make a hat. These hats are like a hat made out of a handkerchief with knots in each corner.
- Pupils can wear their crazy hats while singing the song.

Homework

- Pupil's Audio CD: Pupils listen to the text and the song at home. Explain to pupils that they should listen to tracks 29 and 30 on the CD.
- Activity Book, pages 48-49: Time permitting, some tasks can be done in class.
- Dictation: *clothes, dancer, jacket, shirt, shoes, skirt, socks*
- Optional extra homework: Pupils can copy their written task from Lesson 2 onto paper to display on the wall.

Extra activity

- Ask a volunteer to stand in front of the class. Describe the volunteer's clothes eg *David's shoes are big. David's shirt is white.*
- Ask pairs to stand at the front and make two sentences about their partner's clothes. Make sure all pupils have a turn.

Lesson 3   My clothes are cool.

Aims

- Learn and use new vocabulary: *scarf, T-shirt, boots, dress, jeans, new, Let's play.*
- Learn and use new grammar: possessive pronouns *my, your, his, her, its, our, your, their*

Materials

- Magazine photos of clothing: jacket, shirt, shoes, skirt, socks, boots, dress, jeans, scarf, T-shirt
- A new notebook
- Optional for extra activity: Bingo cards. One piece of paper divided into six boxes for each pupil.

Lead-in

- Revise the words from Lesson 2 with the items of clothing. Put the magazine photos of the clothes on the desk, call out a word and ask volunteers to find the item. Then ask volunteers to call out items for the other pupils to find.
- Revise the possessive 's. Ask a pupil for a pencil. Say, for example, *Tom's pencil is red.* Ask pupils to repeat. Then ask pairs to make sentences about each other in front of the class.
- Check homework. Tell pupils to open their Activity Books at pages 48 and 49. Ask volunteers to read out their answers. Then sing the song from Lesson 2 (CD2: 14).
- Test dictation: *clothes, dancer, jacket, shirt, shoes, skirt, socks.* See the teacher's introduction pages 7-9 for teaching suggestions. Go round the class and check all pupils' dictation.

New vocabulary

- Teach *boots, dress, jeans, scarf, T-shirt* with the items of clothing. Hold up the magazine photo of the boots and say *These are boots.* Ask pupils to repeat. Do the same with the other items. Point out to pupils that *jeans* is plural ie *These are jeans.*

- Hold up the new notebook and ask *What's this?* Elicit *It's a notebook.* Show pupils that the notebook hasn't been written in and explain that it is new. Teach *new.* Say *It's a new notebook. It's new.* Ask pupils to repeat.

- Tell pupils to open their books at page 66 and to look at the vocabulary box. Hold up your book and point to the first picture word. Say the word and ask pupils to repeat. Do the same with all the words. Then read out the new picture words in the vocabulary box in random order and ask pupils to point to the correct pictures.

- Read out the words *Let's play.* Explain the meaning. Ask pupils to say *Let's play.* and then mime they are playing. (eg a board game, basketball)

- Read out all the words again one by one and ask pupils to repeat after you.

A Read.

- Tell pupils to look at the photo of the boy and the girl. Ask pupils to say what clothes the children have got. eg *The girl has got a pink dress.* Ask pupils to find out the names of the children.

- Tell pupils to read the dialogue between the children and to find out who has got a pink scarf. Allow pupils enough time to read the dialogue alone.

- Read out the dialogue one sentence at a time and ask pupils to repeat.

- Ask volunteers to read out a sentence each of the dialogue. Then ask volunteers to act out the dialogue to the class.

B Write.

- Read the example to pupils and ask them find the sentence in the dialogue which gives them the answer *dress.* Tell them to underline the sentence.

- Explain the rest of the task to pupils. Make sure they understand the meanings of all the words. Allow them enough time to complete the task alone. Go round the class helping pupils where necessary.

- Check answers. Ask volunteers to read out the answers.

Answers
1 dress (given)
2 jeans
3 boys
4 scarf
5 boots

C Look and learn.

- Read out the dialogue and ask pupils to repeat. Tell pupils to circle the word *your* and explain the meaning. Draw a line down the middle of the board. On the left write *I, you, he, she, it, we, you, they.*

- Ask pupils to look at the grammar box. Read out the possessive pronouns and explain the meaning. Write the possessive pronouns on the right hand side of the board.

- Read out the example sentences and ask pupils to repeat. Tell them to circle words *Her* and *Our.* Ask volunteers to read out the dialogue and the sentences.

- Practise the grammar. Write this sentence on the board:
I've got a dog. _____ dog is brown.
Ask pupils to find the missing word.
Change the sentence to:
You've got a dog. _____ dog is brown.
Continue with all the possessive pronouns except *its.*
Finally, write:
This is my brown dog. _____ name is Brownie.
Ask pupils to find the missing word.

D Write.

- Read out the example and ask pupils to repeat. Ask pupils to circle *We* in the first sentence. Explain that this word helps them to find the word *our.* They can look at the two columns you wrote on the board for help. Read out all the sentences and check pupils understand the meanings

- Explain the task to pupils. Tell pupils to cross out the words they use from the box as they use them. Allow pupils enough time to complete the task alone. Go round the class helping where necessary.

- Check answers. Write them on the board if necessary.

Answers
1 Our (given)
2 My
3 her
4 their
5 your
6 his

Say it! 2.15

- Write *s* on the board. Ask pupils to say the name of this letter. Explain that the letters *s* sometimes makes an *s* sound and sometimes makes *a z* sound.

- Tell pupils to look at the task. Play the first part of the recording (Listen and say.) asking pupils to repeat the words *socks* and *jeans* each time they hear them (*Socks* and *jeans* will be heard twice.). Ask pupils to tell you which *s* sounded like *s* and which sounded like *z.* Tell them to underline the *s* sound and circle the *z* sound.

- Ask for volunteers to read out the phrase (*Sharks and whales haven't got flippers and masks.*). Play the recording and ask all pupils to repeat. Tell pupils to underline the *s* sound and circle the *z* sounds. (*Sharks and whales haven't got flippers and masks.* will be heard once.)

E Say.

- Read out the speech bubble to pupils, one sentence at a time and ask them to repeat.

- Quickly revise the clothes vocabulary. Describe your own clothes to pupils. Use three sentences as in the example. eg *My shirt is white. My shoes are black. My jacket is blue. I'm cool!*
- Ask volunteers to stand in front of the class and to describe their clothes. Make sure all pupils have a turn.

Extension activity

- Pupils can do the speaking task again, but this time they describe their friend. Explain that they must change *My* to *His* or *Her* and *I'm* to *He's* or *She's*.

F Draw and write.

- Tell pupils to draw a picture of themselves and what they are wearing. Allow them enough time to complete their drawings.
- Explain to pupils that they must write three things about their clothes. Go round the class helping with ideas and spelling where necessary.
- Ask pupils to hold up their books and to show each other their pictures. Ask volunteers to read out their work.

Homework

- Activity Book, pages 50-51: Time permitting, some tasks can be done in class.
- Dictation: *boots, dress, jeans, new, scarf, T-shirt*
- Revision for Test 6:
  Words: *bag, flippers, map, mask, mobile phone, beautiful, Come on!, clothes, dancer, jacket, shirt, shoes, skirt, socks, boots, dress, jeans, new, scarf, T-shirt, Let's play.*
  Grammar: *have got* interrogative, possessive *'s, my, your, his, her, its, our, your, their*

Teacher's Note

Pupils will do Test 6 in the following lesson. After every three units, there is a review which can be done in the same lesson as the test.

Optional activity

Revision for Test 6

- Revise the clothes words. Ask pupils to remember all the clothes they learnt in this unit and write the words on the board. Ask volunteers to draw the clothes next to the words.
- Revise the items from Lesson 1 with the flashcards.
- Revise *Have/Has _____ got?* Write *beautiful* and *new* on the board. Ask volunteers to show you beautiful things and new things in the room. Ask these questions:
  Have you got new shoes?
  Has Jane got a beautiful dress?
  Have they got new jeans?
  Elicit answers.
- Revise *'s* and the possessive pronouns. Ask a volunteer to stand up and say, for example, *Paul's shirt is white. His shirt is white.* Ask pupils to repeat. Do the same with other volunteers. Then draw a line down the middle of the board and write the personal pronouns *I-they* on the left and ask pupils to tell you the possessive pronouns *my-their* to write on the right. Alternatively ask volunteers to write one each on the board.

Extra activity

- Play clothes bingo. Hand out one piece of paper divided into six boxes to each pupil. Tell pupils to draw one item of clothing they have learnt in Unit 6 in each box, meaning they will have six different items. Go round the class helping pupils where necessary.
- When pupils have finished their drawings, explain the rules of the game. You will call out a clothes word and if a pupil has drawn it they can tick the box in pencil. Then you call out another word and so on. When a pupil has ticked all six boxes, he/she shouts *bingo* and hold up his bingo card.
- Pupils can rub out the ticks, and the game can be played again.

Let's remember!

Aims

- Revise vocabulary from Units 4-6
- Revise grammar from Units 4-6

Materials

- Flashcards:
  Unit 4: *drawing, helicopter, pupils, school*
  Unit 6: *bag, flippers, map, mask, mobile phone*

Revision

- Revise the words from the flashcards. Hold up a flashcard and ask pupils to call out the word. Then place the flashcards face down on your desk. Ask a volunteer to choose a flashcard from the desk, turn it over and say what it is.

- Ask pupils to remember all the *classroom objects* they have learnt in units 4-6. Point to real objects to prompt pupils. Do the same for *body parts* and *clothes.*

- Revise the *affirmative* and *negative* of *have got*. Write *I've got a pet.* and *It hasn't got legs.* on the board and ask volunteers to read out the sentences and to guess what your pet is (a fish). Copy the following table onto the board:

I	have got	a pet.
He	haven't got	a tail.
She	has got	
It	hasn't got	

Ask pupils to make sentences with the words across the columns. Make sure they use the correct forms.

- Revise the *interrogative* of *have got*. Ask pupils *Have you got a sister/brother?* and elicit correct answers. Revise all persons. Here are some suggested questions:
  Has a dog got four legs?
  Have they got brown hair?
  Has she got small ears?
  Have we got pencils?

- Revise all forms of *There is/are*. Put a pencil on the desk and say. *Look. There is a pencil.* Ask pupils to repeat. Add another pencil and say. *Look. There are two pencils.* Ask pupils to repeat. Then say *Are there any pencils?* and elicit answer *Yes, there are.* Ask *Is there a ruler?* and elicit answer *No, there isn't.* Repeat the task with other classroom objects.

- Revise the *possessive 's* and the *personal pronouns.* Ask a pupil to hand you a pencil. Say, for example, *This is Andrew's pencil.* Ask pupils to repeat. Then say *It's his pencil*, and ask pupils to repeat. Then ask *Is it my pencil?* And elicit answer *No, it isn't.* Ask the same question with *your, her, our*, and *their.*

Lead-in

- Check homework. Tell pupils to open their Activity Books at pages 50 and 51. Ask volunteers to read out their answers. Ask volunteers to come to the front of the class and to show their drawing for task E. Then quickly check all pupils' books.

- Test dictation: *boots, dress, jeans, new, scarf, T-shirt.* See the teacher's introduction pages 7-9 for teaching suggestions. Go round the class and check all pupils' dictation.

A Find and stick.

- Ask pupils to open their books at page 68 and to look at task A. Ask volunteers to read out the words. Then read out the words again and ask pupils to repeat as a class.

- Show pupils where to find the stickers in their books. Tell them to remove the stickers one at a time and to stick them in the correct boxes. Allow pupils enough time to stick all the stickers. Go round the class helping pupils where necessary.

- Check answers. Ask volunteers to hold up their books and read out the words.

B Write.

- Tell pupils to look at the table. Ask volunteers to tell you the words for each picture.

- Tell pupils to find the words in the box and to write them in the correct column. Tell them to cross through a word in the box when they have used it. Allow them enough time to complete the task alone. Go round the class helping pupils where necessary.

- Check answers.

Answers

Clothes: jacket (given), dress, skirt
Classroom: board, desk, ruler

Extension activity

- Ask pupils to think of two more words for each category in task B. Write their ideas on the board.

- Give pupils a third category: *Beach.* Ask them to think of three objects for the beach. Write their ideas on the board.

C Circle.

- Read out the example and ask pupils why *legs* is the correct answer. Read out all the sentences and make sure that pupils remember the meanings of all the words.

- Explain the rest of the task to pupils. Allow them enough time to complete the task alone. Go round the class helping pupils where necessary.

- Check answers. Ask volunteers to read out their answers.

Answers
1 legs (given)
2 pens
3 hair
4 fish
5 tail
6 notebook

D Write 've got, haven't got, 's got or hasn't got.

- Ask pupils to look at picture 1 and to describe what they can see. Read out the example and ask pupils why 's got is the correct answer. Ask pupils to look at all the pictures and to describe them. Then read out all the sentences and make sure that pupils remember the meanings of all the words.

- Explain the rest of the task to pupils. Allow them enough time to complete the task alone. Go round the class helping pupils where necessary.

- Check answers. Ask volunteers to read out their answers.

Answers
1 's got (given)
2 hasn't got
3 've got
4 's got
5 've got
6 haven't got

E Write

- Tell pupils to look at number 1, the example. Ask them to think about what they have to do in this task. Help them work out that the words in the sentences have been mixed up. They have to put the words in the correct order to make sentences. Ask volunteers to read out the correct sentence.

- Explain the rest of the task to pupils. Do each sentence one at a time. Ask volunteers to read out their answers. Write the answer on the board. Then continue to the next sentence. Go round the class helping pupils where necessary.

- Check answers. Ask volunteers to read out their answers.

Answers
1 There's a rubber on the chair. (given)
2 There aren't fifteen pencils in my bag.
3 Are there any helicopters?
4 I've got a green T-shirt.
5 Has he got two parrots?

F Circle.

- Read out the example and ask pupils why The is the correct answer. Read out all the sentences and make sure that pupils remember the meanings of all the words.

- Explain the rest of the task to pupils. Allow them enough time to complete the task alone. Go round the class helping pupils where necessary.

- Check answers. Ask volunteers to read out their answers.

Answers
1 The (given)
2 Mum's
3 His
4 a
5 Our
6 boy's

Extra activity

Poster: My things

This poster can be used to consolidate and revise vocabulary and grammar of Units 4-6 in a fun and interesting way. Pupils can also play a game with the poster. Follow the procedure outlined on the back of the poster.

Homework

- Pupil's CD: Pupils listen to the songs at home. Explain to pupils that they should listen to tracks 24, 26 and 30 on the CD.

- Activity Book, pages 52-53: Time permitting, some tasks can be done in class.

- Revision for Progress Test 2. Pupils should revise all the vocabulary and grammar from Units 4-6.

Teacher's Note

Pupils will do Progress Test 2 in the following lesson. After the test, you can do the lesson Fun & Games.

Fun & Games

Aims

- Consolidate new vocabulary with fun activities
- Consolidate new grammar with fun activities
- Make a puppet

Materials

- One photocopy of the puppet cutout for each pupil (page 141)
- Scissors, colouring pencils, drinking straws, sticky tape
- Optional for extra activity: 12 quiz cards. Write one question on each card, so they can be shuffled to play again. See Extra activity for questions.

Lead-in

- Tell pupils that today's lesson is all about fun and games. Ask them to open their books at page 70. Ask them what they can see (a boy doing a hand stand).
- Read out the paragraph and ask pupils to follow the words with their fingers. Read it out again one sentence at a time and ask pupils to repeat. Check comprehension with these questions. Encourage pupils to use English for the words they have learnt.
  What's the boy's name? (Tamir)
  Where is Tamir from? (Morocco)

  Show pupils on the map where Morocco is.

- Consolidate vocabulary pupils have learnt using the picture. Here are some suggestions:

  Pupils point to the boy's body parts and name them: *arms, legs, fingers, toes, hair, eyes, ears, nose.*
  Has Tamir got a blue T-shirt?
  Has he got a yellow T-shirt?
  Has he got socks?
  Has he got shoes?
  Has he got a tail?
  How old is Tamir? Guess.
  Is he a pupil?
  Is Tamir at school?
  Is Tamir fat / thin?
  Are there any cats?

Quiz time!

- Ask pupils *What's that?* and elicit *It's a spider.* Read out the question and both answers and make sure pupils understand the meaning. Ask pupils to choose the correct answer (a). Ask volunteers to read out the question and answer.

A Colour.

- Ask pupils to describe what they can see (a girl, a boy and a dog). Ask volunteers to name the clothes the girl is wearing. Then do the same for the boy and the dog.

- Ask pupils to colour in the clothes as they like. Go round the class revising the names of the clothes with individual pupils. Ask *What's that? / What are those?* and elicit answers
- Write the following on the board:
  The girl's T-shirt is _____ .
  The girl's skirt is _____ .
  The girl's shoes are _____ .
  The boy's shirt is _____ .
  The boy's jeans are _____ .
  The boy's shoes are _____ .
  The dog's hat is _____ .
  The dog's scarf is _____ .
  The dog's boots _____ .
  Read out what is on the board. Ask pupils to describe their pictures using the sentences on the board and adding the colours they have used.

B Sing. 2:16

- Tell pupils they are going to learn a song. Explain to pupils that the song is about a funny clown called Freddy.
- Ask pupils to look at the song and find the body words they know. Demonstrate the meaning of *wiggle* using your fingers.
- Play the recording and tell pupils to listen and follow the words with their fingers.
- Read out the song one line at a time and ask pupils to repeat after you.
- Play the recording again. Encourage pupils to sing along. Practise many times until pupils are familiar with the words.
- Pupils can wiggle their fingers and whole bodies while they sing the song.

C Make.

- Tell pupils they are going to make a puppet of Funny Freddy. Tell pupils to look at the picture in task C and explain each stage to them.
  1 Colour in Funny Freddy.
  2 Cut out the puppet.
  3 Stick a drinking straw on the back of the puppet with sticky tape.
  4 The puppet is ready to wiggle for the song.
- Ask pupils to have their colouring pencils ready. Hand out the photocopies of the puppet cutouts and ask pupils to colour it in.
- When all pupils are ready, ask pupils to put their colouring pencils away. Then hand out the scissors. Ask pupils to cut out their puppet. Go round the class helping pupils where necessary. Collect the scissors.
- Hand out one drinking straw to each pupil. Give pupils a piece of sticky tape and show them where to stick the drinking straw on the back of the puppet.
- Ask pupils to hold up their puppets. Encourage them to describe the colours they have used to colour in Funny Freddy. eg
  His nose is red.
  His hair is green.
  His shoes are black.
- Play the song. Pupils can wiggle their puppets as they sing.

Homework

- Pupil's Audio CD: Pupils listen to the song at home. Explain to pupils that they should listen to track 31 on the CD.

- Optional extra homework: Pupils draw and colour their own clowns in their notebooks. They can describe their clowns in the next lesson.

Extra activity

- Play *Simon says*. Explain the rules of the game to pupils:
  You give pupils instructions about their bodies. If the instruction is preceded with the words *Simon says*, pupils must do what you say. If the instruction stands alone, pupils mustn't do anything.
  Any pupils who carry out an instruction when they shouldn't, are out. Touching the wrong body part also means a pupil is out. The winner is the last pupil left who hasn't made any mistakes.

- Ask pupils to stand up. Here are some suggested instructions:
  Simon says touch your nose.
  Simon says touch your hair.
  Simon says wiggle your fingers.
  Touch your ears.
  Wiggle your nose.

- This game can be repeated many times. It's also a good way to finish any lesson if you have a few minutes to spare.

Trek's reporters in Brazil

Brazil

Ask pupils to look at the National Geographic photo on pages 72-73 (use L1) and tell them that it has been taken on the long Copacabana beach in Rio de Janeiro.

Pupils are likely to know that Brazil is famous for football. They will probably know a few famous Brazilian football players' names. Encourage them to name a few (Pele, Rivaldo, Ronaldo, Ronaldhino). Ask them what they know about the Brazilian landscape. Then explain that in Rio there are beautiful long beaches (Copacabana and other smaller ones). Tell them that the city is very colourful and has a big carnival celebration every year. Then tell them about the Amazon forest and river. The forest is enormous, but sadly it is being cut down. This is bad because this forest gives the world a lot of rain. Without the forest we won't have any rain or water. Pupils might know where South America is situated. Ask volunteers to find South America on the classroom map and then show them where Brazil is. Then point to the map at the top of the page to show them. First show them where their own country is on the globe and then point out the area in red where the reporters are. Explain that this is Brazil.

The third country the reporters visit is Brazil. In episode 1, they visit the Copacabana beach in Rio. They meet some children and play beach volleyball with them and then swim in the sea. In episode 2, they want to watch a sporting event, so they go to the stadium and watch the Brazilian National team. In episode 3, the reporters visit the capital of the Amazon area, the city of Manaus. They admire the beautiful theatre and wander around the fruit market. Then they go on a boat ride into the impressive Amazon rain forest.

Fun facts

Here are some facts about Brazil which your pupils will find interesting:

1   Brazil is the largest country in South America.
2   It is the only country in South America where people speak Portuguese.
3   New species of wildlife are often found in Brazil.
4   The Amazon forest makes up half of the rain forests in the world.
5   There are more than two million different kinds of insects in the Amazon.
6   There are many dangerous animals in the Amazon, for example the anaconda snake and the piranha fish.
7   Brazil sells shoes to other countries.
8   Coffee is a very popular drink in Brazil.
9   Samba music is from Brazil.
10 The most popular sport in Brazil is football.
11 Brazil has won the World Cup five times.
12 The 2016 Olympic Games will be held in Rio de Janeiro, Brazil.

Lesson 1 Trek's reporters in Brazil

Aims

- Learn and use new vocabulary: *swim, sea, look at, run, play volleyball, jump, very, everybody*
- Learn and use new grammar: *can, can't*

Materials

- Optional for extra activity: 8 word cards with these words:
  dance
  stand up
  sit down
  run
  clap your hands
  play volleyball
  swim
  jump
- Masks: Trek, Mia, Ty, Leo

Lead-in

- Revise *fantastic, fun, Come on.* and *Let's go.* Draw a beach and a simple beach umbrella on the board. Say *Look. A beach. It's fantastic.* Ask pupils to repeat. Write *fantastic* on the board. Then say *Let's play. It's fun.* Ask pupils to repeat. Write *fun* on the board. Beckon to two pupils and say *Come on.* When they come to the front of the class, say *Let's go* and open the classroom door as if to leave. They should follow you. This could be repeated with another pair. Write *Come on.* and *Let's go.* on the board. Read out the words on the board. Ask pupils to repeat and check they remember the meanings.

- Check homework. Tell pupils to open their Activity Books at pages 52 and 53. Ask volunteers to read out their answers. Then quickly check all pupils' books.

Episode outline

Brazil: Episode 1

Trek receives a new DVD from the reporters who are now in sunny Brazil. They are in Rio de Janeiro on the famous long sandy beach called Copacabana. Ty starts to play beach volleyball with some local children. A girl invites Mia to join in, which she does. Poor Ty has to stop because he is hot and tired. Then Mia sees Leo who is swimming in the sea. Mia and the children all run to join Leo in the sea. But Ty is still too tired to join in.

New vocabulary

- Teach the new words with movements. Say *Look at me!* and put your hands around your eyes as if they are binoculars. Ask pupils to copy and repeat. Then jump and say *jump*. Ask pupils to copy and repeat.

Do the same with *run, play volleyball* and *swim*. Then ask pupils where they swim at the beach. Draw wavy lines for the sea on the board next to the beach and say *Look. The sea.* Ask pupils to repeat.

- Tell pupils to open their books at page 74 and to look at the vocabulary box. Hold up your book and point to the first picture word. Say the word and ask pupils to repeat. Do the same with all the words. Then read out the new picture words in the vocabulary box in random order and ask pupils to point to the correct pictures.

- Read out the words *very* and *everybody*. Explain the meanings. Then say *Jump everybody.* and encourage all pupils to jump. Then say *That's very good! Well done.*

- Read out all the words again one by one and ask pupils to repeat after you.

A Listen and read.

For teachers using the DVD

- Make sure each pupil has a copy of the DVD worksheet found on page 133.

- Please follow the procedure outlined in Unit 1, Lesson 1 on page 31 for teachers using the DVD.

Before you watch

> **Answers**
> 1 on a very long beach in Brazil
> 2 beach volleyball

While you watch

> **Answers**
> 1 play
> 2 run
> 3 jump
> 4 Look at
> 5 swim

After you watch

> **Answers**
> 1 long
> 2 beach volleyball
> 3 in the sea
> 4 Leo, Mia and the children

For teachers using the audio CD 2.17

- Tell pupils to look at the cartoon story. Ask them to find the country Brazil on the classroom map.

- Play the recording. Tell pupils to look at the pictures and follow the speech bubbles with their fingers.

- Play the recording again. Pause after each speech bubble and ask pupils to repeat.

- Check pupils understand the story. Use L1 where necessary.

Is the beach long or short? (long)
What do Ty and Mia play ? (beach volleyball)
Where is Leo? (in the sea)
Who can swim? (Leo, Mia and the children)

- Play the recording again. Then ask volunteers to read out the story.

- Assign characters to volunteers and ask them to act out the story in front of the class. Pupils can wear the character masks.

B Look and learn.

- Read out the dialogue. Read it out again and ask pupils to repeat.

- Ask pupils to look at the grammar box. Explain the meaning of *can* and *can't.* Tell pupils that we can also say *cannot* instead of *can't.* Practise the grammar point. Ask two volunteers to stand at the front of the classroom and to jump up and down. Say *They can jump.* Ask pupils to repeat. Then write these animals on the board:
Kangaroos
Cats
Snakes
Write *can jump / can't jump.* next to the animals and ask volunteers to make sentences.

- Ask pupils to underline *can* and *can't* in the dialogue and sentences. Ask volunteers to read them out.

C Write can or can't.

- Read out the example and ask pupils why *can* is the correct answer.
- Explain the rest of the task to pupils. Tell them to look at the pictures to find the answers. Read out the sentences and make sure pupils remember the meaning of all the words. Allow pupils enough time to complete the task alone. Go round the class helping pupils where necessary.
- Check answers. Write them on the board if necessary.

> **Answers**
> 1 can (given)
> 2 can't
> 3 can
> 4 can't

Say it! 2.18

- Write *can* on the board. Read it out and tell pupils that the *a* sound is short. Say *can* again and ask pupils to repeat. Write *can't* on the board. Read it out and tell pupils that now the *a* sound is longer and that they must remember the *t* sound as well. Say *can't* again and ask pupils to repeat. Practise *can* and *can't* a few times.

- Tell pupils to look at the task. Play the first part of the recording (Listen and say.) asking pupils to repeat the words *can* and *can't* each time they hear them. (*Can* and *can't* will heard twice.)

- Ask for volunteers to read out the sentence. Play the recording and ask all pupils to repeat. (The sentence will be heard once.)

D Sing. 2.19

- Tell pupils they are going to learn a song. Ask pupils if they can dance. Teach *dance* and ask volunteers to demonstrate. Say *They can dance. Very good!* Ask pupils to look at the picture and to describe what the children can do. Elicit *They can dance.* and *They can jump.* Then teach *Clap.* Say *Look at me.* Clap your hands and ask pupils to copy. Then say *We can clap.* Ask pupils to repeat. Then say *Clap your hands.* and ask pupils to do so.

- Teach the instructions *Sit down.* and *Stand up.* Using a chair yourself, demonstrate what you want pupils to do. Say *Sit down.* and do so. Then say *Stand up.* and do so. Do this a few times and ask pupils to copy and repeat.

- Play the recording and tell pupils to listen and follow the words with their fingers.

- Read out the song one line at a time and ask pupils to repeat after you.

- Play the recording again. Encourage pupils to sing along. Practise many times until pupils are familiar with the words.

- Read out the song again line by line and teach pupils the movements. First pupils dance. Then they sit down, stand up, clap their hands and repeat. Then they jump one step to the left, one step to the right, clap their hands and repeat.

Extension activity

- Divide pupils into groups. Tell them that you will play the song and that they can practise the movements in their groups to make a little dance routine. Go round the class making suggestions and helping the groups.

- Each group performs their routine while the other groups sing.

Homework

- Pupil's Audio CD: Pupils listen to the recording of the cartoon story and the song at home. Explain to pupils that they should listen to tracks 32 and 33 on the CD.

- Activity Book, pages 54-55: Time permitting some tasks can be done in class.

- Dictation: *swim, sea, look at, run, play volleyball, jump*

Extra activity

- Ask a volunteer to come to the front of the class and to follow the instruction the pupils read out. Hold up one of the instruction cards eg *Jump.* Pupils read out the word and the volunteer must do the action. The pupils then decide if the volunteer can or can't do the action depending on his//her performance. Elicit *He can jump.* or *He can't jump.*

- Repeat until all pupils have had a turn.

Lesson 2   What a noise!

Aims

- Learn and use new vocabulary: *guitar, recorder, drums, piano, music, sing, What a noise!*
- Learn and use new grammar: *Can you ...? Yes, I can. No, I can't.*

Materials

- Flashcards: drums, guitar, piano, recorder, music, sing

Lead-in

- Revise the words from Lesson 1 with actions. Say *jump* and ask pupils to do the action. Continue with all the action words.
- Revise *can* and *can't*. Say *I can dance*. Then ask volunteers to make their own sentences for things they can do. Then say *I can't swim*. Ask volunteers to make their own sentences for things they can't do.
- Check homework. Tell pupils to open their Activity Books at pages 54 and 55. Ask volunteers to read out their answers. Then quickly check all pupils' books.
- Test dictation: *jump, look at, play volleyball, run, swim, sea*. See the teacher's introduction pages 7-9 for teaching suggestions. Go round the class and check all pupils' dictation.
- Sing the song from lesson 1.

New vocabulary

- Teach the new words with the flashcards. See the teacher's introduction pages 7-9 for teaching suggestions.
- Tell pupils to open their books at page 76 and to look at the vocabulary box. Hold up your book and point to the first picture word. Say the word and ask pupils to repeat. Do the same with all the words. Then read out the new picture words in the vocabulary box in random order and ask pupils to point to the correct pictures.
- Read out the phrase *What a noise!* Explain the meaning. Ask pupils to clap as loudly as they can. Cover your ears and say *What a noise!*
- Read out all the words again one by one and ask pupils to repeat after you.

A Listen and read. 2.20

- Tell pupils that they are going to read about a music lesson in Japan. Show pupils on the map where the country Japan is.
- Ask pupils to look at the photo and to point to the pupils. Then ask them to point to the teacher. Ask pupils to remember the name of the teacher in Australia (Mr Davis). Tell them that the teacher in this lesson is a lady so her title is *Mrs*. Write *Mrs* and *Mr* on the board. Ask pupils to find the teacher's name. (Mrs Chan)
- Play the recording. Tell pupils to follow the text with their fingers.
- Play the recording again. Pause after each sentence and ask pupils to repeat.

- Play the recording again. Then ask volunteers to read out a sentence each of the text.

B Circle.

- Read the example to pupils. Ask them to underline the name *Mrs Chan* in the text.
- Explain the rest of the task to pupils. Tell them to underline the words in the text which give them the answers. Allow them enough time to complete the task alone. Go round the class encouraging and helping pupils where necessary.
- Check answers. Write them on the board if necessary.

Answers
1 Mrs (given)
2 guitar
3 can't
4 fingers

C Look and learn.

- Read out the dialogue. Read it out again and ask pupils to repeat.
- Ask pupils to look at the grammar box. Read out the grammar notes and sentences. Ask pupils to repeat. Explain the meaning of the notes.
- Ask pupils to circle the question and underline the answer in the dialogue and sentences. Ask volunteers to read out the dialogue.
- Practise the questions and short answers. Write *Yes, I can.* and *No, I can't.* on the board. Ask pupils questions about themselves and tell them to choose an answer from the board.
  eg *Can you sing?*
  Can you play the piano?
  Can you play the drums?
  Repeat with names. Remind pupils to use *he* or *she* in their answer.
  eg *Can Mark play the guitar?*
  Can Joanne sing?

D Write.

- Read out the example and ask pupils why *Yes, it can.* is the correct answer.
- Explain the task to pupils. Tell them that for some answers they write what is true for them. Read out the questions. Check that pupils remember the meanings of all the words. Go around the class while pupils answer the questions. Help them find the correct personal pronouns for the answers.
- Check answers. Write them on the board if necessary.

Answers
1 Yes, it can. (given)
2 pupils' own answer
3 pupils' own answer
4 Yes, they can.
5 pupils' own answer
6 No, they can't.

E Listen and number. 🔊 2.21

- Tell pupils to look at the pictures for this task. Ask volunteers to describe what the children in each picture can or can't do.

- Explain to pupils they will hear descriptions of the children in the pictures. Explain that they must write the correct numbers under the pictures. Play the recording for the example. Make sure pupils understand what to do.

- Play the rest of the recording, pausing between questions where necessary. Play the recording again and ask pupils to check their answers.

Listening script
1 Look! That's Natalie. She can jump.
2 This is my sister, Lisa. She's very small. She can sing.
3 There's Pete and that's his brother Jack. They can't play the piano.
4 Can they play beach volleyball? Yes, they can.
5 Look! Holly is in the sea. She can swim.

Answers
First picture 2
Second picture 1(given)
Third picture 3
Fourth picture 4
Fifth picture 5

F Say.

- Read out the example to pupils. Read it out again and ask pupils to repeat after each sentence.

- Ask volunteers to read out the whole example. Then tell pupils that they are going to describe their friends to the rest of the class. Explain that they must introduce their friend, say their name, and then say one thing their friend can do and one their friend can't do. Give pupils a few minutes to discuss in pairs what they are going to say. Go round the room helping with words.

- Ask pairs to stand at the front of the class and talk about each other.

Extension activity

- Pupils can repeat the Speaking task and talk about members of their family.
  eg *My Dad's name is John. He can swim. He can't sing.*

Homework

- Pupil's Audio CD: Pupils listen to the text at home. Explain to pupils that they should listen to track 34 on the CD.

- Activity Book, pages 56-57: Time permitting, some tasks can be done in class.

- Dictation: *guitar, recorder, drums, piano, music, sing*

- Optional extra homework: Pupils can draw their friend and write three sentences about him or her. eg *This is Maria. She can dance. She can't play volleyball.* Pupils' work can be displayed on the wall.

Extra activity

- Play *Simon says*. See page 76 to see how to play it. Use any of these instructions:
  jump
  dance
  stand up
  sit down
  run
  play volleyball
  swim
  sing
  play the drums/piano/recorder/guitar
  clap your hands

Lesson 3   This is my drawing.

Aims

- Learn and use new vocabulary: *listen to, read, ride a bike, watch TV, song, Guess what!*

- Learn and use new grammar: *Present Continuous affirmative (I, you, he, she, it)*

Materials

- Flashcards: drums, guitar, piano, recorder, music, sing

Lead-in

- Revise the words from Lesson 2 with the flashcards. Hold up the flashcards one at a time and choose pupils to call out the word. Then ask a volunteer to take over the role of teacher and do the same with the flashcards.

- Revise *Can you ...?* Ask each pupil one question and elicit answers.

- Check homework. Tell pupils to open their Activity Books at pages 56 and 57. Ask volunteers to read out their answers. Then quickly check all pupils' books.

- Test dictation: *drums, guitar, piano, recorder, music, sing.* See the teacher's introduction pages 7-9 for teaching suggestions. Go round the class and check all pupils' dictation.

New vocabulary

- Teach the new words with actions. Revise *Look at* with your hands around your eyes like binoculars. Then cup your hands behind your ears and say *Listen to*. Ask pupils to copy and repeat. Then open and book and say *I can read*. Ask pupils to copy and repeat. Finally teach *ride a bike* and *watch TV*. Sit on a chair and mime riding a bike. Ask pupils to guess what you are doing. Say *Ride a bike*. Do the same with *watch TV*, by pretending to turn on a TV and changing channel with the remote control.

- Tell pupils to open their books at page 78 and to look at the vocabulary box. For the last word say sing a song and ask pupils if they can work out the meaning. Explain the meaning if necessary. Hold up your book and point to the first picture word. Say the word and ask pupils to repeat. Do the same with all the words. Then read out the new picture words in the vocabulary box in random order and ask pupils to point to the correct pictures.

- Read out the phrase *Guess what!* Explain the meaning and ask pupils to repeat. Mime singing a song and say *This is a great song*.

- Read out all the words again one by one and ask pupils to repeat after you.

A Read.

- Tell pupils to look at the boy and his drawing. Tell pupils to read the first three sentences of the text. Then ask them who the people in the drawing are.

- Write *read a book* on the board and read it out. Then underneath write *I'm reading a book.* Ask pupils to tell you what new things are in this sentence. Underline *I'm* and *ing*. Read out the sentence and ask pupils to repeat. Tell pupils that this is how we talk about something we are doing now.

- Read out the first four sentences of the text to pupils. Ask them what Grandpa is doing. Then tell pupils to read to the end of the text and find out what each member of the family is doing. Then check their comprehension by asking what Mum, Dad, Helen and Grandma are doing.

- Read out the text one sentence at a time. Stop after each sentence and ask pupils to repeat.

- Ask volunteers to read out a sentence each of the text.

Extension activity

- Quickly revise the verb *to be affirmative I, you, he, she* and *it* with pupils. Write *I _____ fantastic.* on the board and ask a pupil to write the missing word in the gap. Do the same with *you, he, she* and *it*.

B Match.

- Read the example to pupils. Ask them to find where the answer is in the text.

- Explain the rest of the task to pupils. Tell them to underline the words in the text which give them the answers. Allow them enough time to complete the task alone. Go round the class encouraging and helping pupils where necessary.

- Check answers. Write them on the board if necessary.

Answers
1 Grandpa (given)
2 Mum
3 Dad
4 Helen
5 Grandma
6 Simon

C Look and learn.

- Read out the dialogue and ask pupils to repeat.

- Ask pupils to look at the grammar box. Read out the grammar notes and sentences. Ask pupils to repeat. Explain the meaning of the notes. Tell them that when we talk about something we are doing now, we use *I'm* then the action word and we add *ing* to the action word. Write this clearly on the board in stages as you explain. Then ask pupils to tell you what we use with *You* and elicit *You're*. Do the same for *He's, She's* and *It's*.

- Ask pupils to circle the person in the dialogue and sentence and underline the action words with *ing*. Check pupils' books individually. Ask pupils to read out the dialogue and the sentence.

- Practise the grammar. Write these sentences on the board.
  I _____ read_____ .
  You _____ sing _____ .
  He _____ is jump_____ .
  Ask volunteers to write the answers in the gaps. Then read out the sentences and ask pupils to repeat.

- Ask pupils to look at the grammar box again. Read out the three action words *ride, run* and *swim*. Then read out *riding, running* and *swimming*. Ask pupils what they notice about the word when *ing* is added. Tell pupils that these are spelling rules that they must learn. Tell pupils that you will give them one minute to learn how to spell *riding, running* and *swimming*. Do a funny count down from 10-1 at the end of the minute so this is fun for pupils. Then ask volunteers to write the words they have just learnt on the board.

D Write.

- Ask pupils to look at the first picture. Read out the example and ask pupils to repeat. Explain that they must use the action word in brackets and change it so it talks about now. Remind pupils that this means putting the *'m, 're* or *'s* with the person and adding *ing* to the action word. Write *'m, 're* and *'s* on the board.

- Ask pupils to look at the second picture. Ask a volunteer to suggest an answer. Elicit *Kate is riding her bike*. Tell pupils to write this in their books. Then write the whole answer on the board so pupils can check their work. Do the same with 3 and 4.

- Check answers. Go round the class helping pupils where necessary.

E Say.

- Read out the example. Read it out again and ask pupils to repeat.

- Ask three volunteers to act out the example. You need at least one girl and one boy. Ask one pupil to mime reading a book and another pupil to mime playing the drums. A third pupil then describes what they are doing. Remind the third pupil to use *he* and *she* correctly.

- Ask pupils for ideas of what they can mime. Write their ideas on the board, eg:
  He's watching TV.
  She's singing.
  He's running.
  She's playing volleyball.
  Then ask three pupils to stand at the front. Two choose an action each to mime from the board. The third pupil then has to describe what they are doing. Repeat with three different pupils.

- Clean the board. Ask pupils to do the task again, but without help from the board. Choose three confident pupils to try first. Prompt where necessary.

F Draw and write.

- Tell pupils to draw a picture of a mum, a dad and a child doing actions they have learnt. It can be their own family or an imaginary one.

- Read out the beginning of sentences and ask pupils what they should write in the gaps. Ask them to finish the sentences. Go round the class helping pupils with the missing parts of the sentences.

- Ask pupils to hold up their books and to show each other their pictures. Ask volunteers to read out their work.

Homework

- Activity Book, pages 58-59: Time permitting, some tasks can be done in class.

- Dictation: *listen to, read, ride a bike, watch TV, song*

- Optional dictation: *ride - riding, run - running, swim - swimming*

- Revision for Test 7:
  Words: *jump, look at, play volleyball, run, swim, sea, very, everybody, drums, guitar, piano, recorder, music, sing, What a noise!, listen to, read, ride a bike, watch TV, song, Guess what!*
  Grammar: *can, can't, Can you …? Yes, I can. No, I can't., Present Continuous affirmative (I, you, he, she, it)*

Teacher's Note

Pupils will do Test 7 in the following lesson. If you don't want to rush into Unit 8, for the rest of the lesson do these activities:

1 Pupils can read out the cartoon story from Unit 7 Lesson 1. Then ask volunteers to act out the cartoon story. Pupils can wear the character masks.
2 Pupils can read out the texts from Lesson 2 and 3.
3 Repeat the Say task from Lesson 2.
4 Sing the song.
5 Play *Simon says*.

Optional activity

Revision for Test 7

- Revise the words from the flashcards. Then write the words on the board. Ask a volunteer to read out a word and come and choose the corresponding flashcard. Practise until all pupils remember the words well.

- Revise the action verbs. Say a verb and ask pupils to do the action.

- Write *can* and *can't* on the board. Then write *A cat* and *A fish* on the board. Ask volunteers to say things that a cat can and can't do and things that a fish can and can't do.

- Pretend to read a book and say *I'm reading*. Ask pupils to repeat. Ask a pupil to pretend to sing. Say *You're singing*. Ask pupils to repeat. Ask a boy to pretend to play volleyball and say *He's playing volleyball*. Ask pupils to repeat. Ask a girl to pretend to swim and say *She's swimming*. Ask pupils to repeat. Then write the sentences on the board. Read them out and ask pupils to repeat.

8

Lesson 1 Trek's reporters in Brazil

Aims

- Learn and use new vocabulary: *baseball, football, basketball, tennis, think, win*
- Learn and use new grammar: *Present Continuous affirmative (we, you, they)*

Materials

- Magazine or Internet pictures of the sports *baseball, basketball, football* and *tennis*
- Optional for Extra activity: one piece of paper for each pupil to draw on

Lead-in

- Revise the action verbs from Unit 7. Ask pupils to mime the instruction. Then write the verb on the board. Use these action verbs: jump, run, play volleyball, swim, sing, read, ride a bike, watch TV.
- Revise the *Present Continuous affirmative*. Write *read* on the board. Open a book and say *Look. I'm reading.* Ask pupils to copy and repeat. Ask a volunteer to write the sentence on the board. Ask volunteers what they must add to *read* to show we are talking about something that is happening now. Elicit *I'm* and *ing*. Circle *I'm* and underline *ing*. Remind pupils that some action verbs have a special spelling with *ing*. Ask volunteers to write the following verbs on the board: *swimming, running, riding*
- Check homework. Tell pupils to open their Activity Books at pages 58 and 59. Ask volunteers to read out their answers. Then quickly check all pupils' books.
- Test dictation: *listen to, read, ride a bike, watch TV, song.* See the teacher's introduction pages 7-9 for teaching suggestions. Go round the class and check all pupils' dictation.

Episode outline

Brazil: Episode 2

The reporters are thinking about which sport to watch in Brazil. Ty likes baseball, Mia likes tennis and Leo likes basketball. Then Mia remembers which sport is very popular in Brazil. She takes Ty and Leo to the football stadium where they watch a match. Brazil wins the match 2-1. Outside the stadium they see a poster of the Amazon and decide to go there.

New vocabulary

- Teach *baseball, basketball, football* and *tennis*. Hold up the picture for baseball and say *Look! Baseball.* Ask pupils to repeat. Do the same with the other sports. Write

the words on the board. Say *Basketball is fantastic!* Then ask pupils to say which sport they like best.

- Tell pupils to open their books at page 80 and to look at the vocabulary box. Hold up your book and point to the first picture word. Say the word and ask pupils to repeat. Do the same with all the sports words. Then read out the new picture words in the vocabulary box in random order and ask pupils to point to the correct pictures.
- Read out *think* and *win*. Explain the meanings. Then say *I'm thinking.* and mime that you are thinking. Ask pupils to copy and repeat. Then ask pupil what football teams want and elicit *win*.
- Read out all the words again one by one and ask pupils to repeat after you.

A Listen and read.

For teachers using the DVD

- Make sure each pupil has a copy of the DVD worksheet found on page 134.
- Please follow the procedure outlined in Unit 1, Lesson 1 on page 31 for teachers using the DVD.

Before you watch

Answers
1 in Brazil
2 football
3 the Amazon

While you watch

Answers
a 9
b 3
c 10
d 2
e 1
f 11
g 7
h 5
i 4
j 8
k 6

After you watch

Answers
1 tennis
2 football
3 2-1
4 Brazil
5 the Amazon

For teachers using the audio CD 2.22

- Tell pupils to look at the cartoon story. Ask them to name the sports the reporters are thinking about in the second picture.

- Play the recording. Tell pupils to look at the pictures and follow the speech bubbles with their fingers.
- Play the recording again. Pause after each speech bubble and ask pupils to repeat.
- Check that pupils understand the story. Use L1 where necessary.
  Which sport is cool? (tennis)
  What sport do the reporters go to watch? (football)
  What's the score? (2-1)
  Which team wins? (Brazil)
  Where do the reporters want to go next? (the Amazon)
- Play the recording again. Then ask volunteers to read out the story.
- Assign characters to volunteers and ask them to act out the story in front of the class. Pupils can wear the masks.

B Look and learn.

- Read out the speech bubble. Read it out again and ask pupils to repeat.
- Ask pupils to look at the grammar box. Explain the meaning. Tell pupils that we use *we're*, *you're* and *they're* before the action verb and then *ing* when we're talking about things happening now. Read out the notes and example sentence in the grammar box and ask pupils to repeat.
- Ask pupils to pretend to be Amber and Chris and to read out the speech bubble.
- Practise the grammar point. Ask four volunteers to stand at the front of the class. Tell them to mime they are playing tennis. Ask them to say what they are doing using *we*. Elicit *We're playing tennis.* Then ask the class to say what they are doing using *they*. Elicit *They're playing tennis.* Then ask two volunteers to stop miming while the other two continue. Ask the first volunteers to say what their friends are doing using *you*. Elicit *You're playing tennis.* Repeat with new volunteers and a different sport.

C Circle.

- Read out the example and ask pupils why *are* is the correct answer.
- Explain the rest of the task to pupils. Read out all the sentences and check pupils understand the meanings. Allow them enough time to complete the task alone. Go round the class helping pupils where necessary.
- Check answers. Write them on the board if necessary.

Answers
1 are (given)
2 winning
3 We're
4 are
5 They're
6 playing

D Listen and match. 2.23

- Read out the names and sports to pupils. Explain

to pupils that they will listen to some children playing different sports. They must match the children to the sports they are playing.
- Play the recording for the example. Make sure pupils understand what to do.
- Play the recording. Pause to allow pupils enough time to write down the answers. Play the recording again and ask pupils to check their answers.

Listening script
What are they playing?
1
This is Sandra. She's playing basketball.
Basketball is fantastic!

2
That's Adam. He's playing baseball. Hello, Adam.
You're great.
Thank you. Baseball is cool!

3
Hello Tim. Hi Paula.
We're playing football.
Football is fantastic!

4
Hello, John.
Hi. I'm playing volleyball. Volleyball is great!

5
There's Katy. She's playing tennis. Hi, Katy.
Hi. Come on. Let's play tennis. It's great!

Answers
1 Sandra: basketball (given)
2 Adam: baseball
3 Tim and Paula: football
4 John: volleyball
5 Katy: tennis

E Say.

- Read out the example ask pupils to repeat after you. Ask all pupils to run on the spot and say together *We're running.*
- Ask pairs to make their own sentences like the one in the example. Allow pairs a minute to choose a sport or action verb. Then ask the pairs to mime their sport or action verb to the class and to say what they are doing.

Extension activity

- Ask pairs to mime a new sport or action verb but not to say anything. Ask another pair to say what they are doing. eg *You're running.*

Extra Activity

- Hand out a piece of paper to each pupil. Ask pupils to draw themselves and their friends playing one of the sports they learnt in this lesson.
- Ask pupils to hold up their drawings and to show them to the class. Ask them to describe what they are doing in the picture. eg *I'm jumping. We're playing basketball.*

Lesson 2   They're having fun.

Aims

- Learn and use new vocabulary: *old, people, rollercoaster, town, sit, stand, have fun*
- Learn and use new grammar: *Present Continuous negative*

Materials

- a new book and an old book

Lead-in

- Revise *baseball, basketball, football* and *tennis* and the *Present Continuous*. Write these sports on the board. Ask pupils which sport is fantastic for them. Elicit eg *Basketball is fantastic!* Then ask pupils to mime a sport you specify. Say for example *You're playing football.*
- Check homework. Tell pupils to open their Activity Books at pages 60 and 61. Ask volunteers to read out their answers. Then quickly check all pupils' books.
- Test dictation: *baseball, basketball, football, tennis.* See the teacher's introduction pages 7-9 for teaching suggestions. Go round the class and check all pupils' dictation.

New vocabulary

- Teach *old, people, sit* and *stand.* Hold up the new book and say *This is a new book.* Ask pupils to remember the meaning of *new.* Then hold up the old book and ask *Is this a new book?* Elicit the answer *No, it isn't.* Say *This is an old book.* Ask pupils to repeat. Write *old* on the board. Draw three stick people on the board and say *Three people.* Ask pupils to repeat. Say *They're standing.* and ask pupils to repeat. Draw two more stick people sitting down. Say *Two people. They're sitting.* and ask pupils to repeat.

- Teach *rollercoaster, town* and *have fun.* Ask pupils in L1 if they like funfairs. Ask them to name a town they know which has got a funfair. Write on the board for example *Dover is a town.* Explain the meaning of *town.* Then write rollercoaster on the board and explain which ride this is. Ask two volunteers to pretend they are on a rollercoaster. Point to the volunteers and say *Look! They're having fun!* Ask pupils to repeat. Do the same with more volunteers.

- Tell pupils to open their books at page 82 and to look at the vocabulary box. Hold up your book and point to the first picture word. Say the word and ask pupils to repeat. Do the same with all the words. Then read out the new picture words in the vocabulary box in random order and ask pupils to point to the correct pictures.

- Read out all the words again one by one and ask pupils to repeat after you.

A Listen and read. 2.24

- Tell pupils that they are going to read about a rollercoaster. Ask pupils to look at the photo and describe what they can see. Help pupils to use English for the words they know, eg *rollercoaster, people, They're sitting, They're having fun.*

- Play the recording. Tell pupils to follow the text with their fingers.

- Play the recording again. Pause after each sentence and ask pupils to repeat.

- Play the recording again. Then ask volunteers to read out a sentence each of the text.

B Write Yes or No.

- Read the example to pupils. Ask them to underline the sentence in the text which gives them the answer.

- Explain the rest of the task to pupils. Tell them to underline the words in the text which give them the answers. Allow them enough time to complete the task alone. Go round the class encouraging and helping pupils where necessary.

- Check answers. Write them on the board if necessary.

Answers
1 No (given)
2 Yes
3 No
4 Yes
5 Yes

C Look and learn.

- Ask pupils to look at the picture. Ask pupils *Is Amber happy?* and elicit answer *No, she isn't.* Read out the speech bubble. Read it out again and ask pupils to repeat.

- Ask pupils to look at the grammar box. Read out the grammar notes and sentences. Ask pupils to repeat. Explain the meaning of the notes.

- Ask pupils to underline the words that we need in the grammar sentences to show something is not happening now. Ask volunteers to read out the sentences. Do the same for the speech bubble.

- Practise the grammar. Write affirmative sentences on the board. Ask pupils to make the sentences negative. eg *I'm running.*
  You're listening to music.
  He's playing football.
  We're having fun.
  Ask pupils to say something about themselves which they are not doing. Say *I'm not singing.* Ask volunteers to make their own sentences.

D Write.

- Read out the example and explain to pupils that they have to write the action verb in brackets in the right form. Tell them to use the grammar box for help. Read out the example and ask pupils to repeat.

- Explain the rest of the task to pupils. Read out all the sentences and check pupils understand the meanings. Allow them enough time to complete the task alone. Go round the class helping pupils where necessary.

- Check answers. Write the answers on the board.

Answers
1 isn't riding (given)
2 aren't swimming
3 'm not watching
4 aren't listening
5 isn't standing

Say it! 2.25

- Write *y* on the board. Ask pupils to say the name of this letter. Write *Yes* on the board and ask volunteers to read it out. Then write *happy* on the board and ask volunteers to read it out too. Ask pupils if the *y* has got the same sound in both words. Help them work out that a *y* at the beginning of a word sounds different from a *y* at the end. Read out the words *yes* and *happy* a few times and ask pupils to repeat.

- Tell pupils to look at the task. Play the first part of the recording (Listen and say.) asking pupils to repeat the words *happy* and *yes* each time they hear them. (*Happy* and *yes* will be heard twice.)

- Ask for volunteers to read out the sentence. Play the recording and ask all pupils to repeat. (The sentence will be heard once.)

E Sing. 2.26

- Tell pupils they are going to learn a song. Explain to pupils that the song is about a rollercoaster and when they sing they can pretend they are riding one.

- Ask pupils to look at the picture and describe what they can see. Encourage them to use English for words they know.

- Play the recording and tell pupils to listen and follow

the words with their fingers.

- Read out the song one line at a time and ask pupils to repeat after you.

- Play the recording again. Encourage pupils to sing along. Practise many times until pupils are familiar with the words.

- Pupils can sing and pretend they are riding a rollercoaster at the same time. If possible line the chairs up in pairs in the classroom to look like a rollercoaster.

Homework

- Pupil's Audio CD: Pupils listen to the text and the song at home. Explain to pupils that they should listen to tracks 36 and 37 on the CD.

- Activity Book, pages 62-63: Time permitting, some tasks can be done in class.

- Dictation: *old, people, rollercoaster, town, sit, stand, have fun*

Extra activity

- Play *Simon says*. See page 76 for how to play it. Use the *Present Continuous*:

  You're playing volleyball/tennis/basketball/football/baseball.

  You're having fun!
  You aren't having fun.
  You're jumping.
  You're sitting.
  You aren't sitting.
  You're standing.
  You aren't standing.
  You're riding a rollercoaster.

Lesson 3   Are they playing?

Aims

- Learn and use new vocabulary: *climb, cook, dance, kick, rock*

- Learn and use new grammar: *Present Continuous interrogative*

Materials

- flashcards: climb, cook, dance, kick, rock

Lead-in

- Revise *stand, sit* and the *Present Continuous negative*. Ask half the class to stand up. Say *You aren't sitting.* Look at the other half of the class and say *You aren't standing.* Ask pupils to repeat. Then ask volunteers to say things they aren't doing eg, *I'm not jumping.* Write some words on the board to help pupils, *run, sing, swim, play volleyball.*

- Check homework. Tell pupils to open their Activity Books at pages 62 and 63. Ask volunteers to read out their answers. Then quickly check all pupils' books.

- Test dictation: *old, people, rollercoaster, town, sit, stand, have fun*. See the teacher's introduction pages 7-9 for teaching suggestions. Go round the class and check all pupils' dictation.

New vocabulary

- Teach the new words with the flashcards. See the teacher's introduction pages 7-9 for teaching suggestions.

- Tell pupils to open their books at page 84 and to look at the vocabulary box. Hold up your book and point to the first picture word. Say the word and ask pupils to repeat. Do the same with all the words. Then read out the new picture words in the vocabulary box in random order and ask pupils to point to the correct pictures.

- Read out all the words again one by one and ask pupils to repeat after you.

A Read.

- Tell pupils to look at the photos. Ask them to tell you in English what they think the children are doing. eg *They're climbing. They're cooking. They're standing. He's playing football*.

- Tell pupils to read paragraph 1 to find out the children's names. Then ask them to read paragraph 2 and see who has got a birthday. For paragraph 3, ask pupils to find out who Cindy is. For paragraph 4, ask pupils to find out the name of the boy who is playing football.

- Read out the paragraphs. Pause after each sentence and ask pupils to repeat.

- Ask volunteers to read out a sentence each of the paragraphs.

B Match.

- Read the example to pupils. Ask them to say which paragraph has got the answer in it. Then ask them to underline the sentences which give them the answer.

- Explain the rest of the task to pupils. Tell them to underline the words in the text which give them the answers. Allow them enough time to complete the task alone. Go round the class encouraging and helping pupils where necessary.

- Check answers. Write them on the board if necessary.

Answers
1 Tina and Lori are climbing a rock. (given)
2 Ann is standing.
3 Luke and Cindy are playing.
4 Sam is kicking the ball.

C Look and learn.

- Ask pupils what they think Chris is doing. They are likely to know that this is Wii tennis. Elicit *He's playing tennis. He's playing a computer game*. Read out the dialogue and ask pupils to repeat.

- Ask pupils to look at the grammar box. Read out the grammar notes and sentences. Ask pupils to repeat. Explain the meaning of the notes.

- Ask pupils to circle the question and underline the short answer in the dialogue and in the sentences.

- Practise the grammar. Give volunteers instructions and ask other pupils to answer your questions. eg (volunteers sing) *Are they singing?* (volunteer boy jumps) *Is he jumping?* (volunteer girl plays tennis) *Is she playing football?*

D Write.

- Read out the example and ask pupils why *they are* is the correct answer. Tell them to check the grammar notes to help them find the correct short answers. Remind pupils to think carefully about which personal pronoun to use in the answer.

- Explain the task to pupils. Read out the questions. Check pupils remember the meanings of all the words. Allow pupils enough time to complete the task. Go round the class helping pupils where necessary.

- Check answers. Write them on the board if necessary.

Answers
1 they are (given)
2 we aren't
3 it isn't
4 she is
5 he isn't

E Say.

- Read out the dialogue to pupils and ask them to repeat. Tell them that they are going to play the same guessing game.

- Ask three volunteers to come to the front of the class. Whisper in the ear of two volunteers *You're swimming*. They must then mime that they are swimming. The third volunteer must guess what they are doing. Help the volunteer if necessary. Say the question *Are you swimming?* and ask the other volunteers to answers *Yes, we are*.

- Repeat with three new volunteers. Continue until all pupils have had a go.

Extension activity

- Divide the class into pairs. They can take turns to mime and ask questions using their own ideas. Go round the class listening to pairs and helping where necessary.

- Ask each pairs to perform one mime and question to the class.

F Draw and write.

- Ask pupils to draw two of their friends doing something that they have learnt so far. Go round the class suggesting ideas for the drawings.

- When pupils have finished their drawings, ask them to complete the sentences. Help with spelling where necessary.

- Ask volunteers to hold up and read out their work.

Homework

- Activity Book, pages 64-65: Time permitting, some tasks can be done in class.
- Dictation: *climb, cook, dance, kick, rock*
- Revision for Test 8:
  Words: *baseball, basketball, football, tennis, think, win, old, people, rollercoaster, town, sit, stand, have fun, climb, cook, dance, kick, rock*
  Grammar: *Present Continuous affirmative, negative and interrogative*

Teacher's Note

Pupils will do Test 8 in the following lesson. If you don't want to rush into Unit 9, for the rest of the lesson do these activities:
1 Pupils can read out the cartoon story from Unit 8 Lesson 1. Then ask volunteers to act out the cartoon story.
2 Pupils can read out the texts from Lesson 2 and Lesson 3.
3 Repeat the *Say* task from Lesson 3.
4 Sing the song.
5 Play the spelling game.

Optional activity

Revision for Test 8

- Revise the sports and action words. Say *You're playing baseball.* and ask pupils to mime the action. Do the same for *basketball, football, tennis, think, win, sit, stand, have fun, climb, cook, dance* and *kick*.

- Write *old, people, rollercoaster, town* and *rock* on the board. Ask pupils to remember the meanings of these words. Ask volunteers to draw pictures for the words.

- Revise the *Present Continuous*. Write *cook* on the board. Ask a boy to pretend he is cooking. Say *He's cooking.* Ask a volunteer to write this sentence on the board. Then ask the boy to stop and stand still. Say *He isn't cooking.* Ask another volunteer to write this sentence on the board. Then ask the class *Is he cooking?* and elicit short answer *No, he isn't.* Ask volunteers to write the question and short answer on the board. Ask the boy to start to 'cook' again. Ask *Is he cooking?* and elicit *Yes, he is.* Ask a volunteer to write this short answer on the board. Read out all the sentences and ask pupils to repeat.

- Ask pupils what we do if we change *He* to *I.* Make the appropriate changes on the board. Read out the sentences and ask pupils to repeat. Do the same with all persons.

Extra Activity

- Play a spelling game. Divide the class into two teams, Team A and Team B. Divide the board into two columns. Write A on the left and B on the right. A pupil from Team A comes to the board. You say a word and the pupil must spell it correctly. Team mates can advise and help in English only. Correct spelling wins one point. Then a pupil from Team B must spell a word. The team with the most points wins. The words get gradually more difficult.

sit	*football*
win	*baseball*
fun	*basketball*
old	*stand*
tennis	*town*
cook	*dance*
rock	*people*
kick	*climb*
think	*rollercoaster*

- Play the spelling game again. This time pupils can choose an easy word or a difficult word. An easy word scores one point, whereas a difficult word scores two points.

9

Lesson 1   Trek's reporters in Brazil

Aims

- Learn and use new vocabulary: *boat, market, cinema, theatre, city, Be careful!*
- Learn and use new grammar: *What are you doing?*

Materials

- Flashcards: boat, market, cinema, theatre, city
- Masks: Trek, Ty, Mia, Leo

Lead-in

- Revise *climb, cook, dance* and *kick*. Say a word and ask pupils mime the action.
- Revise the *Present Continuous interrogative*. Ask a volunteer to jump up and down. Ask pupils *Is he jumping?* and elicit answer *Yes, he is.* Then ask a different volunteer to pretend to swim? Ask pupils *Is she singing?* and elicit answer *No, she isn't.* Repeat with these actions and questions:

  (2 pupils play volleyball) *Are they playing tennis?*

  (1 pupil reads) *Are you reading?* (pupil answers with *I*)

  (2 pupils play guitars) *Are you playing the piano?* (pupils answer with *we*)

- Check homework. Tell pupils to open their Activity Books at pages 64 and 65. Ask volunteers to read out their answers. Then quickly check all pupils' books.
- Test dictation: *climb, cook, dance, kick, rock.* See the teacher's introduction pages 7-9 for teaching suggestions. Go round the class and check all pupils' dictation.

Episode outline

Brazil: Episode 3

The reporters are finishing their trip to Brazil. They fly to the Amazon, landing in the city of Manaus. In the city, they admire the theatre building. Next they visit the market where Ty slips on a banana skin. Then Ty and Leo decide to go on a river boat ride to the Amazon forest. Mia joins them. They think the Amazon is fantastic. Trek liked the DVD and thinks Brazil is great.

New vocabulary

- Teach the new words with the flashcards. See the teacher's introduction pages 7-9 for teaching suggestions.
- Tell pupils to open their books at page 86 and to look at the vocabulary box. Hold up your book and point to the first picture word. Say the word and ask pupils to repeat. Do the same with all the words. Then read out the new picture words in the vocabulary box in random order and ask pupils to point to the correct pictures.

- Read out the phrase *Be careful!* Explain the meaning. Ask a volunteer to pretend to slip on a banana skin. Say *Be careful!* Ask pupils to repeat. Tell pupils to practise this in pairs for a few minutes.
- Read out all the words again one by one and ask pupils to repeat after you.

A Listen and read.

For teachers using the DVD

- Make sure each pupil has a copy of the DVD worksheet found on page 135.
- Please follow the procedure outlined in Unit 1, Lesson 1 on page 31 for teachers using the DVD.

Before you watch

> **Answers**
> 1 in a city in the Amazon
> 2 by plane
> 3 a banana peel
> 4 a boat

While you watch

> **Answers**
> a 5
> b 2
> c 6
> d 1
> e 3
> f 4

After you watch

> **Answers**
> 1 Leo
> 2 Leo
> 3 They're standing in a boat.
> 4 Mia
> 5 big

For teachers using the audio CD 2.27

- Tell pupils to look at the cartoon story. Ask pupils to look at the story and find the frame where Ty slips on a banana skin (frame 3). Ask pupils what they would say to Ty (Be careful, Ty!).
- Play the recording. Tell pupils to look at the pictures and follow the speech bubbles with their fingers.
- Play the recording again. Pause after each speech bubble and ask pupils to repeat.
- Check pupils understand the story. Use L1 where necessary.
  Who thinks the theatre is a cinema? (Leo)
  Who thinks the market is great? (Leo)
  What are Ty and Leo doing? (They're standing in a boat.)
  Who gets on the boat last? (Mia)
  Is the Amazon big or small? (big)

- Play the recording again. Then ask volunteers to read out the story.
- Assign characters to volunteers and ask them to act out the story in front of the class. Pupils can wear the character masks.

Extra activity

- Listen again to all three episodes of the mini story. Play the recordings from Lesson 1 of units 7, 8 and 9. Ask pupils to follow the speech bubbles with their fingers.
- Divide the class into three groups, one group for each episode. Assign roles to pupils in each group. Then ask each group to act out their episode in front of the class. Pupils can wear the character masks.

B Look and learn.

- Read out the dialogue. Read it out again and ask pupils to repeat.
- Ask pupils to look at the grammar box. Read out the grammar notes and sentences. Ask pupils to repeat. Explain the meaning of the notes.
- Ask pupils to circle the question and underline the answer in the grammar sentences and the dialogue. Ask volunteers to read out the sentences.
- Practise the grammar. Ask volunteers to mime a sport they have learnt. Ask volunteers questions and elicit answers. eg *What are you doing? I'm playing basketball/ volleyball/baseball/tennis/football.*
  Pupils can do the same in pairs. Go round the class listening and helping where necessary.

C Write.

- Read out the question for number 1 and ask pupils to read out the answer. Explain that they must look at the person in the answer in order to complete the question.
- Explain the rest of the task to pupils. Check pupils remember the meanings of all the words. Allow them enough time to complete the task alone. Go round the class helping pupils where necessary.
- Check answers. Ask pairs to read out the questions and answers.

Answers
1 are you (given)
2 is he
3 is she
4 are they
5 are you

Say it! 2.28

- Write *t* and *h* on the board. Ask pupils to say the name of these letters. Then write *th* on the board. Tell them the sounds *th* make together. Say *theatre* and ask pupils to repeat. Then say *this* and ask pupils to repeat. Ask pupils if they notice the difference in the sound of *th* in *theatre* (θ) and in *this* (δ).
- Tell pupils to look at the task. Play the first part of the recording (Listen and say) asking pupils to repeat the words *theatre* and *there* each time they hear them (*theatre* and *there* will be heard twice).

- Ask for volunteers to read out the sentence. Play the recording and ask all pupils to repeat (the sentence will be heard once).

D Listen and tick. 2.29

- Tell pupils that they are going to listen to descriptions of what some children are doing. Explain that they must listen carefully and tick the correct box. First ask pupils what the children in each picture are doing. eg 1 *What is he doing? He's sitting. He's standing.*
- Play the recording for the example. Make sure pupils understand what to do.
- Play the recording pausing between numbers where necessary. Play the recording again and ask pupils to check their answers.
- Check answers.

Listening script
1
What are you doing?
I'm sitting.

2
What are Steve and Todd doing?
They're watching TV.

3
What is Nina doing?
She's playing baseball.

4
What are you doing?
We're riding a rollercoaster.

Answers
Pupils tick the following pictures.
1 1st picture (given)
2 2nd picture
3 1st picture
4 1st picture

E Say.

- Read out the dialogue and ask pupils to repeat. Tell pupils that they are going to mime any action they like as they did with sports earlier. Ask pupils to remember the actions they have learnt and write a list on the board for ideas.
  eg *read*
  sing
  swim
  run
  jump
  play the piano/drums/recorder/guitar
  stand
  sit
  kick
  climb
  dance
  cook

- Ask pupils to work in pairs and think of one mime each. They must then practise their questions and answers. Go round the class helping where necessary.

- Ask pairs to come to the front of the class, perform the mimes, questions and answers.

Homework

- Pupil's Audio CD: Pupils listen to the cartoon story at home. Explain to pupils that they should listen to track 38 on the CD.

- Activity Book, pages 66-67. Time permitting some tasks can be done in class.

- Dictation: *city, cinema, theatre, market, boat*

Lesson 2   It's New Year!

Aims

- Learn and use new vocabulary: *colours, dragon, fireworks, sky, New Year*

- Learn and use new grammar: *Imperative*

Materials

- Flashcards: city, cinema, theatre, market, boat
- Some colouring pencils
- Magazine or Internet pictures of a Chinese dragon and fireworks
- Optional for Extension activity: a toy spider

Lead-in

- Revise the words from Lesson 1. Stick the flashcards on the board. Call out the words one at a time and ask volunteers to come to the board and point to the correct flashcard.

- Ask a pupil *What are you doing*? Elicit *I'm sitting.* Then ask another pupil *What is he doing?* and point to a boy. Elicit *He's sitting.* Continue with *What are they doing?* pointing to two pupils. *What are you doing?* asking two pupils to answer. *What is she doing*? pointing to a girl.

- Check homework. Tell pupils to open their Activity Books at pages 66 and 67. Ask volunteers to read out their answers. Then quickly check all pupils' books.

- Test dictation: *boat, market, cinema, theatre, city*. See the teacher's introduction pages 7-9 for teaching suggestions. Go round the class and check all pupils' dictation.

New vocabulary

- Teach the new words. Hold up the two pictures and ask pupils to tell you in L1 what they can see. Point to the dragon and say *It's a dragon.* Ask pupils to repeat. Write *dragon* on the board. Do the same for *They're fireworks.* Ask pupils where we see fireworks. Point upwards and say *Fireworks are in the sky.* Write *sky* on the board. Then write *colours* on the board and ask pupils what colours fireworks are. Write the colours they tell you underneath colours.

- Tell pupils to open their books at page 88 and to look at the vocabulary box. Hold up your book and point to the first picture word. Say the word and ask pupils to repeat. Do the same with all the words. Then read out the new picture words in the vocabulary box in random order and ask pupils to point to the correct pictures.

- Read out the words *New Year*. Explain the meaning. Ask pupils how they celebrate New Year in their country. Explain that in China they have dragons and fireworks.

- Read out all the words again one by one and ask pupils to repeat after you.

A Listen and read. ⊙ 2.30

Background information
Chinese New Year

The Chinese New Year is not celebrated on the 1st of January as in other countries. Every year it falls on a different date somewhere between 21st January and 20th February. The Chinese New Year nowadays is also called Spring Festival and is the most important holiday in China. The celebrations last for 15 days. At the turn of the new year, there are firework displays in all cities. There are also a lot of dancing dragon performances during this time. The dragon represents prosperity, good luck and good fortune.

- Tell pupils that they are going to read about Chinese New Year. Ask pupils to look at the photo say what colours the dragon is.

- Play the recording. Tell pupils to follow the text with their fingers.

- Play the recording again. Stop after each sentence and ask pupils to repeat.

- Play the recording again. Then ask volunteers to read out a sentence each of the text.

B Write.

- Read the example to pupils. Ask them to find the sentence in the first paragraph which gives them the answer.

- Explain the rest of the task to pupils. Tell them to underline the sentences in the text which give them the answers. Allow them enough time to complete the task alone. Go round the class encouraging and helping pupils where necessary.

- Check answers. Write them on the board if necessary.

Answers
1 dragon (given)
2 Music
3 happy
4 New year
5 fireworks

C Look and learn.

- Read out the speech bubble. Read it out again and ask pupils to repeat. Explain to pupils that Amber and Chris are giving each other orders.

- Ask pupils to look at the grammar box. Read out the grammar notes. Explain that when we want someone to do something we say the action verb eg *Look!* When we want someone not to do something we say *Don't* and the action verb eg *Don't look.*

- Practise the grammar. Give the pupils instructions to follow:
  Stand up.   *Run.*
  Jump.   *Don't run.*
  Don't jump.   *Sit down.*

D Circle.

- Ask pupils to look at the pictures and describe what they can see. Explain that they must look at the pictures and decide if the instruction is to do something or not to do something. Read out the example and ask pupils to repeat.

- Explain the task to pupils. Check pupils remember the meanings of all the words. Allow them enough time to complete the task alone. Go round the class helping pupils where necessary.

- Check answers. Ask pupils to read out their answers.

Answers
1 Don't sit (given)
2 Don't swim
3 Dance
4 Look

Extension activity

- Put a chair at the front of the class. Ask a volunteer to sit on the chair. Say *Stand up.* Then place the toy spider on the chair. Ask the volunteer to act as if to sit down and say worriedly *Don't sit on the chair!*

- Ask pairs to act out this short role play. They can practise for a few minutes first and then perform for the class.

E Sing. 2.31

- Tell pupils they are going to learn a song. Explain to pupils that the song is about fireworks on New Year's Eve. Ask them if there are fireworks in their country on New Year's Eve.

- Ask pupils to look at the picture and say what colours they can see.

- Play the recording and tell pupils to listen and follow the words with their fingers.

- Read out the song one line at a time and ask pupils to repeat after you.

- Play the recording again. Encourage pupils to sing along. Practise many times until pupils are familiar with the words.

Extra activity

- Divide the class into two groups. Hold a singing competition. Ask the first group to stand at the front of the class and sing the song. Award them a mark out of ten. Then ask the second group to sing at the front of the class and award them a mark out of ten.

- The singing competition can also be held for pairs or individuals rather like *Pop Idol.* Choose a panel of judges from the pupils who can award marks for singing and performance. This can be held at the beginning of the next lesson so pairs can practise at home with the pupil's audio CD. They can choose any song from the units that they prefer.

Homework

- Pupil's Audio CD: Pupils listen to the text and the song at home. Explain to pupils that they should listen to tracks 39 and 40 on the CD.

- Activity Book, pages 68-69: Time permitting some tasks can be done in class.

- Dictation: *colours, dragon, fireworks, sky, New Year*

- Optional extra homework: pupils can copy the song onto paper and draw fireworks. Their work can be displayed on the classroom wall.

Lesson 3   Let's go to London!

Aims

- Learn and use new vocabulary: *buy, park, picnic, river, shop, lots of, ride, thing*

- Learn and use new grammar: *Let's*

Materials

- An A3 size piece of white card. A black marker.

- Optional for extra activity: word cards:
  city, cinema, theatre, market, boat, dragon, fireworks, sky, park, picnic, river, shop

Lead-in

- Revise the words from Lesson 2. Write *New Year* on the board and ask pupils to remember words they learnt which are connected to Chinese New Year (dragon, fireworks, sky, colours). Ask volunteers to write the words on the board.

- Revise the *Imperative.* Give pupils instructions to follow eg *Swim. Don't swim. Read your book. Don't read your book. Dance. Don't dance.*

- Check homework. Tell pupils to open their Activity Books at pages 68 and 69. Ask volunteers to read out their answers. Then sing the song from Lesson 2.

- Test dictation: *colours, dragon, fireworks, sky, New Year.* See the teacher's introduction pages 7-9 for teaching suggestions. Go round the class and check all pupils' dictation.

New vocabulary

- Teach the words *park, river* and *shop*. Draw a simple map of a town on the board. Then draw two roads which cross in the middle. Write *My town* above the map. Then tell pupils that you are going to draw three things in your town and that they should guess what they are in L1.

Draw a round park and put a tree and flower in it.

Draw a square building and give it a sign that says *Cool clothes!*

Draw a blue river under one road. Erase part of the road at the river and draw an arch for a bridge.

Help pupils guess the things. Then teach *park, shop* and *river*. Point to the places, say the word and ask pupils to repeat. eg *This is a shop.*

- Teach *buy* and picnic. Say *I'm in a clothes shop. What can I buy? A dress or an apple?* Ask pupils to answer and elicit *A dress.* Write *buy* on the board. Repeat *What can I buy?* Ask pupils to work out what the word *buy* means. Then say *I'm in the park. I'm having a picnic.* Ask pupils if they know the word *picnic.* If not explain, the meaning. Write *picnic* on the board. Read out all the new words and ask pupils to repeat.

- Tell pupils to open their books at page 90 and to look at the vocabulary box. Hold up your book and point to the first picture word. Say the word and ask pupils to repeat. Do the same with all the words. Then read out the new picture words in the vocabulary box in random order and ask pupils to point to the correct pictures.

- Read out the words *lots of, ride* and *thing*. Ask one pupil to *stand up* and say *Look! One pupil.* Then ask all the pupils to stand up and say Look! *Lots of pupils.* Ask pupils to repeat. Then gather a few pens, pencils, books, notebooks and other things in the classroom and say *Lots of things.* For *ride* use L1 to explain meaning.

- Read out all the words again one by one and ask pupils to repeat after you.

A Read.

> **Background Information**
>
> **London**
>
> London is the capital city of England and the UK. London is one of the biggest cities in Europe. Its population is about 14 million people together with the metropolitan area. London was the first city in the world to have an underground railway, known as 'The Tube'. The river Thames flows through the city and is the longest river in England and the second largest in the UK. London is a very popular destination for tourists with more than 26 million visitors every year.
>
> There are many interesting places to visit in London like Buckingham Palace (the home of the royal family), Hyde Park, the London Zoo, The London Eye, the British Museum, Madame Tussauds, Big Ben and many others. There are over 100 theatres in London. London is also great for shopping.

- Tell pupils to look at the poster of London. Ask them if they know where London is. Show them on the world map.

- Ask pupils to read the poster and choose two places they would like to visit in London. Allow pupils enough time to read the poster alone. Ask pupils to tell you the places they have chosen.

- Read out the poster one sentence at a time and ask pupils to repeat.

- Ask volunteers to read out a sentence each of the poster.

B Circle.

- Read the example to pupils and ask them to find the sentence in the poster which gives them the answer *city*. Tell them to underline the sentence.

- Explain the rest of the task to pupils. Make sure they understand the meanings of all the words. Allow them enough time to complete the task alone. Go round the class helping pupils where necessary.

- Check answers. Ask volunteers to read out the answers.

> **Answers**
> 1 city (given)
> 2 shops
> 3 picnic
> 4 long
> 5 go

C Look and learn.

- Read out the dialogue and ask pupils to repeat.

- Ask pupils to look at the grammar box. Read out the sentences and explain the meaning. Tell pupils that we use *Let's* to suggest doing something. Read out the example sentences and ask pupils to repeat.

- Practise the grammar. Say *Let's dance.* And encourage pupils to dance. Then ask pupils to make their own suggestions and the class acts them out.

D Write.

- Explain to pupils that the words of some sentences have been mixed up and that they have to write the words in the correct order to make sentences. Read out the example and ask pupils to repeat.

- Make sure pupils have understood the task. Allow them enough time to complete the task alone. Go round the class helping where necessary.

- Check answers. Ask pupils to read out their sentences.

> **Answers**
> 1 Let's go to London! (given)
> 2 Let's have a picnic!
> 3 Let's go to the cinema!
> 4 Let's see the fireworks!

E Say.

- Read out the dialogue and ask pupil to repeat.
- Tell pupils that they are going to make a map of a city. Hold up the piece of card and tell them that they are going to draw the map on it. Ask them to tell you what places they want on their map. Write their suggestions on the board.

  a park
  a cinema
  a theatre
  shops
  a river
  a school

- Draw some boxes on the map with the black marker. Then ask pupils to gather round and ask each pupil to draw something in one of the boxes on the map with the marker. If there are more pupils than boxes, they can draw something twice in one box.
- Ask pupils to sit down again. Hold up the poster, look at it, think for a while and then say *Let's go to school!* Ask pupils to answer *Yes. OK.* or *Oh no!*
- Ask pairs to hold up the map and make one suggestion each about what to do in their town. Ask pupils to look at the dialogue and replace the words in orange with their own choices. Write these verbs on the board for help.

  go
  buy
  have
  play
  swim

F Draw and write.

- Ask pupils to draw their own small poster in their books. Explain that they should draw at least three things. Allow them enough time to draw their posters.
- Ask pupils to finish the sentences under the poster. Read out the sentences to make sure they understand the meanings. Go round the class helping with spelling where necessary.
- Ask pupils to hold up their books and to show each other their posters. Ask volunteers to read out their sentences.

Homework

- Activity Book, pages 70-71: Time permitting, some task can be done in class.
- Dictation: *buy, park, picnic, river, shop*
- Revision for Test 9:
  Words: *city, cinema, theatre, market, boat, Be careful!, colours, dragon, fireworks, sky, New Year, buy, park, picnic, river, shop, lots of, ride, thing*
  Grammar: *What are you doing?*
  Imperative
  Let's

Teacher's Note

Pupils will do Test 9 in the following lesson. After every three units there is a review which can be done in the same lesson as the test.

Optional activity

Revision for Test 9

- Revise the city words (*city, cinema, theatre, market, boat, park, picnic, river, shop*). Ask pupils to remember all the city words they learnt in this unit and write the words on the board. Ask pupils to spell out the words.
- Revise the New Year words. Ask pupils to write the words they remember on the board.
- Revise *What are you doing?* Write the question on the board. Write *are you* in a different colour. Then say *What am I doing?*. Ask a volunteer to erase *are you* and replace the words with *am I*. Ask other volunteer to do the same for *is he/she/it* and *are we/you/they*.
- Revise the *Imperative* and *Let's*. Ask a volunteer to give the class an instruction (eg *Jump!*). Then ask another volunteer to tell the class not to do what the other volunteer ordered (eg *Don't jump*). Then suggest to pupils that they sing the song. Say *Let's sing!* If there is time, finish the revision with one of the songs from units 7-9.

Extra activity

- Play hangman with nouns from Units 7-9. See Unit 1 Lesson 3 for instructions.

Let's remember!

Aims
- Revise vocabulary from Units 7-9
- Revise grammar from Units 7-9

Materials
- Flashcards:

Unit 7: *drums, guitar, piano, recorder, music, sing*

Unit 8: *climb, cook, dance, kick, rock*

Unit 9: *city, cinema, theatre, market, boat*

Lead-in
- Check homework. Tell pupils to open their Activity Books at pages 70 and 71. Ask volunteers to read out their answers. Then quickly check all pupils' books.
- Test dictation: *buy, park, picnic, river, shop*. See the teacher's introduction pages 7-9 for teaching suggestions. Go round the class and check all pupils' dictation.

Revision
- Revise the words from the flashcards. Hold up a flashcard and ask pupils to call out the word. Stick the flashcard on the board. When all the flashcards are on the board, ask volunteers to come to the board, point to a flashcard of their choice and say the word. Repeat, but when a flashcard has been pointed to, remove it from the board.
- Ask pupils to remember all the sports they have learnt. They can search the vocabulary boxes at the beginning of each lesson to help them remember. Write them on the board, asking pupils to spell the words. Do the same for music words and city words.
- Revise the Present Continuous. Write *I'm singing.* and *I'm not singing.* on the board and ask volunteers to read out the sentences. Then write *You _____ singing.* and *You _____ singing.* on the board and ask volunteers to complete the sentences. Do the same with all persons. Then ask *Are you singing?* and elicit answers. Ask questions with different persons eg *Is he sitting? Are they standing? Are you listening?* and elicit answers.
- Revise the *Imperative* and *can, can't* and *Can you?* Ask volunteers to follow instructions, eg *dance.* Then say *Can he dance?* and elicit answers. Write on the board. *He can/can't dance.* Here are some suggested instructions:
swim
run
play the piano
play football
- Revise *Let's.* Write *Let's _____ .* on the board. Ask pupils to tell you suggestions for things they can do in their town, eg *Let's go to the shops. Let's go on a bus ride. Let's play football in the park.*

A Find and stick.
- Ask pupils to open their books at page 92 and to look at task A. Ask volunteers to read out the words. Then read out the words again and ask pupils to repeat as a class.
- Show pupils where to find the stickers in their books. Tell them to remove the stickers one at a time and to stick them in the correct boxes. Allow pupils enough time to stick all the stickers. Go round the class helping pupils where necessary.
- Check answers. Ask volunteers to hold up their books and read out the words.

B Write.
- Tell pupils to look at the crossword. Ask volunteers to tell you the words for each picture. Write the words on the board in capitals asking pupils to spell them.
- Tell pupils to complete the crossword on their own using capitals. Allow them enough time to complete the task alone. Go round the class helping pupils where necessary.
- Check answers. Write them on the board if necessary.

Answers
1 TENNIS (given)
2 FOOTBALL
3 GUITAR
4 BASKETBALL
5 DRUMS
6 RECORDER

C Circle.
- Read out the example and ask pupils why *listen to* is the correct answer. Read out all the sentences and make sure that pupils remember the meanings of all the words.
- Explain the rest of the task to pupils. Allow them enough time to complete the task alone.
- Go round the class helping pupils where necessary.
- Check answers. Ask volunteers to read out their answers.

Answers
1 listen to (given)
2 piano
3 reading
4 swim
5 market
6 climb

D Circle.
- Read out the example and ask pupils why *watching* is the correct answer. Read out all the sentences and make sure that pupils remember the meanings of all the words.
- Explain the rest of the task to pupils. Allow them enough time to complete the task alone.

- Go round the class helping pupils where necessary.
- Check answers. Ask volunteers to read out their answers.

Answers
1 watching (given)
2 Is
3 aren't
4 isn't
5 'm not
6 playing

E Write can or can't.

- Read out the example and ask pupils why *can't* is the correct answer. Read out all the sentences and make sure that pupils remember the meanings of all the words.
- Explain the rest of the task to pupils. Allow them enough time to complete the task alone.
- Go round the class helping pupils where necessary.
- Check answers. Ask volunteers to read out their answers.

Answers
1 can't (given)
2 can't
3 can
4 can
5 can't
6 can

F Write.

- Explain to pupils that the words in the box are the ones missing from the sentences. Tell them that when they have used a word to cross it through. Read out the first sentence and ask pupils to repeat. Ask them why *Let's* is the correct answer.
- Ask pupils to complete the task. Allow them enough time to complete the task alone. Go round the class helping pupils where necessary.
- Check answers. Ask volunteers to read out their answers.

Answers
1 Let's (given)
2 Don't
3 Let's
4 Look
5 Dance
6 Don't

Extra activity

Poster: Hobbies

This poster can be used to consolidate and revise vocabulary and grammar of Units 7-9 in a fun and interesting way. Pupils can also play a game with the poster. Follow the procedure outlined on the back of the poster.

Homework

- Pupil's Audio CD: pupils listen to the songs at home. Explain to pupils that they should listen to tracks 33, 37 and 40 on the CD.
- Activity Book, pages 72-73: Time permitting, some tasks can be done in class.
- Revision for Progress Test 3. Pupils should revise all the vocabulary and grammar from Units 7-9.

Teacher's Note

The pupils will do Progress Test 3 in the following lesson. After the test, you can do the lesson *Fun & Games*.

Fun & Games

Aims

- Consolidate new vocabulary with fun activities
- Consolidate new grammar with fun activities
- Make a board game

Materials

- One photocopy of the board game cutout and four players for each pupil (page 143)
- Scissors, colouring pencils
- Dice for each group

Lead-in

- Tell pupils that today's lesson is all about fun and games. Ask them to open their books at page 94. Ask them what they can see (a girl riding a bike).
- Read out the paragraph and ask pupils to follow the words with their fingers. Read it out again one sentence at a time and ask pupils to repeat. Check comprehension with these questions. Encourage pupils to use English for the words they have learnt.
  What is the girl's name? (Kay)
  What is she doing? (She's riding a bike.)
  Is she having fun? (Yes, she is.)
  Is she at the beach? (No, she isn't. She's in the park.)
- Consolidate vocabulary pupils have learnt using the picture. Here are some suggestions:

Kay can ride a bike.
Can you ride a bike?
What sports can you play?
Kay's town has got a park.
Has your town got a park?
What has your town got?

Quiz time!

- Tell pupils to look at the small picture. Read out the question and both answers and make sure pupils understand the meaning. Ask pupils to choose the correct answer (a). Ask a volunteer to read out the question and answer.

A Find.

- Tell pupils they are going to do a fun task. Ask them to look at the picture and tell them that they have to find the right route for Trek to find his friends (Ty, Mia, Leo) who are at the beach. Allow pupils enough time to find the route. Then volunteers can hold up their books and show which route is the correct.

B Sing. 2:32

- Tell pupils they are going to learn a song. Explain to pupils that the song is about what people are doing in a park.
- Play the recording and tell pupils to listen and follow the words with their fingers.
- Read out the song one line at a time and ask pupils to repeat after you.
- Play the recording again. Encourage pupils to sing along. Practise many times until pupils are familiar with the words.
- Pupils can do actions and sing the song again. They can pretend to ride a bike and kick a ball. They can then clap for *sing the song* and *have fun*.

C Make.

- Tell pupils they are going to make a board game. Tell pupils to look at the pictures in task C and explain each stage to them.

1 Colour in the pictures and number the boxes.
2 Cut out the board game.
3 Cut out the counters.
4 Fold the flaps of the counters back so they stand up.
5 Play the game in pairs.

- Ask pupils to have their colouring pencils ready. Hand out the photocopies of the board game cutouts and ask pupils to colour in the picture and number the boxes.
- When all pupils are ready, ask them to put their colouring pencils away. Then hand out the scissors. Ask pupils to cut out their board games. Go round the class helping pupils where necessary. Then ask pupils to cut out the players.
- Collect the scissors. Show pupils how to fold the flap back on the players so they stand up. Help them with the folding where necessary.

Rules

The game can be played by two to four players. The players throw the dice and move their counters forward the number of squares the dice shows. If they land on a picture they must say what the picture shows. If they don't know the word, they move back one square. The winner is the first player to reach the star. Players don't have to throw an exact number to reach the star.

- Divide pupils into groups of two or four. Explain the rules of the game to pupils. Ask each group to choose a board they are going to use, and which player they want to be. Hand out one dice per group. Tell them they can start playing. Go round the class encouraging pupils to remember the words.
- Pupils can play again. Tell the groups to change boards and players, so they all get a chance to use what they have made. Collect in the dice.

Homework

- Pupil's Audio CD: pupils listen to the song at home. Explain to pupils that they should listen to track 41 on the CD.

- Optional extra homework: Pupils can play the board game with a family member at home.

Extra activity

- Play an alphabet game. Ask pupils to call out the alphabet and as they do so write the capital letters on the board. Then ask volunteers to write the lower case letters next to the capitals.

- Explain to pupils that they are going to play a game with the letters. The game starts with the first pupil at the front of the class. This pupil must think of a word beginning with A. The next pupil must think of a word beginning with B and so on. The game continues round and round the class until all the letters have been used.

Ask pupils to look at the National Geographic photo on pages 96-97 (use L1) and tell them that it is a photo of the island of Santorini.

Pupils are likely to know that Greece is famous for its history, beautiful islands and archaeological sites. They will probably know a few famous places. Encourage them to name a few (the Acropolis, Mount Olympus, Crete, Rhodes, etc). Ask them what they know about the Greek landscape. Then explain that in Greece, there are islands, mountains, plains and forests. In the capital city of Athens, there is the famous temple, the Parthenon, on the Acropolis. Athens is a very busy city. The countryside is quieter and there are many forests. There are also many islands in Greece. Crete is the largest island. It has plains, beaches, forests and mountains. It's also got the famous site of Knossos. The famous White Mountains on the east of the island are home to many plants and animals. Particularly well-known are the wild goats which are called Kri Kri. Pupils might know where Greece is situated. Ask volunteers to find Europe on the classroom map and then show them where Greece is. Then point to the map at the top of the page to show them.

The fourth country the reporters visit is Greece. In episode 1, they meet Mr Nikou and his son George in Athens. Trek sees on his TV the National Guard in traditional dress in front of the parliament building. The reporters go back to Mr Nikou's house where they meet his wife and daughters. George shows them around his house. In episode 2, they go to the island of Hydra to visit George's grandma. She is delighted to see them and can't stop hugging her grandson George and her son Mr Nikou. Ty admires her cooking. In episode 3, the reporters leave Athens and fly to Crete. They go on a hike in the White Mountains. They see some Kri Kri goats and a dragonfly. Ty gets scared because he thinks it's a dragon. The episode ends with a beautiful sunset over the sea, and the moon just coming up.

Fun facts

Here are some facts about Greece which your pupils will find interesting:

1   Greece is also called Hellas.

2   There are more than a thousand islands in Greece.

3   Most of Greece is mountains.

4   Mount Olympus is the highest mountain in Greece.

5   Many islands are in fact the tops of mountains.

6   There are turtles in the sea around Greece. They are endangered.

7   There are brown bears in the forests. They are endangered too.

8   Greek food is said to be very healthy.

9   Greece won the European Football Championship in 2004.

10   The most popular sport in Greece is football.

11   The Olympic Games were held in Greece in 2004.

12   Greek mythology is well-known all over the world.

10

Lesson 1   Trek's reporters in Greece

Aims

- Learn and use new vocabulary: *glass, bedroom, living room, kitchen, man, reporter, I'm sorry. Welcome to ...*
- Learn and use new grammar: *plural nouns*

Materials

- A glass
- One piece of blank paper for each pupil
- Masks: Trek, Mia, Ty, Leo

Lead-in

- Revise *baby, bus, fox* and *beach*. Write the words on the board and ask pupils to remember the meanings. Ask volunteers to draw pictures next to the words.
- Check homework. Tell pupils to open their Activity Books at pages 72 and 73. Ask volunteers to read out their answers. Then quickly check all pupils' books.

Episode outline

Greece: Episode 1

Trek's little sister Tessy asks him what he is watching on TV. He explains that it is a DVD from the reporters who are in Greece. The TV screen shows the National Guard in front of Syntagma square in Athens. The reporters have arranged to meet Mr Nikou and his son George in Athens. Ty notices that Mr Nikou is very tall. They go home with George and his dad and meet his mum and little baby sisters. Mia admires the living room. Ty and Leo go to George's bedroom where they play basketball. Ty accidentally hits Leo on the head with the ball. Then they all eat in the kitchen.

New vocabulary

- Draw a large square on the board. Divide it into four boxes. Then add a roof so you have a house. Say *Look! It's a house.* Draw a bed in one room upstairs. Point to the room and say *A bedroom.* Ask pupils to repeat. Draw a TV and sofa in a room downstairs and say *A living room.* Ask pupils to repeat. Then draw a table in the other room and say *A kitchen.* Ask pupils to repeat. Practise the rooms a few times. Ask volunteers to come to the board, point to the rooms and name them.
- Teach *man* and *glass*. Ask a pupil *What's your grandpa's name?* Ask *Is your grandpa a baby?* Elicit *No, he isn't.* Say *Your grandpa is a man.* Write *man* on the board and ask pupils to read it out. Teach *glass* with the glass you have brought. Hold up the glass and say *Look. A glass.* Ask pupils to repeat.

- Tell pupils to open their books at page 98 and to look at the vocabulary box. Hold up your book and point to the first picture word. Say the word and ask pupils to repeat. Do the same with all the words. Teach *reporter.* Ask pupils to tell you the names of the reporters in *Happy Trails.* Remind them of the meaning if necessary. Then read out the new picture words in the vocabulary box in random order and ask pupils to point to the correct pictures.
- Read out the words *I'm sorry.* and *Welcome to.* Explain the meanings. Ask pupils to tell you when they would apologize with *I'm sorry.* Then ask how they would welcome someone to their house. Elicit *Welcome to my house.* Ask pupils to repeat.
- Read out all the words again one by one and ask pupils to repeat after you.

A Listen and read.

For teachers using the DVD

- Make sure each pupil has a copy of the DVD worksheet found on page 136.
- Please follow the procedure outlined in Unit 1, Lesson 1 on page 31 for teachers using the DVD.

Before you watch

Answers
1 Trek's sister
2 in Greece
3 The Nikou family

While you watch

Answers
1 men
2 babies
3 bedroom
4 living room
5 sorry
6 kitchen

After you watch

Answers
1 tall
2 George
3 No. They're babies.
4 a ball
5 Welcome to Greece!

For teachers using the audio CD 2.33

- Tell pupils to look at the cartoon story. Ask them to find the country Greece on the classroom map.
- Play the recording. Tell pupils to look at the pictures and follow the speech bubbles with their fingers.

- Play the recording again. Pause after each speech bubble and ask pupils to repeat.

- Check pupils understand the story. Use L1 where necessary.
  Is Mr Nikou tall or short? (tall)
  What's the boy's name? (George)
  Are his sisters big? (No. They are babies.)
  What hits Leo on the head? (a ball)
  What does Mrs Nikou say in the kitchen? (Welcome to Greece!)

- Play the recording again. Then ask volunteers to read out the story.

- Assign characters to volunteers and ask them to act out the story in front of the class. Pupils can wear the character masks.

B Look and learn.

- Read out the dialogue. Read it out again and ask pupils to repeat.

- Ask pupils to look at the grammar box. Explain that for some words when there is more than one, we add *es* but their spelling changes. Read out the words on the left and ask pupils to repeat. Explain the meanings and spelling rules.
  y = ies
  s, ss, x, ch, o = es
  Then tell pupils that for some words when there is more than one, we don't add *es* but their spelling changes completely. Read out the words on the right and ask pupils to repeat. Explain the meanings.

- Ask pupils to find the plural words in the dialogue and to circle them (women, men).

C Write.

- Ask pupils to look at picture 1. Ask them to count the ostriches (one on the left, two on the right). Explain that on the left they write the word for one thing, but on the right they must write the word for more than one thing.

- Explain the rest of the task to pupils. Tell them to look at the pictures and to tell you what they can see. Help them remember words if necessary. Then ask pupils to complete the task. Allow them enough time to complete the task alone. Go round the class helping pupils where necessary.

- Check answers. Read out the words and ask pupils to repeat to practise pronunciation.

Answers
1 ostrich / ostriches (given)
2 woman / women
3 fly / flies
4 octopus / octopuses
5 tomato / tomatoes

D Listen and circle. 2.34

- Explain to pupils that Ty is looking for everyone in George's house. Read out the sentences and check pupils understand the meanings. Then explain that they must listen carefully and circle the room each person is in.

- Play the recording for the example. Make sure pupils understand what to do.

- Play the recording. Pause between numbers where necessary. Play the recording again and ask pupils to check their answers.

Listening script
1
Ty: Mrs Nikou is watching TV.
Mrs Nikou: My TV is in the kitchen.
Ty: Cool! A TV in the kitchen! I've got a TV in my bedroom.

2
Ty: Mr Nikou is in the bedroom.
Mr Nikou: Yes, I'm reading my book.
Ty: Your bedroom is blue! My living room is blue too.

3
Ty: Hi, George. What are you doing?
George: I'm playing basketball in my bedroom. I can't play basketball in the living room.
Ty: Basketball in the bedroom! That's fantastic!

4
Ty: Look! The babies are in the living room.
Mia: Yes. I'm in the living room too. I'm playing with the babies.

5
Ty: Leo! Leo! Is he in the kitchen? Oh, there you are! You're in the living room too.
Leo: This living room is very big.

Answers
1 kitchen (given)
2 bedroom
3 bedroom
4 living room
5 living room

E Say.

- Tell pupils you want them to draw a picture of their house. Hand out a piece of blank paper to each pupil. Allow them enough time to draw.

- When pupils have finished their drawings, read out the example. Read it out again and ask pupils to repeat after each sentence.

- Tell pupils that you want them to describe their houses too. Write these words on the board to help them:
  my house
  kitchen
  bedroom
  living room
  big
  small
  beautiful
  nice
  great
  Ask a volunteer to hold up his picture and to describe it. Prompt where necessary. Make sure all pupils have a turn.

Lesson 2   Sandy is making cakes.

Aims

- Learn and use new vocabulary: *butter, chocolate, flour, milk, face, make*
- Learn and use new grammar: *some, any*

Materials

- Flashcards: butter, chocolate, flour, milk, face

Lead-in

- Revise the words from Lesson 1 on the board. Ask a volunteer to draw a square house on the board and four rooms. Ask pupils to call out the names of the rooms so the volunteer can label them. Encourage pupils to call out the spelling.
- Revise the plural words from Lesson 1. First write the singular words on the left:

baby	tomato
bus	man
glass	woman
fox	child
beach	foot

Then ask pupils to tell you the plural. Ask them to call out the spelling.

- Check homework. Tell pupils to open their Activity Books at pages 74 and 75. Ask volunteers to read out their answers. Then quickly check all pupils' books.
- Test dictation: *bedroom, kitchen, living room*. See the teacher's introduction pages 7-9 for teaching suggestions. Go round the class and check all pupils' dictation.

New vocabulary

- Teach the new words with the flashcards. See the teacher's introduction pages 7-9 for teaching suggestions.
- Tell pupils to open their books at page 100 and to look at the vocabulary box. Hold up your book and point to the first picture word. Say the word and ask pupils to repeat. Do the same with all the words. Then read out the

new picture words in the vocabulary box in random order and ask pupils to point to the correct pictures.

- Read out the verb *make*. Explain the meaning. Say *Let's make a cake!* and ask pupils to repeat.
- Read out all the words again one by one and ask pupils to repeat after you.

A Listen and read. ⊙ 2.35

- Ask pupils to look at the photo and to say what the little girl is making (cakes). Revise *pink* and *brown* with the question *What colours are the cakes?*
- Play the recording. Tell pupils to follow the text with their fingers.
- Play the recording again. Pause after each sentence and ask pupils to repeat.
- Play the recording again. Then ask volunteers to read out a sentence each of the text.

B Write Yes or No.

- Read the example to pupils. Ask them to find the sentence in the text which gives the answer *Yes*.
- Explain the rest of the task to pupils. Tell them to underline the words in the text which give them the answers. Allow them enough time to complete the task alone. Go round the class encouraging and helping pupils where necessary.
- Check answers.

Answers
1 Yes (given)
2 No
3 Yes
4 Yes
5 Yes

C Look and learn.

- Read out the dialogue. Read it out again and ask pupils to repeat.
- Ask pupils to look at the grammar box. Read out the grammar notes and sentences. Ask pupils to repeat. Explain that when we have got something we say *some* if we don't want to say an exact number. When we haven't got anything we say *any* and we also use *any* in questions.
- Ask pupils to underline *any* in the dialogue. Ask volunteers to read out the dialogue.
- Practise the grammar. Write these sentences on the board. Ask pupils to read them out and fill in the gaps with *some* or *any*.
  Have cakes got _____ eggs?
  I've got _____ cool toys.
  She hasn't got _____ brothers or sisters.

D Write some or any.

- Read out the example and ask pupils why *any* is the correct answer.

- Explain the task to pupils. Read out the sentences. Check pupils remember the meanings of all the words. Allow enough time for pupils to complete the task alone.

- Check answers. Ask volunteers to read out the sentences.

Answers
1 any (given)
2 some
3 some
4 any
5 some
6 any

E Sing. 🔊 2.36

- Tell pupils they are going to learn a song. Teach pupils *Rub your tummy*. Point to your tummy and say *tummy*. Ask pupils to repeat. Then rub your tummy and say *Rub your tummy*. Ask pupils to copy and repeat.

- Ask pupils to look at the pictures and say what ingredients they can see. Elicit *chocolate* and *milk*.

- Play the recording and tell pupils to listen and follow the words with their fingers.

- Read out the song one line at a time and ask pupils to repeat after you.

- Play the recording again. Encourage pupils to sing along. Practise many times until pupils are familiar with the words. Pupils can rub their tummies as they sing the song.

Homework

- Pupil's Audio CD: Pupils listen to the text and the song at home. Explain to pupils that they should listen to tracks 43 and 44 on the CD.

- Activity Book, pages 76-77: Time permitting, some tasks can be done in class.

- Dictation: *butter, chocolate, flour, milk, face*

Lesson 3   Where are the oranges?

Aims

- Learn and use new vocabulary: *basket, carrot, cheese, orange, potato, sweets*

- Learn and use new grammar: *Where, prepositions of place (in, on, in front of, behind, next to, under)*

Materials

- Flashcards: butter, chocolate, flour, milk, face

- A basket, a carrot, some cheese, an orange, a potato, some sweets

Lead-in

- Revise the words from Lesson 2 with the flashcards. Hold up the flashcards one at a time and choose pupils to call out the word. Then ask a volunteer to take over the role of teacher and do the same with the flashcards.

- Revise *some* and *any*. Hold up the *chocolate* flashcard and say:
  Have we got any chocolate?
  Yes, we have. We've got some chocolate.
  Ask pupils to repeat. Then hide the chocolate flashcard and say:
  Have we got any chocolate?
  No, we haven't. We haven't got any chocolate.

- Check homework. Tell pupils to open their Activity Books at pages 76 and 77. Ask volunteers to read out their answers. Then quickly check all pupils' books.

- Test dictation: *butter, chocolate, flour, milk, face*. See the teacher's introduction pages 7-9 for teaching suggestions. Go round the class and check all pupils' dictation.

New vocabulary

- Teach the new words with the objects. Say *I'm going to the shops*. Hold up the basket. Say *Look. I've got a basket. Let's buy a carrot*. Hold up the carrot and say the word. Ask pupils to repeat. Do the same mini dialogue with some cheese, an orange, a potato and some sweets

- Teach the *prepositions of place*. Put the basket on a chair. Say *The basket is on the chair*. Repeat *on*. Ask pupils to repeat. Put the carrot in the basket. Say *The carrot is in the basket*. Repeat *in*. Ask pupils to repeat. Continue with the carrot for *in front of, behind, under* and *next to*.

- Tell pupils to open their books at page 102 and to look at the vocabulary box. Hold up your book and point to the first picture word. Say the word and ask pupils to repeat. Do the same with all the words. Then read out the new picture words in the vocabulary box in random order and ask pupils to point to the correct pictures.

- Read out all the words again one by one and ask pupils to repeat after you.

A Read.

- Tell pupils to look at the photo and to describe what they can see. Ask pupils to read the dialogue and to find which item Mum doesn't buy.

- Read out the text one sentence at a time. Pause after each sentence and ask pupils to repeat.

- Ask volunteers to read out a sentence each of the text. Then ask pupils to practise the dialogue in pairs. Move around the classroom listening and helping. Pairs can then perform the dialogue in front of the class.

B Write.

- Read the example to pupils. Ask them to find where the answer is in the text.

- Explain the rest of the task to pupils. Tell them to underline the words in the text which give them the answers. Allow them enough time to complete the task alone. Go round the class encouraging and helping pupils where necessary.

- Check answers. Write them on the board if necessary.

Answers
1 carrots (given)
2 eggs
3 cheese
4 basket

C Look and learn.

- Read out the dialogue and ask pupils to repeat.

- Ask pupils to look at the grammar box. Read out the grammar notes and sentences. Ask pupils to repeat. Explain the meaning of the notes.

- Practise the grammar. Remind pupils of the *prepositions of place* with the basket and carrot as in the Lead-in.

D Circle.

- Ask pupils to look at the first picture. Read out the example and ask pupils to repeat. Explain that they must look at the picture to work out the answer.

- Ask pupils to look at the other pictures and to say what they can see. Explain the task to pupils. Allow them enough time to complete the task alone. Go round the class helping pupils where necessary.

- Check answers. Ask volunteers to read out their answers.

Answers
1 in (given)
2 behind
3 under
4 next to

Say it! ◎ 2.37

- Write *w* on the board. Read it out and ask pupils to repeat. Play the first part of the recording (Listen and say) asking pupils to repeat the words *Wendy* and *sweets* each time they hear them (*Wendy* and *sweets* will be heard twice).

- Ask for volunteers to read out the question. Play the recording and ask all pupils to repeat (the phrase will be heard once).

E Say.

- Read out the example. Read it out again and ask pupils to repeat. Ask pupils to draw items in their own basket on the right in task F. Tell them not to write anything yet. They should draw three items from the lesson.

- Allow pupils enough time to finish their drawings. Then ask volunteers to hold up their books and to describe their shopping baskets. Prompt where necessary.

F Draw and write.

- Tell pupils to now write what is in their baskets. Allow pupils enough time to finish the task. Then ask pupils to read out their work.

Homework

- Activity Book, pages 78-79: Time permitting, some tasks can be done in class.

- Dictation: *basket, carrot, cheese, orange, potato, sweets*

- Optional extra homework: Pupils can copy the picture and three sentences from task F onto a piece of paper to be displayed on the classroom wall.

- Revision for Test 10:
Words: *bedroom, kitchen, living room, man, glass, reporter, I'm sorry. Welcome to ..., butter, chocolate, flour, milk, face, make, basket, carrot, cheese, orange, potato, sweets*
Grammar: *plural nouns, some, any, Where, prepositions of place*

Teacher's Note

Pupils will do Test 10 in the following lesson. If you don't want to rush into Unit 11, for the rest of the lesson do these activities:
1 Pupils can read out the cartoon story from Unit 10 Lesson 1. Then ask volunteers to act out the cartoon story.
2 Pupils can read out the texts from Lessons 2 and 3.
3 Repeat the *Say* task from Lesson 3.
4 Sing the song.
5 Hand out pieces of paper and ask pupils to draw their own shopping baskets. They can talk about what is in the baskets and what the colours and numbers are.
eg *There are two carrots in my basket. They're orange.*

Optional activity

Revision for Test 10

- Revise the words from the flashcards. Then write the words on the board. Ask a volunteer to read out a word and come and choose the corresponding flashcard. Practise until all pupils remember the words well.

- Revise the other *food* words. Hold up the item of food and ask pupils to call out the word.

- Revise the rooms of a house. Ask volunteers to tell you the names of three rooms they have learnt. Test if they can spell them.

- Write the plurals on the board. Say a word in singular and ask pupils to call out the plural eg *man-men, foot-feet, baby-babies*. Check spelling on the board.

- Revise *some* and *any*. Ask four pupils to stand up at the front of the class and look happy. Say *Look. They've got some friends*. Ask pupils to repeat. Then ask three pupils to sit down. Ask the remaining pupil to look sad. Say *He hasn't got any friends*. Ask pupils to repeat. Write the two sentences on the board. Underline *some* and *any*. Then ask pupils which word we use in a question and elicit *any*. Ask a pupil to think of a question and write it on the board. Eg *Has Mark got any friends?*

- Revise the prepositions of place. Ask pupils to all hold a pen. Give pupils instructions where to put the pen and ask them to follow them:
Put the pen on the desk / in your bag / under your chair / next to your book / behind your friend / in front of your fingers.

11

Lesson 1　Trek's reporters in Greece

Aims

- Learn and use new vocabulary: *work, love, Monday, Tuesday, Wednesday, Thursday, Friday, Saturday, Sunday*
- Learn and use new grammar: *Present Simple affirmative (I, you, he, she, it)*

Materials

- Optional for Extra activity: one piece of paper for each pupil to draw on
- Masks: Mia, Ty, Leo

Lead-in

- Revise the *food words* from Unit 10. Say a word eg *orange* and ask a pupil to draw it on the board. Continue with *carrot, cheese, potato, sweets, butter, chocolate, flour* and *milk*.
- Revise the prepositions of place. Put a pen on the desk and ask *Where's the pen?* Elicit *It's on the desk*. Write *on* on the board. Practise *in, under, behind, next to* and *in front of* with the pen in different places. Write the prepositions of place on the board.
- Check homework. Tell pupils to open their Activity Books at pages 78 and 79 Ask volunteers to read out their answers. Then quickly check all pupils' books.
- Test dictation: *basket, carrot, cheese, orange, potato, sweets*. See the teacher's introduction pages 7-9 for teaching suggestions. Go round the class and check all pupils' dictation.

Episode outline

Greece: Episode 2

It's Saturday. The reporters are going to the island of Hydra on Mr Nikou's boat. They go to visit George's grandma who is a hospitable warm-hearted lady. Leo chats to George on the journey. At the port, George's grandma meets them and hugs George. He is a little embarrassed. At his grandma's house, they all talk about cooking. Ty especially enjoys the cakes George's grandma has made. Then George's grandma hugs her son Mr Nikou. He is very embarrassed. Everyone laughs.

New vocabulary

- Teach the days of the week. Ask pupils what day it is and then tell them the day in English. Then say all the days from Monday to Sunday and ask pupils to repeat one at a time. Write the days on the board.

- Tell pupils to open their books at page 104 and to look at the vocabulary box. Hold up your book and point to the picture words. Help pupils work out the meanings from the pictures. Say the words and ask pupils to repeat.
- Read out the days of the week and ask pupils to repeat.
- Read out all the words again one by one and ask pupils to repeat after you.

A Listen and read.

For teachers using the DVD

- Make sure each pupil has a copy of the DVD worksheet found on page 137.
- Please follow the procedure outlined in Unit 1, Lesson 1 on page 31 for teachers using the DVD.

Before you watch

Answers
1 because it's Saturday
2 by boat
3 Mr Nikou and George

While you watch

Answers
a 10
b 4
c 6
d 11
e 1
f 8
g 12
h 2
i 7
j 5
k 9
l 3

After you watch

Answers
1 Saturday
2 George's grandma
3 the cakes
4 because she loves her son (Mr Nikou) and her grandson (George)

For teachers using the audio CD 2.38

- Tell pupils to look at the cartoon story. Ask them to find and underline the days of the week in the story.
- Play the recording. Tell pupils to look at the pictures and follow the speech bubbles with their fingers.
- Play the recording again. Pause after each speech bubble and ask pupils to repeat.
- Check pupils understand the story. Use L1 where necessary.

What day is it? (Saturday)
Who do the reporters visit? (George's grandma)
What does Ty enjoy? (the cakes)
Why is George's grandma happy? (because she loves her son and grandson)

- Play the recording again. Then ask volunteers to read out the story.

- Assign characters to volunteers and ask them to act out the story in front of the class. Pupils can wear the character masks.

B Look and learn.

- Read out the speech bubble. Read it out again and ask pupils to repeat.

- Ask pupils to look at the grammar box. Tell pupils they are learning how to talk about things they do every day. Tell them that the verb stays the same except for *he, she* and *it* where we add an *s*. Point out the spelling changes. Read out the words and example sentence in the grammar box and ask pupils to repeat.

- Ask pupils to pretend to be Amber and Chris and to read out the speech bubble. Ask pupils to circle the verbs.

- Practise the grammar point. Write *On Monday I play basketball.* on the board. Read it out and ask pupils to repeat. Then change *I* to *you*. Ask pupils if the verb needs to change (no). Then change *you* to *he*. Ask pupils if the verb needs to change. Elicit that *play* becomes *plays*. Read out the sentence and ask pupils to repeat.

C Circle.

- Read out the example and ask pupils why *love* is the correct answer.

- Explain the rest of the task to pupils. Read out all the sentences and check pupils understand the meanings. Point out that a name is the same as using *he* or *she* and *My cat* is the same as using *it*. Allow them enough time to complete the task alone. Go round the class helping pupils where necessary.

- Check answers. Ask volunteers to read out the answers. Write them on the board if necessary.

Answers
1 love (given)
2 go
3 rides
4 climbs
5 plays
6 buy

Say it! 2: 39

- Write *g* on the board. Explain that there are two ways of pronouncing *g*. Say *good* and ask pupils to repeat. Then say *George* and ask pupils to repeat. Play the first part of the recording (Listen and say) asking pupils to repeat the words *George* and *great* each time they hear them (*George* and *great* will be heard twice).

- Ask for volunteers to read out the sentence. Play the recording and ask all pupils to repeat (the sentence will be heard once).

D Sing. 2: 40

- Tell pupils they are going to learn a song. Explain to pupils that the song is about the days of the week.

- Ask pupils to look at the picture and describe what they can see. Encourage them to use English for words they know.

- Play the recording and tell pupils to listen and follow the words with their fingers.

- Read out the song one line at a time and ask pupils to repeat after you.

- Play the recording again. Encourage pupils to sing along. Practise many times until pupils are familiar with the words.

- Pupils can stand in a circle and sing.

Homework

- Pupil's Audio CD: Pupils listen to the cartoon story and the song at home. Explain to pupils that they should listen to tracks 45 and 46 on the CD.

- Activity Book, pages 80-81: Time permitting, some tasks can be done in class.

- Dictation: *Monday, Tuesday, Wednesday, Thursday, Friday, Saturday, Sunday*

Extra activity

- Hand out a piece of paper to each pupil. Ask pupils to write a day of the week at the top of their choice. Then ask them to draw what they do on that day. Tell them to draw something they can describe in English.

- Ask pupils to hold up their drawings and to show them to the class. Ask them to describe what they do on that day of the week, eg *On Monday I play football*. Then ask another pupil to say what the pupil does, eg *On Monday he plays football*.

Lesson 2   We love snow.

Aims

- Learn and use new vocabulary: *snow, castle, breakfast, eat, get up, wear*

- Learn and use new grammar: *Present Simple affirmative (we, you, they)*

Lead-in

- Revise the days of the week. Ask pupils to recite the days of the week as a class. Then ask pupils to recite them individually.

- Revise the *Present Simple affirmative*. Ask a pupil to say which sport he loves. Elicit for example *I love football*. Ask pupils to repeat. Write *I love football.* on the board. Then write *He _____ football.* underneath. Ask pupils to fill in the missing word (*loves*). Remind them of spelling changes with *watch* and *go*.

- Check homework. Tell pupils to open their Activity Books at pages 80 and 81. Ask volunteers to read out their answers. Then quickly check all pupils' books.

- Test dictation: *Monday, Tuesday, Wednesday, Thursday, Friday, Saturday, Sunday*. See the teacher's introduction pages 7-9 for teaching suggestions. Go round the class and check all pupils' dictation.

New vocabulary

- Teach *castle* and *snow*. Draw a simple castle with turrets on the board and say *Look! A castle.* Then draw round flakes of snow falling around the castle and say *snow*. Point to the castle and say *castle* and then point to the snow and say *snow*. Ask pupils to repeat.

- Ask pupils in L1 what they do after they wake up. Elicit they get up. Then ask pupils in L1 what they do next. Elicit they eat breakfast. Then ask what they wear. Say these sentences and ask pupils to repeat.
I get up.
I eat breakfast.
I wear a jacket.
Then write the sentences on the board. Circle the new words and explain the meanings if necessary.

- Tell pupils to open their books at page 106 and to look at the vocabulary box. Hold up your book and point to the first word. Say the word and ask pupils to repeat. Do the same with all the words. Then read out the new words in the vocabulary box in random order and ask pupils to point to the correct pictures.

- Read out all the words again one by one and ask pupils to repeat after you.

A Listen and read. 2: 41

- Tell pupils that they are going to read about a snow castle. Ask pupils to look at the photo and describe what they can see. Help pupils to use English for the words they know.

- Play the recording. Tell pupils to follow the text with their fingers.

- Play the recording again. Pause after each sentence and ask pupils to repeat.

- Play the recording again. Then ask volunteers to read out a sentence each of the text.

B Match.

- Read the example to pupils. Explain to pupils that they should read the sentences and match it to the correct pictures. Allow them enough time to complete the task alone. Go round the class encouraging and helping pupils where necessary.

- Check answers. Ask pupils to read out the sentences and then hold up their books and point to the corresponding pictures.

C Look and learn.

- Ask pupils to look at the picture. Ask pupils what Amber and Chris are doing. Read out the dialogue. Read it out again and ask pupils to repeat.

- Ask pupils to look at the grammar box. Read out the grammar notes and sentence. Ask pupils to repeat. Explain the meaning of the notes.

- Ask pupils to circle the verbs in the grammar sentence and dialogue.

- Practise the grammar. Ask pupils in pairs to say things they love, eg *We love cats.* Allow pairs a few minutes to think about what they are going to say.

D Write.

- Read out the example and explain to pupils that they have to put the words in the correct order to make sentences. Read out the example and ask pupils to repeat.

- Go through all the sentences and check that pupils understand the meanings. Allow them enough time to complete the task alone. Go round the class helping pupils where necessary.

- Check answers. Ask pupils to read out their sentences. Write answers on the board if necessary.

Answers
1 We make great cakes. (given)
2 They eat oranges.
3 You play in the snow.
4 They watch TV in the bedroom.

E Listen and number. 2: 42

- Ask pupils to look at the pictures and to say what they can see. Explain that they are going to hear descriptions of the pictures and that they must put the correct number under each picture.

- Play the recording for the example. Make sure pupils understand what to do.

- Play the recording. Pause to allow pupils enough time to write down the answers. Play the recording again and ask pupils to check their answers.

- Check answers. Ask pupils to repeat what they heard about the pictures, eg *They eat sweets.*

Listening script
1
Sally and Tina love sweets. They eat lots of sweets.
2
Mum and Dad work on Saturday. They're reporters.
3
Nick and Tom eat apples. They love red apples.
4
My sisters make a cake on Sunday. It's yummy!
5
Mary's mum and dad love hats. They wear blue hats.
6
My brothers play the drums. They're playing the drums now. What a noise!

F Say.

- Read out the example and ask pupils to repeat after you. Tell pupils that they are going to say what they do on Saturday and Sunday. Explain that they can use the given words for help if they want to.

- Ask pupils to practise what they are going to say in pairs. Remind them to replace the words in orange with their own choices. Then ask volunteers to stand up and say what they do on Saturday and Sunday.

Extension activity

- Ask volunteers one at a time to repeat their sentences. Then ask pupils to say what the volunteers said using *He* or *She*.
  eg *On Saturday I play basketball.*
  On Saturday he plays basketball.

Homework

- Pupil's Audio CD: Pupils listen to the text. Explain to pupils that they should listen to track 47 on the CD.

- Activity Book, pages 82-83: Time permitting, some tasks can be done in class.

- Dictation: *snow, castle, breakfast, eat, get up, wear*

Lesson 3   I'm from Paris.

Aims

- Learn and use new vocabulary: *crisps, maths, popcorn, scooter, English, like, live, at the weekend*

- Learn and use new grammar: *Present Simple negative*

Materials

- A packet of crisps, a packet of popcorn

- A magazine or Internet picture of a scooter

- Optional for extra activity: photocopies of ten by ten square grids for pupils to make wordsearches.

Lead-in

- Revise the Present Simple. Say *On Monday I get up. I eat breakfast. I go to school.* Ask pupils to repeat. Then ask volunteers to say what they do on Tuesday, Wednesday and so on. Write *I eat breakfast.* on the board. Then write *They eat breakfast.* on the board. Ask pupils to read the sentences out. Then write *She _____ breakfast.* on the board. Ask a volunteer to write the missing word in the gap. Make sure pupils remember the *s* for the third person.

- Check homework. Tell pupils to open their Activity Books at page 82 and 83. Ask volunteers to read out their answers. Then quickly check all pupils' books.

- Test dictation: *castle, snow, breakfast, eat, get up, wear.* See the teacher's introduction pages 7-9 for teaching suggestions. Go round the class and check all pupils' dictation.

New vocabulary

- Teach *crisps* and *popcorn* with the packets you have brought. Hold up the packets and say *Look. Crisps and popcorn.* Ask pupils to repeat. Then teach *scooter* with the picture. Ask pupils if they have got a scooter. Finally teach *maths* and *English.* Ask pupils if they like the subjects maths and English in L1. Say *I love maths.* and *I love English.* Ask pupils to repeat. Write the new words on the board. Read them out and ask pupils to repeat.

- Tell pupils to open their books at page 108 and to look at the vocabulary box. Hold up your book and point to the first picture word. Say the word and ask pupils to repeat. Do the same with all the words. Then read out the new picture words in the vocabulary box in random order and ask pupils to point to the correct pictures.

- Read out the words *like, live* and *at the weekend* and explain the meanings. Say these example sentences and ask pupils to repeat:
  I like dogs.
  I live in London.
  At the weekend I swim.

- Read out all the words again one by one and ask pupils to repeat after you.

A Read.

Background information

Paris is the capital city of France. It is situated on the river Seine. The population of the metropolitan area of Paris is about 12 million, and it is one of the most populated areas of Europe. A popular nickname of this city is 'The City of Light' which was given to the city firstly because it was (and still is) a centre of education and ideas and secondly because it had street lights very early on. Famous landmarks in Paris are the Eiffel Tower, the Louvre Museum and the Notre Dame Cathedral.

The Eiffel Tower was built in 1887 to 1889 by an engineer called Gustave Eiffel. It is 324 metres tall. Six million people visit the Eiffel Tower every year.

- Tell pupils to look at the pictures. Ask them to tell you in English what the boy is riding (a scooter). Ask them if they now where the Eiffel Tower is (Paris). Tell pupils they are going to read an email from a boy who lives in Paris, France. Show pupils where this is on the classroom map.

- Tell pupils to read sentence 1 to find out the boy's name (John). Then ask them to read to the end of the paragraph. Ask *Has John got a brother? Has John got a sister?* (No, he hasn't). Ask pupils to then read the rest of the text and to find out two things he doesn't like (bikes and English).

- Read out the email. Stop after each sentence and ask pupils to repeat.
- Ask volunteers to read out a sentence each of the email.

B Circle.

- Read the example to pupils. Ask them to say which paragraph has the answer in it. Then ask them to underline the sentences that give them the answer.
- Explain the rest of the task to pupils. Tell them to underline the words in the text which give them the answers. Allow them enough time to complete the task alone. Go round the class encouraging and helping pupils where necessary.
- Check answers. Ask pupils to read out the sentences.

Answers
1 friends (given)
2 cinema
3 popcorn
4 scooter
5 maths

C Look and learn.

- Ask pupils why Chris's teacher, Mr Fry, looks angry (Chris has drawn a funny drawing of him.). Read out the thought bubble and ask pupils to repeat.
- Ask pupils to look at the grammar box. Read out the grammar notes and sentences. Ask pupils to repeat. Explain the meaning of the notes.
- Ask pupils to circle the verb and underline the word that makes it negative in the speech bubble and example sentence.
- Practise the grammar. Write these sentences on the board and ask pupils to say the opposite.
  I like chocolate.
  He likes maths.
  Write the opposite sentences on the board.

D Write don't or doesn't.

- Read out the example and ask pupils why *don't* is the correct answer. Remind pupils to think carefully about the person in each sentence to help them find the answer.
- Explain the task to pupils. Read out the sentences. Check pupils remember the meanings of all the words. Allow pupils enough time to complete the task. Go round the class helping pupils where necessary.
- Check answers. Ask pupils to read out the sentences.

Answers
1 don't (given)
2 don't
3 don't
4 doesn't
5 don't
6 doesn't

E Say.

- Read out the dialogue to pupils and ask them to repeat. Tell them that they are going to work in pairs. Explain that they have to think of one thing they like and one thing they don't like. They say two sentences about themselves and two sentences about their friend. They should use the dialogue to help them. Remind pupils to replace the words in orange with their own choices.
- Allow pupils enough time to work out in pairs what they are going to say. Go around the class helping where necessary.
- Ask a pair to stand at the front of the class and say their sentences. Continue until all pairs have had a turn.

F Write.

- Tell pupils they are going to write their own emails. Ask them if they have computers at home and if they have seen an email. Briefly explain what an email is.
- Read through the email and ask pupils to suggest what they could write in the gaps. Write a few of their ideas on the board. Then ask pupils to complete their emails on their own.
- Ask volunteers to hold up and read out their work.

Homework

- Activity Book, pages 84-85: Time permitting, some task can be done in class.
- Dictation: *crisps, maths, popcorn, scooter, English*
- Optional extra homework: Pupils can copy their email onto a piece of paper to be displayed on the classroom wall.
- Revision for Test 11:
  Words: *work, love, Monday, Tuesday, Wednesday, Thursday, Friday, Saturday, Sunday, castle, snow, breakfast, eat, get up, wear, crisps, maths, popcorn, scooter, English, like, live, at the weekend*
  Grammar: *Present Simple affirmative and negative*

Revision for Test 11

- Revise the days of the week. Ask volunteers to write the days on the board. Circle *Saturday* and *Sunday* and then ask a volunteer to write *at the weekend* on the board too.

- Write *get up, eat, wear, work, love, like*, and *live* on the board. Ask pupils the meaning of each verb. Ask volunteers to make sentences with each verb eg *I eat apples. I like maths. Dad works on Monday.*

- Write *castle, snow, breakfast, crisps, maths, popcorn, scooter* and *English* on the board. Ask pupils which of these things they can eat. Ask them the meanings of the other words.

- Revise the Present Simple. Say *I like maths.* Ask pupils to repeat. Say *He likes maths.* Ask pupils to repeat. Ask them to say what is different in the second sentence (*he* and *likes*). Remind them about the *s* at the end of the verb the verb for *he, she* and *it*. Then say *I don't like maths.* Ask pupils to repeat. Then ask pupils how to say the same for *he*. Elicit *He doesn't like maths.* Write all four sentences on the board.

Teacher's Note

The pupils will do Test 11 in the following lesson. If you don't want to rush into Unit 12, for the rest of the lesson do these activities:

1 Pupils can read out the cartoon story from Unit 11 Lesson 1. Then ask volunteers to act out the cartoon story.
2 Pupils can read out the texts from Lesson 2 and Lesson 3.
3 Repeat the *Say* task from Lesson 3.
4 Sing the song.
5 Make new wordsearches with words from the whole unit.

- Pupils can make their own wordsearches with the days of the week. Hand out a grid of ten squares by ten squares to each pupil. Show them how to fill in the grid with the days of the week. Tell them to use capital letters. Go round the class helping with spelling where necessary. Then tell pupils to fill in the other boxes with any letters they like.

- Pupils can swap wordsearches and then find each other's words.

12

Lesson 1   Trek's reporters in Greece

Aims

- Learn and use new vocabulary: *cave, dragonfly, goat, island, panda, sun, moon*
- Learn and use new grammar: *Present Simple interrogative*

Materials

- Flashcards: cave, dragonfly, goat, island, panda, sun, moon
- Masks: Trek, Ty, Mia, Leo

Lead-in

- Revise the words *crisps, maths, popcorn, scooter* and *English*. Write the words on the board and ask pupils to say which two are *food*, which is a *toy* and which two are *lessons*.

- Revise the Present Simple affirmative and negative. Say *I like maths*. Ask pupils to repeat. Say *I don't like parrots*. Ask pupils to repeat. Then ask volunteers to make two sentences of their own. Write your sentences on the board. Then change *I* to *He*. Ask pupils what other changes must now be made to the sentences.

- Check homework. Tell pupils to open their Activity Books at pages 84 and 85. Ask volunteers to read out their answers. Then quickly check all pupils' books.

- Test dictation: *crisps, maths, popcorn, scooter, English*. See the teacher's introduction pages 7-9 for teaching suggestions. Go round the class and check all pupils' dictation.

Episode outline

Greece: Episode 3

The reporters are finishing their trip to Greece. They say goodbye to George and his dad. They fly to Crete, where they go hiking in the White Mountains. In the mountains, they see the local wild goats – the Kri Kri. They also see a dragonfly and Ty gets scared as he mistakes it for a dragon and thinks it will eat him. At the end of the trip, the reporters admire the sunset and the moon coming up. Trek liked the DVD and thinks Greece is great.

New vocabulary

- Teach the new words with the flashcards. See the teacher's introduction pages 7-9 for teaching suggestions.

- Tell pupils to open their books at page 110 and to look at the vocabulary box. Hold up your book and point to the first picture word. Say the word and ask pupils to repeat. Do the same with all the words. Then read out the new picture words in the vocabulary box in random order and ask pupils to point to the correct pictures.

- Read out all the words again one by one and ask pupils to repeat after you.

A Listen and read.

For teachers using the DVD

- Make sure each pupil has a copy of the DVD worksheet found on page 138.

- Please follow the procedure outlined in Unit 1, Lesson 1 on page 31 for teachers using the DVD.

Before you watch

Answers
1 Mr Nikou and his son George
2 They are on an island (Crete).

While you watch

Answers
1 island
2 goats
3 caves
4 dragonfly
5 pandas
6 insect
7 sun
8 moon

After you watch

Answers
1 goats
2 a dragonfly
3 the sun
4 Yes

For teachers using the audio 2.43

- Tell pupils to look at the cartoon story. Ask pupils to find the new things they have learnt in the pictures.

- Play the recording. Tell pupils to look at the pictures and follow the speech bubbles with their fingers.

- Play the recording again. Pause after each speech bubble and ask pupils to repeat.

- Check pupils understand the story. Use L1 where necessary.
  What animals are Kri Kri? (goats)
  What is Ty scared of? (a dragonfly)
  What does Mia say is beautiful? (the sun)
  Does Trek like Greece? (Yes)

- Play the recording again. Then ask volunteers to read out the story.

- Assign characters to volunteers and ask them to act out the story in front of the class. Pupils can wear the character masks.

Extra activity

- Listen again to all three episodes of the story. Play the recordings from Lesson 1 of Units 10, 11 and 12. Ask pupils to follow the speech bubbles with their fingers.

- Divide the class into three groups, one group for each episode. Assign roles to pupils in each group. Then ask each group to act out their episode in front of the class. Pupils can again wear the character masks.

B Look and learn.

- Read out the dialogue. Read it out again and ask pupils to repeat.

- Ask pupils to look at the grammar box. Read out the grammar notes and sentences. Ask pupils to repeat. Explain the meaning of the notes.

- Ask pupils to circle the question and underline the answer in the grammar sentences and the dialogue. Ask volunteers to read out the sentences.

- Practise the grammar. Ask volunteers questions and ask them to answer. First write *Yes, I do.* and *No, I don't.* on the board.
  Do you like popcorn?
  Do you like insects?
  Do you play baseball?
  Do you eat worms?
  Write *Yes, he/she does.* and *No, he/she doesn't.* on the board. Then ask the questions in the third person, eg *Does Maria eat worms?*

C Write.

- Read out the question for number 1 and ask pupils to read out the answer. Explain that they must look at the beginning of the answer and the person in order to complete the answer.

- Explain the rest of the task to pupils. Check that pupils remember the meanings of all the words. Allow them enough time to complete the task alone. Go round the class helping pupils where necessary.

- Check answers. Ask pairs to read out the questions and answers.

Answers
1 doesn't (given)
2 don't
3 does
4 do
5 doesn't

D Listen and tick. 2.44

- Tell pupils that they are going to listen to descriptions of some pictures. Explain that they must listen carefully and tick the correct box. First ask pupils what each picture shows.

- Play the recording for the example. Make sure pupils understand what to do.

- Play the recording pausing between numbers where necessary. Play the recording again and ask pupils to check their answers.

Listening script

1
Look! Do you like my drawing?
Is it a dragonfly?
No, it isn't. It's a dragon. It's a small dragon!

2
That's my dad.
Wow! That's a big mountain behind your dad.
It isn't a mountain. It's a cave. Dad likes caves.

3
Do you like my photo?
Yes, I do. The goats are nice. They aren't white.
No, they aren't. They're brown goats. They're Kri Kri.

4
Wow! Look at the moon in the sky. It's very white.
Where's the moon?
It's next to the sun.

Answers
Pupils tick the following pictures.
1 2nd picture (given)
2 1st picture
3 1st picture
4 1st picture

E Say.

- Read out the dialogue and ask pupils to repeat. Tell pupils that they are going to ask each other questions about the pictures. First ask pupils what they can see in the pictures.

- Ask pupils to work in pairs and ask each other questions. Remind pupils to replace the words in orange with their own choices. Go round the class helping where necessary.

- Ask pairs to come to the front of the class and to perform their questions and answers.

Extension activity

Pupils can repeat the speaking task E, but this time ask about each other's family and friends.
eg *Does your mum like popcorn?*
Does your friend like snakes?

Homework

- Pupil's Audio CD: Pupils listen to the cartoon story at home. Explain to pupils that they should listen to track 48 on the CD.

- Activity Book, pages 86-87: Time permitting, some tasks can be done in class.

- Dictation: *cave, dragonfly, goat, island, panda, sun, moon*

Lesson 2   What do they do every day?

Aims
- Learn and use new vocabulary: *morning, afternoon, night, laugh, go to bed, study, lucky, at ... o'clock*
- Learn and use new grammar: *What do you do?*

Materials
- Flashcards: cave, dragonfly, goat, island, panda, sun, moon

Lead-in
- Revise the words from Lesson 1. Stick the flashcards on the board. Call out the words one at a time and ask volunteers to come to the board and point to the correct flashcard.
- Ask a pupil *Do you like dragonflies?* Elicit *Yes, I do.* or *No, I don't*. Then ask another pupil *Does (pupil's name) like dragonflies?* and elicit answer.
- Check homework. Tell pupils to open their Activity Books at pages 86 and 87. Ask volunteers to read out their answers. Then quickly check all pupils' books.
- Test dictation: *cave, dragonfly, goat, island, panda, sun, moon*. See the teacher's introduction pages 7-9 for teaching suggestions. Go round the class and check all pupils' dictation.

New vocabulary
- Teach the new words. Say *I get up*. Ask pupils to repeat. Ask pupils in L1 if they get up in the morning or afternoon. Elicit *morning*. Say *I get up in the morning.* and ask pupils to repeat. Then teach *afternoon* and *night*. Write *morning, afternoon* and *night* on the board. Say *I study maths in the afternoon*. Ask pupils to repeat. Then yawn and say *I go to bed at night*. Ask pupils to repeat. Then teach *laugh*. Laugh out loud and say *I laugh! I laugh every day!* Ask pupils to copy and repeat.
- Tell pupils to open their books at page 112 and to look at the vocabulary box. Hold up your book and point to the first picture word. Say the word and ask pupils to repeat. Do the same with all the words. Then read out the new picture words in the vocabulary box in random order and ask pupils to point to the correct pictures.
- Read out the words *lucky* and *at ... o'clock*. Explain the meanings. Say *Ben gets up at 10 o'clock every day*. Ask pupils to repeat. Then say *Lucky Ben!* Ask pupils to repeat.
- Read out all the words again one by one and ask pupils to repeat after you.

A Listen and read. 🔊 2.45
- Ask pupils to look at the photo. Ask them to count the children. Then ask them what these children are doing. Explain that they are going to read about what these children do every day.
- Play the recording. Tell pupils to follow the text with their fingers.

- Play the recording again pausing after each sentence and ask pupils to repeat. Explain the meaning if necessary.
- Play the recording again. Then ask volunteers to read out a sentence each of the text.

B Match.
- Read the example to pupils. Ask them to find the sentence in the text which gives them the answer.
- Explain the rest of the task to pupils. Tell them to underline the sentences in the text which give them the answers. Allow them enough time to complete the task alone. Go round the class encouraging and helping pupils where necessary.
- Check answers. Ask pupils to read out their sentences.

Answers
1 These children are friends. (given)
2 They get up at 8 o'clock.
3 They go to the beach.
4 Gary has fun with his friends.
5 Gary goes to bed at 10 o'clock.

C Look and learn.
- Read out the speech bubbles. Read them out again and ask pupils to repeat. Ask pupils who they think the woman is (Amber's mum). Ask them why they think Amber's mum looks cross (because they are dirty).
- Ask pupils to look at the grammar box. Read out the grammar notes. Explain the meanings of the time words.
- Practise the grammar. Write these phrases on the board:
  get up
  eat breakfast
  watch TV
  play in my bedroom
  go to bed
- Ask pupils these questions. Tell them to use the ideas on the board to answer.
  What do you do in the morning/afternoon?
  What do you do every day?
  What do you do at 7 o'clock.
  What do you do at night?

D Circle.
- Read out the example and ask pupils why *does* is the correct answer.
- Explain the task to pupils. Check pupils remember the meanings of all the words. Allow them enough time to complete the task alone.
- Check answers. Ask pupils to read out their answers.

Answers
1 does (given)
2 in
3 he
4 do
5 at

Say it! 2.46

- Write *o* on the board. Ask pupils to say the name of this letter. Then write *oo* on the board. Tell them the sounds *oo* make together. Say *moon* and ask pupils to repeat.
- Tell pupils to look at the task. Play the first part of the recording (Listen and say.) asking pupils to repeat the words *look* and *afternoon* each time they hear them. (*Look* and *afternoon* will be heard twice.)
- Ask for volunteers to read out the sentence. Play the recording and ask all pupils to repeat. (The sentence will be heard once.)

E Sing. 2.47

- Tell pupils they are going to learn a song. Ask pupils to look at the pictures and to describe what they can see.
- Play the recording and tell pupils to listen and follow the words with their fingers.
- Read out the song one line at a time and ask pupils to repeat after you.
- Play the recording again. Encourage pupils to sing along. Practise many times until pupils are familiar with the words. Pupils can mime the actions as they sing.

Homework

- Pupil's Audio CD: Pupils listen to the text and the song at home. Explain to pupils that they should listen to tracks 49 and 50 on the CD.
- Activity Book, pages 88-89: Time permitting, some tasks can be done in class.
- Dictation: *morning, afternoon, night, laugh, go to bed, study*

Extra activity

- Teach pupils to tell the time. Draw a clock face on the board. Draw hands on the clock to show one o'clock. Say *It's one o'clock*. Ask pupils to repeat. Do the same up to twelve o'clock.

Lesson 3   It's our favourite season.

Aims

- Learn and use new vocabulary: *spring, summer, autumn, winter, hot, cold, favourite, holiday, season*
- Learn and use new grammar: *What? Where? When? Who?*

Lead-in

- Revise the words and grammar from Lesson 2. Write *morning, afternoon* and *night* on the board. Ask pupils *What do you do in the morning?* Elicit answers, eg *I get up*. Ask *What do you do in the afternoon?* and *What do you do at night?* Elicit answers.

- Sing the song from Lesson 2.
- Check homework. Tell pupils to open their Activity Books at pages 88 and 89. Ask volunteers to read out their answers. Then sing the song from Lesson 2.
- Test dictation: *morning, afternoon, night, laugh, go to bed, study*. See the teacher's introduction pages 7-9 for teaching suggestions. Go round the class and check all pupils' dictation.

New vocabulary

- Teach the seasons. Ask pupils in L1 what their favourite season is. Teach *spring, summer, autumn* and *winter* explaining the meanings. Draw a tree on the board. Draw leaves on it. Say *summer*. Draw some leaves falling off. Say *autumn*. Then erase all the leaves. Say *winter*. Then draw a blossom on the tree and say *spring*.
- Tell pupils to open their books at page 114 and to look at the vocabulary box. Hold up your book and point to the first word. Say the word and ask pupils to repeat. Do the same with all the words. Explain the meanings of *hot, cold, favourite, holiday* and *season*. Then read out the new words in the vocabulary box in random order and ask pupils to point to the correct word.
- Read out all the words again one by one and ask pupils to repeat after you.

A Read.

- Tell pupils that they are going to read a poster about seasons which these children have made.
- Ask pupils to read the poster and choose their favourite season. Then read out the poster one sentence at a time and ask pupils to repeat.
- Ask volunteers to read out a sentence each of the poster.

B Circle.

- Tell pupils to look at the pictures in order to circle the correct words. Read the example to pupils and ask them to repeat.
- Explain the rest of the task to pupils. Make sure they understand the meanings of all the words. Allow them enough time to complete the task alone. Go round the class helping pupils where necessary.
- Check answers. Ask volunteers to read out the answers.

Answers
1 flowers (given)
2 island
3 on holiday
4 autumn

C Look and learn.

- Read out the dialogue and ask pupils to repeat.
- Ask pupils to look at the grammar box. Read out the sentences and explain the meanings of the Wh- question words. Read out the example question and answer and ask pupils to repeat.

- Practise the grammar. Ask these questions and elicit answers:
  What is that? (point to a pencil)
  Where do you live?
  When do you go to bed?
  Who is your best friend?

D Write Who, What, Where or When.

- Read the example to pupils and explain that to find the correct question word they must look at the answer.

- Make sure pupils have understood the task. Read the sentences and make sure pupils understand the meanings of the words. Allow pupils enough time to complete the task alone. Go round the class helping where necessary.

- Check answers. Ask pupils to read out their sentences.

Answers
1 What (given)
2 Who
3 Where
4 When

E Say.

- Read out the dialogue and ask pupils to repeat. Explain to pupils that they are going to hold the same dialogue with their friends, but they have to use answers which are true for them. Remind pupils to replace the words in orange with their own choices.

- Ask two volunteers to stand at the front of the class. They can hold their books for help. Ask one pupil to ask the questions and the other to answer. Prompt where necessary. Repeat until all pupils have had a turn.

F Draw and write.

- Tell pupils to draw their friend in their books. Allow them enough time to draw their friend.

- Then tell pupils to fill in the missing information about their friends. Read out the sentences and ask pupils for suggestions to go in the gaps. Then allow pupils enough time to complete the sentences. Go round the class helping with spelling where necessary.

- Ask pupils to hold up their books and to show each other their work. Ask volunteers to read out their work.

Homework

- Activity Book, pages 90-91: Time permitting, some tasks can be done in class.

- Dictation: *spring, summer, autumn, winter, hot, cold, favourite, holiday, season*

- Revision for Test 12:
  Words: *cave, dragonfly, goat, island, panda, sun, moon, morning, afternoon, night, laugh, go to bed, study, lucky, at ... o'clock, spring, summer, autumn, winter, hot, cold, favourite, holiday, season*
  Grammar: *Present Simple interrogative*
  What do you do?
  What, Where, When, Who?

Optional activity

Revision for Test 12

- Revise the seasons. Ask pupils to tell you the seasons in English and write them on the board. Then ask pupils the times of the day and elicit *morning, afternoon, night*. Write these on the board too. Ask pupils these questions which contain new vocabulary.
  When do you got to bed.
  What is your favourite season.
  What is a hot/cold season?
  When do you study?
  Do you study at three o'clock?
  Are you lucky every day?

- Revise the words from Lesson 1 with the flashcards.

- Revise the Present Simple interrogative. Ask pupils these questions and elicit answers:
  Do you like cats?
  Does Ty like dragons?
  Do the reporters like Greece?
  Do we like English?

- Revise *What, Where, When* and *Who*. Ask pupils to remember the meanings of these words. Then ask volunteers to think of a question to go with each *Wh-* word. Write the questions on the board and elicit answers.
  eg *Where do you live?*
  Who is that boy?
  What is your favourite animal?
  When do you get up?

Teacher's Note

Pupils will do Test 12 in the following lesson. After every three units, there is a review which can be done in the same lesson as the test.

Extra activity

- Play hangman with words from Units 10-12. See Unit 1 Lesson 3 for instructions.

Let's remember!

Aims
- Revise vocabulary from Units 10-12
- Revise grammar from Units 10-12

Materials
- Flashcards:

Unit 10: *butter, chocolate, flour, milk, face*

Unit 12: *cave, dragonfly, goat, island, panda, sun, moon*

Lead-in
- Check homework. Tell pupils to open their Activity Books at pages 90 and 91. Ask volunteers to read out their answers. Then quickly check all pupils' books.
- Test dictation: *spring, summer, autumn, winter, hot, cold, favourite, holiday, season.* See the teacher's introduction pages 7-9 for teaching suggestions. Go round the class and check all pupils' dictation.

Revision
- Revise the words from the flashcards. Hold up a flashcard and ask pupils to call out the word. Then place the flashcards face down on your desk. Ask a volunteer to choose a flashcard from the desk, turn it over and say what it is. Then revise all the food words (*carrot, cheese, orange, potato, sweets, crisps, popcorn*). Say the words and ask pupils to draw them on the board.
- Ask pupils to remember the *days of the week*, *times of the day* and *the seasons*. Ask volunteers to write them on the board. Do the same for *rooms*.
- Revise the *affirmative* and *negative* of the *Present Simple*. Copy the following table onto the board:

I	like	maths
He	don't like	English
They	likes	dragons
We	doesn't like	snakes

Ask pupils to make sentences with the words across the columns. Make sure they use the correct forms.

- Revise the *prepositions of place*. Draw a box on the board. Ask volunteers to draw things in the place you say.

  Draw some popcorn on the box.
  Draw some crisps in the box.
  Draw two men next to the box.
  Draw a tall woman behind the box.
  Draw an ant in front of the box.
  Draw a ball under the box.

A Find and stick.
- Ask pupils to open their books at page 116 and to look at task A. Ask volunteers to read out the words. Then read out the words again and ask pupils to repeat as a class.
- Show pupils where to find the stickers in their books. Tell them to remove the stickers one at a time and to stick them in the correct boxes. Allow pupils enough time to stick all the stickers. Go round the class helping pupils where necessary.
- Check answers. Ask volunteers to hold up their books and read out the words.

B Write.
- Tell pupils to look at the table. Explain the headings if necessary. Ask volunteers to read out the words in the box.
- Tell pupils to write the words in the correct column. Allow them enough time to complete the task alone. Go round the class helping pupils where necessary.
- Check answers.

Answers
Days: Friday (given), Wednesday, Sunday
Seasons: autumn, spring, winter
House: bedroom, kitchen, living room

Extension activity
- Ask pupils to think of one more word for days and seasons. Write their ideas on the board. Ask pupils to remember two kinds of houses they learnt in the book (*igloo* and *castle*).
- Give pupils a third category: *Food*. Ask them to think of three things for food. Write their ideas on the board.

C Circle.
- Read out the example and ask pupils why *moon* is the correct answer. Read out all the sentences and make sure that pupils remember the meanings of all the words.
- Explain the rest of the task to pupils. Allow them enough time to complete the task alone. Go round the class helping pupils where necessary.
- Check answers. Ask volunteers to read out their answers.

Answers
1 moon (given)
2 Who
3 hot
4 breakfast
5 favourite
6 sweets

D Circle.

- Read out the example and ask pupils why *glasses* is the correct answer. Read out all the sentences and make sure that pupils remember the meanings of all the words.

- Explain the rest of the task to pupils. Allow them enough time to complete the task alone. Go round the class helping pupils where necessary.

- Check answers. Ask volunteers to read out their answers.

Answers
1 glasses (given)
2 any
3 some
4 men
5 potatoes
6 some

E Match.

- Tell pupils to look at the pictures of *Mr Green* and *his car*. Explain that they have to look at where he is and match the pictures to the correct sentences. Read out the sentences and ask pupils to repeat. Make sure they remember the meanings.

- Allow pupils enough time to complete the task alone. Go round the class helping pupils where necessary.

- Check answers. Ask volunteers to read out their answers.

Answers
1 He's in his car. (given)
2 He's on his car.
3 He's in front of his car.
4 He's behind his car.
5 He's under his car.
6 He's next to his car.

F Write.

- Read out the example and ask pupils why *love* is the correct answer. Read out all the sentences and make sure that pupils remember the meanings of all the words.

- Explain the rest of the task to pupils. Allow them enough time to complete the task alone. Go round the class helping pupils where necessary.

- Check answers. Ask volunteers to read out their answers. Write the answers on the board.

Answers
1 love (given)
2 doesn't ride
3 Do, study
4 don't
5 goes
6 does, work

Extra activity

Poster: I like chocolate!

This poster can be used to consolidate and revise vocabulary and grammar of Units 10-12 in a fun and interesting way. Pupils can also play a game with the poster. Follow the procedure outlined on the back of the poster.

Homework

- Pupil's Audio CD: pupils listen to the songs at home. Explain to pupils that they should listen to tracks 44, 46 and 50 on the CD.

- Activity Book, pages 92-93: Time permitting, some tasks can be done in class.

- Revision for Progress Test 4. Pupils should revise all the vocabulary and grammar from Units 10-12.

Teacher's Note

The pupils will do Progress Test 4 in the following lesson. After the test, you can do the lesson *Fun & Games*.

Fun & Games ..

Aims

- Consolidate new vocabulary with fun activities
- Consolidate new grammar with fun activities
- Make a mobile

Materials

- One photocopy of the whale cutouts for each pupil (page 145)
- One paper plate for each pupil with a hole in the middle
- Scissors, colouring pencils, string, sticky tape, glue

Lead-in

- Tell pupils that today's lesson is all about fun and games. Ask them to open their books at page 118. Ask them what they can see (*a boy and a girl at an aquarium looking at a whale*).
- Read out the paragraph and ask pupils to follow the words with their fingers. Read it out again one sentence at a time and ask pupils to repeat. Check comprehension with these questions. Encourage pupils to use English for the words they have learnt.
  What's the season? (summer)
  What are the children's names? (Tina and Jim)
  What colour is the whale? (white)
- Consolidate vocabulary pupils have learnt using the picture. Here are some suggestions:
  What do you do on holiday?
  What season do you like?
  What days are the weekend?
  Do whales live on islands?
  What animals live on islands?
  Is it hot or cold?
  What food do children like?

Quiz time!

- Ask pupils *What's that?* and elicit *It's a whale.* Read out the question and both answers and make sure pupils understand the meaning. Ask pupils to choose the correct answer (b). Ask volunteer to read out the question and answer. Tell pupils that whales aren't fish because they breathe air, are warm-blooded, and give birth to babies, and not eggs.

A Match.

- Ask pupils *Who can you see?* Elicit *George, Ty, Mia* and *Leo*. Tell pupils they have to follow the paths to see what the characters like.
- Ask pupils to follow the paths. Then ask them to say what the characters like.
  George likes islands.
  Ty likes his bedroom.
  Mia likes whales.
  Leo likes goats.

B Chant. 2:48

- Tell pupils they are going to learn a chant. Explain to pupils that the chant is about holidays. Play the recording and tell pupils to listen and follow the words with their fingers.
- Read out the chant one line at a time and ask pupils to repeat after you. Play the recording again. Encourage pupils to chant along. Practise many times until pupils are familiar with the words.
- Pupils can clap while they do the chant. They can also make the shapes of the letters with their bodies when they hear H-O-L-I-D-A-Y.

C Make.

- Tell pupils they are going to make a whale mobile. Tell pupils to look at the pictures in task C and explain each stage to them.

1 Colour in the whales.

2 Cut out the whales. Stick the whales together with a piece of string in between each whale.

3 Thread a piece of string through the middle of a paper plate. Tie a knot at the end of the string.

4 Stick the strings which are attached to the whales on three points around the edge of the paper plate so the whales hang downwards.

5 The mobile is ready to hang up.

- Ask pupils to have their colouring pencils ready. Hand out the photocopies of the whale cutouts and ask pupils to colour them in.
- When all pupils are ready, ask them to put their colouring pencils away. Then hand out the scissors. Ask pupils to cut out their whales. Go round the class helping pupils where necessary. Collect on the scissors. Then give each pupil three pieces of string and some glue. Show them how to stick the whales together with the string in the middle. Secure the string firmly with sticky tape if necessary. Collect in the glue.
- Hand out a plate and a long piece of string to each pupil. Show pupils how to tie a knot on one end of the string, helping if necessary. Then show them how to thread the string through the plate. Secure the knot with sticky tape if necessary.
- Show pupils where to stick the whales around the edges of the plate. Give each pupil three pieces of sticky tape and help them stick the whales on.
- Pupils can hang their mobiles up at home.

Extra activity

- Ask pupils which songs they liked best in *Happy Trails 1*. Play their favourite songs.

Play 1

Little Red Riding Hood

The story

This play is based on the traditional fairy tale *Little Red Riding Hood* written by the Brothers Grimm. In this play, however, Grandma is a modern lady who loves dancing. The hunter chases off the wolf and returns to dance with Grandma.

Aims

- Consolidate vocabulary and grammar from Units 1-6
- Put on a play

Materials

- Props and costumes (see below)

Teaching the play

- Ask pupils if they know the fairy tale *Little Red Riding Hood.* Allow them a few minutes to talk about it in L1.

- Ask pupils to look at pages 120-121 in their books. Explain that this is a play about *Little Red Riding Hood.* Tell them that they are first going to listen to the play and then learn it so they can perform it themselves.

- Hold up your book and point to the main characters in the play. Read out the names of the characters and ask pupils to point to the correct pictures. Then read them out again one at a time and ask pupils to repeat. Ask pupils to look at the story and find the characters.

- Read out the new vocabulary words and ask pupils to repeat. Explain the meaning of *bad.*

- Play the recording to pupils (CD2: 49). Ask them to follow the words with their fingers as they listen. Ask pupils these questions for each frame to check comprehension. Use L1 if necessary but encourage pupils to use words they know in English.

    1 *How many apples are there? (six)*
    2 *Which small animals does Little Red Riding Hood meet in the forest? (rabbits and birds)*
    3 *Which bad animal does she meet? (a wolf)*
    4 *What does she pick for Grandma? (flowers)*
    5 *Where does the wolf go? (to Grandma's house)*
    6 *Why is the wolf surprised? (because Grandma is modern)*
    7 *Where does the wolf hide Grandma? (in the wardrobe)*
    8 *Has the wolf got big eyes and ears? (Yes, he has.)*
    9 *Is the wolf hungry? (Yes, he is.)*
    10 *Who is at the door? (the hunter)*
    11 *What does the hunter do? (he chases away the wolf)*
    12 *Who is a great dancer? (Grandma)*

- Play the recording again. Stop after each sentence for pupils to repeat. Then assign roles and ask pupils to read out their parts. Change pupils' roles and repeat. Make sure all pupils have a turn at reading.

Let's sing! 🔘 2:49

My family is cool
My family is great.
So come on and celebrate!

Mum is cool.
Dad is cool.
Brothers and sisters.
We're so cool!

Putting on the play

Pupils can perform the play in the classroom for each other. The play can also be performed for parents and other pupils in a large classroom or hall. Props and costumes are optional.

Characters

These are the main roles for this play. Assign them to more confident pupils.
Mum
Little Red Riding Hood
The wolf
Grandma
The hunter

These are the minor roles for this play. Assign them to less confident pupils.
two rabbits
two birds

The song can be sung by the whole class. If your class is large, pupils without roles can form a class choir.

Props and costumes

Mum
- an apron

Little Red Riding Hood
- a red cape
- a basket of apples

The wolf
- a grey T-shirt/sweatshirt or grey tracksuit
- wolf ears

Grandma
- a dress
- a bead necklace
- a feather hairband

The hunter
- a winter jacket
- a winter hat
- jeans

Rabbits
- rabbit ears
- Optional: White T-shirt

Birds

- beaks
- Optional: Yellow T-shirt

Choir

- matching T-shirts and trousers, eg blue jeans and red tops

How to make the props

Wolf ears

Cut two triangles 15cm long out of grey card. Staple the card ears next to each other along a thick piece of elastic. The elastic should be long enough to fit firmly round a pupil's head. Tie the ends of the elastic. Fold the ears along the edge of the elastic so that they stick up.

Rabbit ears

Cut two triangles 10cm long out of white card. Staple the card ears next to each other along a thick piece of elastic. The elastic should be long enough to fit firmly round a pupil's head. Tie the ends of the elastic. Fold the ears along the edge of the elastic so that they stick up.

Feather hairband

Staple a feather onto a thick piece of elastic. The elastic should be long enough to fit firmly round the top of a pupil's head above the ears. Tie the ends of the elastic.

Beaks

Cut a triangle 10cm long with a 20cm base out of orange card. Bend the two bottom corners together, overlap 2 cm and staple. This creates a beak shape which pupils wear over their noses. Staple a piece of elastic onto the sides of the beak long enough to fit round a pupil's head.

Stage directions

Scene 1 (frames 1-4)

- On the left side of the stage. Mum hands the basket of apples to Little Red Riding Hood. They both wave goodbye. Little Red Riding Hood moves to centre stage. Mum leaves the stage.

- The birds and rabbits enter the stage from the right and go to the centre of the stage. They talk to Little Red Riding Hood. Little Red Riding Hood is picking flowers. Then the wolf appears on tiptoe from the left coming up behind Little Red Riding Hood. The rabbits and birds run/fly away to the right side of the stage. The wolf then leaves from the right.

Scene 2 (frames 5-12)

- Grandma is in her house in the centre of the stage. She is dancing to music. The wolf enters from the left and stands outside the door. He puts on a little girl voice. He opens the doors and is surprised to see Grandma dancing. The music stops. He loses the little girl voice. He takes Grandma's beads and feather hairband, puts them on and locks Grandma into the wardrobe.

- Little Red Riding Hood enters the stage from the left. She goes into the house and looks surprised to see her Grandma looking so different. The wolf puts on a grandma voice. But then he pounces on Little Red Riding Hood, losing the voice. Little Red Riding Hood steps backwards, looking scared.

- Then the hunter runs in from the left of the stage. He enters the house and shouts angrily at the wolf. The wolf runs off the stage to the left. Little Red Riding Hood opens the wardrobe door and hugs her grandma.

- The music starts again. The hunter dances with Grandma. The rabbits and birds come back on stage from the left. They dance with Little Red Riding Hood.

- The choir enters and stands at the front. Mum and the wolf come back on stage. The characters stand behind the choir and they all sing the song.

Play 2

The Hare and the Tortoise

The story

This play is based on the traditional fable *The Hare and the Tortoise* written by Aesop. In this play however, the hare thinks he is a cool guy with a scooter and sunglasses. But the tortoise turns out to be the cool guy who holds a party for all his friends after winning the race. The hare eats humble pie and is a waiter at the party.

Aims

• Consolidate vocabulary and grammar from Units 7-12
• Put on a play

Materials

• Props and costumes (see below)

Teaching the play

• Ask pupils if they know the fable of *The Hare and the Tortoise*. Allow them a few minutes to talk about it in L1.

• Ask pupils to look at pages 122-123 in their books. Explain that this is a play about *The Hare and the Tortoise*. Tell them that they are first going to listen to the play and then learn it so they can perform it themselves.

• Hold up your book and point to the main characters in the play. Read out the names of the characters and ask pupils to point to the correct pictures. Then read them out again one at a time and ask pupils to repeat. Ask pupils to look at the story and find the characters.

• Read out the new words and ask pupils to repeat. Explain the meaning of *stop*.

• Play the recording to pupils (CD2: 50). Ask them to follow the words with their fingers as they listen. Ask pupils these questions for each frame to check comprehension. Use L1 but encourage pupils to use English words they know.

   1 What three animals do we first see? (a rabbit, a bird and a fox)
   2 Who is their friend? (the tortoise)
   3 What is the hare riding? (a scooter)
   4 Can the tortoise run? (No, he can't.)
   5 When is the race? (Saturday at 9 o'clock in the morning)
   6 Is the hare fast? (Yes, he is.)
   7 Does the tortoise stop? (No, he doesn't.)
   8 Does the hare sleep? (Yes, he does.)
   9 Who wins the race? (the tortoise)
   10 Can the tortoise dance? (Yes, he can.)

• Play the recording again. Stop after each sentence for pupils to repeat. Then assign roles and ask pupils to read out their parts. Change pupils' roles and repeat. Make sure all pupils have a turn at reading.

Let's sing! 🔊 2: 50

Rub your tummy.
Rub your tummy.
Milk and chocolate today!

Rub your tummy.
Rub your tummy.
Milk and cakes today!

Yummy yummy yummy!
Come on rub your tummy!
Yummy yummy yummy!

Putting on the play

Pupils can perform the play in the classroom for each other. The play can also be performed for parents and other pupils in a large classroom or hall. Props and costumes are optional.

Characters

These are the main roles for this play. Assign them to more confident pupils.
The hare
The tortoise
The bird
The fox
The rabbit

These are the minor roles for this play. Assign them to less confident pupils.
woodland animals

The song can be sung by the whole class. If your class is large, pupils without roles can form a class choir.

Props and costumes

The hare
• a scooter
• grey T-shirt/sweatshirt
• sunglasses
• a tray

The tortoise
• a shell
• green T-shirt/sweatshirt
• a baseball cap
• a medal

The bird
• a yellow T-shirt/sweatshirt
• a beak

The fox
• a red T-shirt/sweatshirt
• fox ears
• a whistle

The rabbit

- a white T-shirt/sweatshirt
- rabbit ears
- a finishing line

Woodland animals

- brown T-shirt/sweatshirt
- animal ears

Choir

- matching T-shirts and trousers, eg blue jeans and red tops

How to make the props

Hare ears

Cut two triangles 15cm long out of grey card. Staple the card ears next to each other along a thick piece of elastic. The elastic should be long enough to fit firmly round a pupil's head. Tie the ends of the elastic. Fold the ears along the edge of the elastic so that they stick up.

Rabbit ears

Cut two triangles 10cm long out of white card. Staple the card ears next to each other along a thick piece of elastic. The elastic should be long enough to fit firmly round a pupil's head. Tie the ends of the elastic. Fold the ears along the edge of the elastic so that they stick up.

Woodland animals ears

Cut two triangles 10cm long out of brown card. Staple the card ears next to each other along a thick piece of elastic. The elastic should be long enough to fit firmly round a pupil's head. Tie the ends of the elastic. Fold the ears along the edge of the elastic so that they stick up.

Tortoise shell

Cut a large oval shape 35cm long out of green card. Draw tortoise shell shapes on the card and colour them brown. Make two holes in the middle of the card, 5cm in from the edge. Thread a piece of elastic through the holes which is long enough to tie firmly round the pupil's tummy.

Beak

Cut a triangle 10cm long with a 20cm base out of orange card. Bend the two bottom corners together, overlap 2 cm and staple. This creates a beak shape which pupils wear over their noses. Staple a piece of elastic onto the sides of the beak long enough to fit round a pupils head.

The finishing line

Cut a metre of string for the rabbit and fox to hold between them.

The medal

Cut out a round piece of the card, yellow or gold and write the number 1 on the front. Put a hole in the top and thread a 60cm piece of string through the hole. Tie the string at the end.

Stage directions

Scene 1 (frames 1-4)

- The bird, fox and rabbit walk up to centre stage from different directions and greet each other. The tortoise enters from the right and everybody waves.
- The hare enters on his scooter from the left. He takes off his sunglasses and shows off. The fox is cross. Only the tortoise stays calm. The rabbit claps his hands at the thought of a race.
- The hare puts his sunglasses back on and rides off on his scooter. As he goes he suggests the race. The tortoise calls after him accepting the challenge.

Scene 2 (frames 5-11)

- The hare runs onto the right side of the stage towards the back where the tortoise and other animals are waiting. The fox blows the whistle and the race begins. The hare runs to the left of the stage towards the front. The tortoise walks slowly towards the left side of the stage.
- The animals leave the stage from the right. The hare takes off his sunglasses and looks back at the tortoise. He lies down and falls asleep. The tortoise walks by slowly and speaks quietly so as not to wake him up.
- The woodland animals enter the stage from the right at the front now. The fox and rabbit hold a finishing line which the tortoise walks through. Everybody cheers. The bird gives the tortoise a medal. The noise wakes the hare up. He stands up and runs to the finishing line where the tortoise is waiting with a medal around his neck.

Scene 3 (frame 12)

- Everybody is in the centre stage. There is music. The tortoise is dancing as are the woodland animals. The fox is the DJ. The hare is serving food to the rabbits.
- The choir enters and stands at the front. The characters stand behind the choir and they all sing the song.

Christmas

Materials

- one piece of red card and one piece of green card for each pupil sized roughly A5
- one star template for each pupil (page 147)
- scissors

Lead-in

- Tell pupils that today's lesson is about *Christmas*. Ask pupils what they do at Christmas and what decorations they have in their houses in L1.

New vocabulary

- Ask pupils to open their books at page 124. Ask them to look at the vocabulary pictures at the top and to say what they can see. Read out the new words one at a time. Ask pupils to repeat and point to the pictures.
- Ask pupils to look at the photo and to describe what they can see. Encourage them to use English for the words they know.
- Read out the paragraph to pupils. Ask them to follow the words with their fingers as you read. Ask pupils these questions to check comprehension.

  Are there lots of lights? (Yes, there are.)
  Is Santa Claus there? (Yes, he is.)
  Is the star small? (No, it isn't. It's big.)

A Read.

- Tell pupils to read the text about Christmas and ask them in LI if they decorate their homes outside. Then read out the text one sentence at a time and ask pupils to repeat.
- Ask volunteers to read out a sentence each of the text.

B Match.

- Ask pupils to look at the pictures and match them to the words. When they have finished ask pupils to read out the words.

C Colour.

- Revise the colours *red, yellow, blue* and *orange*. Point to objects in the classroom which are these colours, say the words and ask pupils to repeat.

- Ask pupils what they can see in the picture. Elicit *Santa Claus, a Christmas tree, a star* and *two presents*. Ask pupils to colour the picture. Explain that they should look at the numbers for each colour and colour the sections accordingly.
- When pupils have finished their pictures ask them to hold up their books and show each other their work.

D Make.

- Tell pupils they are going to make a Christmas star. Explain each stage to pupils and help them where necessary.

Star instructions:

1 Hand out the star template and scissors to each pupil. Pupils first cut out the stars and then trace round them on theirs pieces of card so they have two stars.

2 Pupils cut out their stars.

3 Collect the scissors. Cut half way up the red star and half way down the green star for each pupil. See template. More dexterous pupils can probably manage this themselves.

4 Show pupils how to slot the stars together.

- Pupils can hold up their stars and say the colours, eg *This star is green and red.*

Carnival

Aims

- Learn and use carnival vocabulary: *costume, monster*
- Draw a carnival costume

Materials

- one piece of paper for each pupil
- colouring pencils

Lead-in

- Tell pupils that today's lesson is about *Carnival time*. Ask pupils what they do at Carnival time and what costumes they like to wear.

New vocabulary

- Ask pupils to open their books at page 125. Ask them to look at the vocabulary pictures at the top and to say what they can see. Read out the new words one at a time. Ask pupils to repeat and point to the pictures.

- Ask pupils to look at the photo and to describe what they can see. Encourage them to use English for the words they know. Ask them to tell you the colours of the children's costumes and hats.

- Read out the paragraph to pupils. Ask them to follow the words with their fingers as you read. Ask pupils these questions to check comprehension.

  Is the monster orange? (No, it isn't. It's green.)
  Has it got big eyes? (Yes, it has.)
  Are the costumes fantastic? (Yes, they are.)

A Read.

- Tell pupils to read the text about Carnival and ask them in LI if they have seen a street parade or taken part in one. Then read out the text one sentence at a time and ask pupils to repeat.

- Ask volunteers to read out a sentence each of the text.

B Match.

- Ask pupils to look at the pictures and match them to the words. When they have finished ask pupils to read out the words.

C Find and circle.

- Tell pupils that these two pictures look the same but there are five differences between them. Explain that they should circle the differences in the second picture.

- Allow pupils enough time to find the five differences. When they have found them ask them to say what they are.

D Draw.

- Tell pupils they are going to draw a carnival costume. Explain that they can draw a costume they have or a costume they imagined. Hand out a piece of paper to each pupil.

- Ask pupils to draw and colour. Move around the classroom asking them to tell you the colours in English.

- Ask pupils to describe their pictures, eg:
  This is my carnival costume. It's a … .
  The drawings can be displayed on the classroom wall.

Easter

Materials

- one photocopy of the Easter basket cutout for each pupil (page 149)
- sticky tape
- colouring pencils

Lead-in

- Tell pupils that today's lesson is about *Easter.* Ask pupils what they do at Easter and what traditions they have in L1.

New vocabulary

- Ask pupils to open their books at page 126. Ask them to look at the vocabulary pictures at the top and to say what they can see. Read out the new words one at a time. Ask pupils to repeat and point to the pictures. Explain that *paint* the substance and the *paint* the action is the same word in English.

- Ask pupils to look at the photo and to describe what they can see. Encourage them to use English for the words they know. They could count the eggs and say what colours they are.

- Read out the paragraph to pupils. Ask them to follow the words with their fingers as you read. Ask pupils these questions to check comprehension:
  What is the season? (spring)
  Is Donna on holiday? (Yes, she is.)
  How many red eggs are there? (three)

A Read.

- Tell pupils to read the text about Easter and ask them what their favourite colour for Easter eggs is. Then read out the text one sentence at a time and ask pupils to repeat.

- Ask volunteers to read out a sentence each of the text.

B Write.

- Ask pupils to read the sentences. Tell them that the answers are in the paragraph. Read out the sentences to check pupils understand the meanings. Then ask pupils to read the paragraph again on their own to find the answers.

- Allow pupils enough time to write the missing words in the gaps. Move around the class helping where necessary.
- Check answers. Ask pupils to read out their sentences.

Answers
1 Easter (given)
2 eggs
3 brush
4 fingers

C Circle and count the eggs.

- Tell pupils that there are some eggs hidden in the picture. Ask them to look for them, circle them and then count them.

- Ask pupils to say where the eggs are. Encourage them to use English when they can.

Answers
Grandpa has got one red egg.
Grandma has got one red egg.
Mum has got an egg for the baby.
There is an egg on the baby's T-shirt.
The cat is eating a broken egg.
The dog has got a chocolate egg.
There are two eggs in the nest.
There are eight eggs hidden in the picture.

D Make.

- Tell pupils they are going to make an Easter basket which they can put little chocolate eggs in. Explain each stage to pupils and help them where necessary.

Easter basket instructions:

1 Hand an Easter basket cutout to each pupil. Tell them to colour it in as they like.

2 Hand out the scissors. Pupils cut out the baskets and handle.

3 Collect the scissors. Show pupils where to fold the sides of the basket and help them stick the sides with sticky tape. Then help them stick the handle on with sticky tape.

- Pupils can take their baskets home and fill them with little chocolate eggs for Easter.

1 Cartoon DVD Worksheet 1

Before you watch

Look at page 26 of Happy Trails 1 Pupil's Book and do the task below.

1   Point to the characters and say their names.
2   Point to Trek's mum.
3   Point to the elephant and fly and say the words.
4   Where's Trek?
5   Where are Trek's reporters?

While you watch

Who says these things? Tick (✔).

	Trek	Trek's mum	Mia	Leo	Ty
1 A photo and a DVD.					
2 Wow! Africa!					
3 Fantastic!					
4 Look! An elephant!					
5 Oh yes! A baby!					
6 Oh no! A fly.					
7 Look, a baby and mum.					

After you watch

1   What has Trek got?
2   Where are the reporters?
3   What animals do they see?
4   What do you think is behind the car?

2 Cartoon DVD Worksheet 2 🐾

Before you watch

Look at page 32 of Happy Trails 1 Pupil's Book and answer the questions.

1 Where are Ty, Mia and Leo?

_____

2 Why are Ty, Mia and Leo scared?

_____

While you watch

Watch the DVD and complete the sentences with these words.

> big   funny   short   small   tall

1 Lions are _____ .
2 I'm _____ .
3 Look! Giraffes. They're _____ .
4 The baby is _____ .
5 The monkeys are _____ .

After you watch

Answer the questions.

1 How many lions are there?

2 Are the lions big or small?

3 What animals do they see next?

4 Which animals are funny?

5 What does the small monkey take?

3 Cartoon DVD Worksheet 3

Before you watch

Look at page 38 of Happy Trails 1 Pupil's Book and answer the questions.

1 How did Ty get his camera back?

_____

2 Where are the reporters?

_____

While you watch

Watch the DVD and number the sentences in the correct order.

a Look. That mountain is big! ⬭

b Africa is cool! ⬭

c It's a penguin. ⬭

d It's an ostrich. ⬭

e My camera! Thanks! This bird is big. ⬭

f This bird is small! ⬭

g Goodbye! ⬭

h This beach is nice. Look! A whale! It's big too. ⬭

After you watch

Answer the questions.

1 What has the ostrich found?

2 Is the mountain big or small?

3 Which three animals do they see?

4 Which animals are big?

5 What does Trek say about Africa?

4 Cartoon DVD Worksheet 4

Before you watch

Look at page 50 of Happy Trails 1 Pupil's Book and answer the questions.

1 Who is with Trek?
a Trek's dad b Trek's mum

2 Where are Trek's reporters?
a in a bus   b in a helicopter

3 What is Mr Davis?
a a pupil   b a teacher

While you watch

Watch the DVD and number the pictures in the correct order.

After you watch

Answer the questions.

1 How do the reporters get to the school?

2 How many pupils are there?

3 What is the teacher's name?

4 How many drawings are there?

Cartoon DVD Worksheet 5

Before you watch

Look at page 56 of Happy Trails 1 Pupil's Book and answer the questions.

1 Who are Trek's reporters with?

_____

2 What's the name of the green animal on the tree?

_____

3 Which animals live only in Australia?

_____

While you watch

Watch the DVD and circle the correct words.

1 Let's see / go the animals.
2 A tree frog. It's got green / red eyes.
3 Look! A koala. It has got a long / big nose.
4 Look! A kangaroo. It's got a long nose / tail.
5 I've got big eyes / ears too.

After you watch

Answer the questions.

1 What are the pupils going to see?

2 Which animal has got red eyes?

3 What colour eyes has the pupil got?

4 What has the koala got?

5 What has the kangaroo got?

6 Cartoon DVD Worksheet 6

Before you watch

Look at page 62 of Happy Trails 1 Pupil's Book and answer the questions.

1 Who is Mia saying goodbye to?

_____

2 What are Trek's reporters wearing in the sea?

_____

3 Does Trek like Australia?

_____

While you watch

Who says these things? Tick (✔).

		Trek	Mia	Leo	Ty
1	Goodbye!				
2	Have you got a map, Ty?				
3	I've got my mask, my flippers and my camera. Come on!				
4	Those fish are beautiful! Oh! An octopus!				
5	It's my mobile phone. It's Mr Davis! He says goodbye!				
6	Australia is great!				

After you watch

Answer the questions.

1 Who has got the map?

2 Where are the masks?

3 What are the fish like?

4 What surprises Ty?

5 Who telephones Leo?

Cartoon DVD Worksheet 7

Before you watch

Look at page 74 of Happy Trails 1 Pupil's Book and answer the questions.

1 Where are Trek's reporters?

_____

2 What are the kids and Ty playing?

_____

While you watch

Watch the DVD and complete the sentences with these words.

> jump   look at   play   run   swim

1 Look! I can _____ beach volleyball!
2 I can _____ .
3 She can _____ .
4 _____ Leo! He's in the sea.
5 We can _____ . Hooray!

After you watch

Answer the questions.

1 Is the beach long or short?

2 What do Ty and Mia play?

3 Where is Leo?

4 Who can swim?

Cartoon DVD Worksheet 8

Before you watch

Look at page 80 of Happy Trails 1 Pupil's Book and answer the questions.

1   Where are Trek's reporters?

_____

2   What sport are they watching?

_____

3   Where are they going next?

_____

While you watch

Watch the DVD and number the sentences in the correct order.

a   Football is fantastic!   ◯

b   Tennis is cool.   ◯

c   Look! The Amazon.   ◯

d   Baseball is great.   ◯

e   We're thinking.   ◯

f   Let's go to the Amazon!   ◯

g   Look. It's Brazil. They're winning.   ◯

h   Hey! This is Brazil. Come on!   ◯

i   Basketball is nice.   ◯

j   Hooray! It's 2-1.   ◯

k   Football! Well done Mia!   ◯

After you watch

Answer the questions.

1   Which sport is cool?

2   What sport do the reporters go to watch?

3   What's the score?

4   Which team wins?

Cartoon DVD Worksheet 9

Before you watch

Look at page 86 of Happy Trails 1 Pupil's Book and answer the questions.

1   Where are Trek's reporters now?

_____

2   How do they travel there?

_____

3   What is Ty going to step on?

_____

4   What else do the reporters travel in?

_____

While you watch

Watch the DVD and number the pictures in the correct order.

After you watch

Answer the questions.

1   Who thinks the theatre is a cinema?

2   Who thinks the market is great?

3   What are Ty and Leo doing?

4   Who gets on the boat last?

5   Is the Amazon big or small?

10 Cartoon DVD Worksheet 10 🐾

Before you watch

Look at page 98 of Happy Trails 1 Pupil's Book and answer the questions.

1 Who is Tessy?

_____

2 Where are Trek's reporters now?

_____

3 Who are the reporters visiting?

_____

While you watch

Watch the DVD and circle the correct words.

1 I'm watching a DVD. Look at those reporters / men, Tessy.
2 This is my mum. The babies / baby are my sisters.
3 This is my house / bedroom.
4 Your living room / glasses are nice.
5 Oh no! I'm nice / sorry, Leo.
6 Come to the living room / kitchen!

After you watch

Answer the questions.

1 Is Mr Nikou tall or short?

2 What's the boy's name?

3 Are his sisters big?

4 What hits Leo on the head?

5 What does Mrs Nikou say in the kitchen?

11 Cartoon DVD Worksheet 11

Before you watch

Look at page 104 of Happy Trails 1 Pupil's Book and answer the questions.

1 Why is George happy?

_____

2 How are Trek's reporters travelling to grandma's house?

_____

3 Who does grandma love very much?

_____

While you watch

Watch the DVD and number the sentences in the correct order.

a Yummy! Your grandma makes great cakes. ⬭

b On Saturday I go to grandma's house. ⬭

c George, I love you! ⬭

d I'm happy. I love my boy! ⬭

e Hooray! It's Saturday! ⬭

f I cook on Monday and Tuesday. ⬭

g OK, OK Mum! I love you too! ⬭

h Hello, Mr Nikou. Hi, George! ⬭

i OK, OK grandma! I love you too! ⬭

j On Friday I work, but I have fun on Saturday and Sunday. ⬭

k And Wednesday and Thursday and Friday! ⬭

l Let's go! ⬭

After you watch

Answer the questions.

1 What day is it?

2 Who do the reporters visit?

3 What does Ty enjoy?

4 Why is George's grandma happy?

12 Cartoon DVD Worksheet 12

Before you watch

Look at page 110 of Happy Trails 1 Pupil's Book and answer the questions.

1 Who are Trek's reporters saying goodbye to?

_____

2 Where are Trek's reporters now?

_____

While you watch

Watch the DVD and complete the sentences with these words.

caves   dragonfly   goats   insect
island   moon   pandas   sun

1 Yes, I do. It's a beautiful _____ .

2 Look! Two _____! They are Kri Kri!

3 Do they live in _____ ?

4 Look! I can see a _____ .

5 A dragon! Oh no! Does it eat _____ ?

6 No, it doesn't! It's an _____ .

7 Look at the _____ Trek. It's beautiful!

8 Look at the _____ too. Do you like Greece, Trek?

After you watch

Answer the questions.

1 What animals are Kri Kri?

2 What is Ty scared of?

3 What does Mia say is beautiful?

4 Does Trek like Greece?

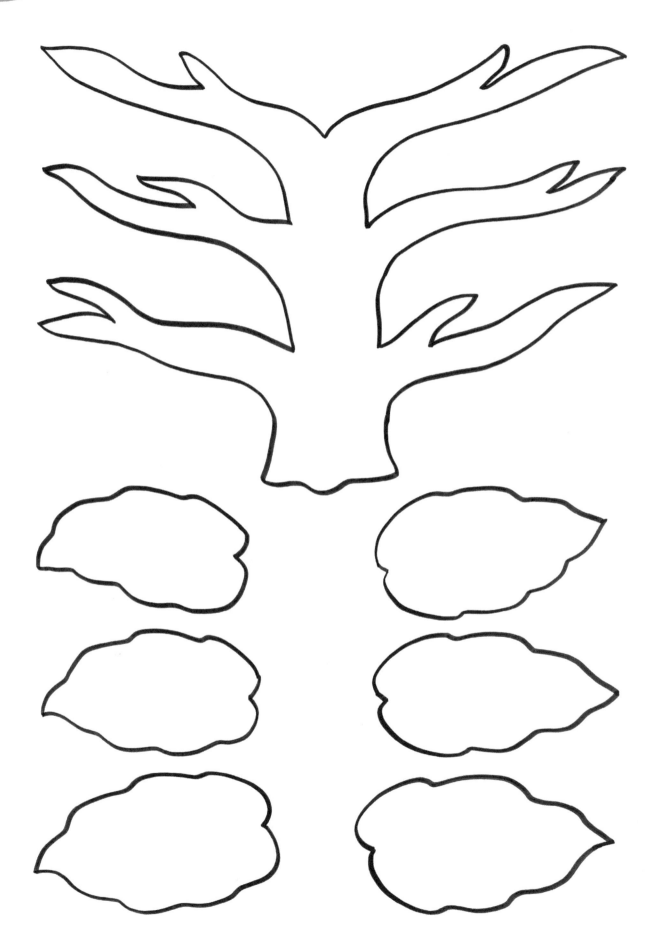

Christmas

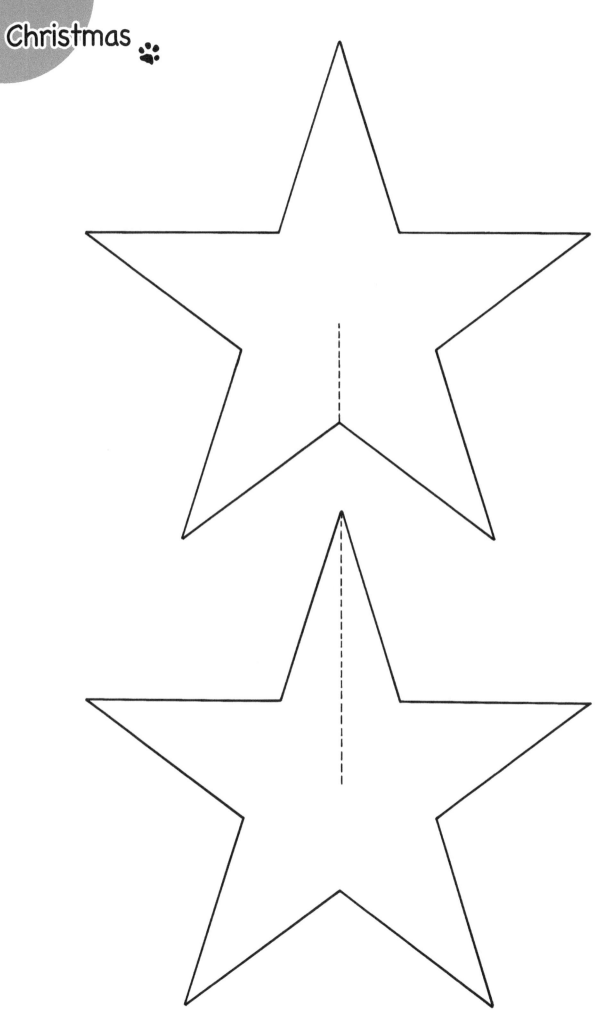

Easter

Activity Book Key

Alphabet (page 4)
A
Aa (given) Bb Cc Dd

B
1 **B**OY
2 DOG (given)
3 **CA**R
4 **A**NT

C
Pupil's own answer

Alphabet (page 5)
A

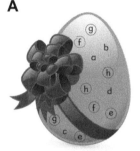

B

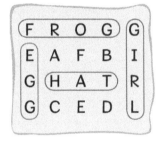

C
How (given)
Fine

Alphabet (page 6)
A
Ll (given) Jj Kk Ll

B [CIRCLE]

C
name (given), How, thank

Alphabet (page 7)
A

B
1 NEST (given)
2 OCTOPUS
3 PENCIL
4 MONKEY

C
octopus
monkey

Alphabet (page 8)
A
Qq (given) Rr Ss Tt

B [CIRCLE]

C
here (given), Thanks, welcome, Wow

Alphabet (page 9)
A
u (given), v, W, x, Y, z

B [CIRCLE]

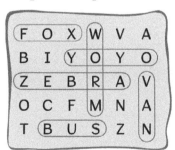

Alphabet (page 10)
A
B (given), D, E, G, J, K, N, P, Q, T, U, W, Y
a, c, f, h, i, l, m, o, r, s, v, x, z

B

A (given) B, C, D, E, F, G
H, I, J, K, L, M, N
O, P, Q, R, S, T, U
V,W
X, Y, Z

Colours
A

1e (given) 2j 3i 4c 5b 6h 7g 8a 9d 10f

B

1 **white** (given)
2 **gr**ee**n**
3 ye**llow**
4 **p**ink
5 **br**own
6 **red**
7 **bl**ue
8 **pur**ple
9 **or**ange
10 **bl**ack

Numbers
A [CIRCLE & WRITE]

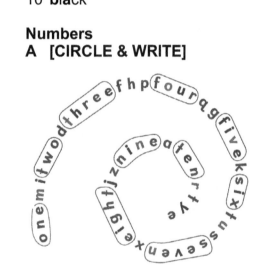

one	_six_
two	_seven_
three	_eight_
four	_nine_
five	_ten_

B

1 one (given)
2 two
3 three
4 four
5 five
6 six
7 seven
8 eight
9 nine
10 ten

Trek & his Reporters
A

1 **Mi**a (given)
2 **Ty**
3 **L**e**o**
4 **Tr**ek

B

What's your name? My name's Trek. (given)
How old are you? I'm nine.
How are you? Fine, thanks.

Unit 1

Lesson 1
A

1 baby (given)
2 fly
3 mum
4 elephant
5 photo

B

1 **fly** (given)
2 **el**e**ph**ant
3 **mum**
4 b**aby**
5 **ph**oto

C

a

baby (given)
fly
hat
monkey
photo

an

ant (given)
egg
elephant
insect
octopus

D

1 a spider (given)
2 an octopus
3 a girl
4 an ant / an insect
5 a yo-yo

E

fantastic (given), ele**ph**ant

Lesson 2
A

1 family (given)
2 brother
3 house

4 sister
5 igloo
6 dad

B

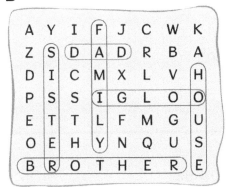

1 dad (given)
2 igloo
3 sister
4 family
5 house
6 brother

C
1 is (given)
2 are
3 is
4 is
5 is
6 am

D
1 'm (given)
2 's
3 's
4 're
5 's
6 'm

E
family (given)
family
cool
cool
brothers, **sisters**
cool

Lesson 3
A
1 My best friend is seven. (given)
2 My grandma is nice.
3 My grandpa is great.
4 My mum is cool.

B

C
1 We're (given)
2 They're
3 You're
4 We're
5 You're
6 They're

D
1 They're monkeys. (given)
2 We're brothers.
3 They're best friends.
4 You're my grandma.
5 We're sisters.
6 You're my grandpa.

E
name (given), am, years, from

Unit 2

Lesson 1
A
1 tall (given)
2 lion
3 giraffe
4 camera
5 short
6 small

B
1 a big lion (given)
2 a short boy
3 a tall giraffe
4 a small camera
5 a short giraffe
6 a tall boy
7 a big camera
8 a small lion

C
1 giraffe (given), giraffes (given)
2 elephant, elephants
3 lion, lions

4 tiger, tigers
5 monkey, monkeys
6 zebra, zebras

D
1 three (given)
2 one (Pupils should colour one yo-yo.)
3 one (Pupils should colour one egg.)
4 five (Pupils should colour five cars.)

E
sister
She's **si**x
She's **sh**ort

Lesson 2
A
1 **toys** (given)
2 **robo**t
3 **comp**uter game
4 ba**ll**
5 **sk**ateboard

B
1 robots (given)
2 balls
3 computer games
4 skateboards
5 toys
C
1 You aren't tall. (given)
2 It isn't a skateboard.
3 They aren't big hats.
4 We aren't girls.
5 He isn't short.

D
1 It isn't a skateboard. (given)
2 They aren't dogs.
3 I'm not a girl.
4 It isn't big.
5 We aren't friends.
6 They aren't photos.

E
1 It's a skateboard. (given)
2 It's a robot.
3 It's a ball.
4 It's a yo-yo.

Lesson 3
A
Pupils draw accordingly.

B
1 BIRTHDAY CAKE
2 PARTY (given)
3 TEDDY BEAR
4 PRESENT

C
1 Yes, it is. (given)
2 No, they aren't.
3 Yes, she is.
4 No, he isn't.
5 No, it isn't.

D
1 Are, am (given)
2 Is, isn't
3 Is, is
4 Am, aren't
5 Are, are

E
Happy (given) **B**irthda**y**
A **tedd**y **b**ear
w**elcom**e

Unit 3

Lesson 1
A
1 beach (given)
2 mountain
3 ostrich
4 penguin
5 whale
6 bird

B

1 mountain (given)
2 whales
3 beach
4 bird
5 penguins
6 ostrich

C
1 This is (given)
2 That's
3 This is
4 That's
5 That's
6 This is

D
1 That's (given)
2 This is
3 This is
4 That's

E
ostri**ch** (given), **c**ar, **c**ar, bea**ch**, **C**ool

Lesson 2
A
1 hungry (given)
2 meerkat
3 snake
4 animals
5 food
6 lizard

B
1 HUNGRY (given)
2 SNAKE
3 LIZARD
4 ANIMALS
5 MEERKAT
6 FOOD

C
1 Those (given)
2 These
3 Those
4 Those
5 These

D
1 Those (given)
2 These
3 These
4 These
5 Those
6 Those

E
s**nake** (given)
hi**ss**
l**io**n
r**oa**r
p**e**ng**ui**n
w**obb**le

Lesson 3
A

B
1 tree (given)
2 flower
3 rabbit
4 shark
5 dolphin

C
1 What's this? (given)
2 What are these?
3 What's that?
4 What are those?

D
1 that, It's (given)
2 those, They're
3 this, It's
4 those, They're
5 this, It's

E
1 a dolphin (given)
2 a flower
3 a rabbit
4 a shark
5 a tree
6 a beach

REVIEW 1 (Units 1-3)

A

Animals, Birds & Fish
giraffe (given)
dolphin
lion
penguin
rabbit
shark

Family
brother
grandpa
mum

Toys
ball
skateboard
teddy bear

B
1 an, igloo (given)
2 a camera
3 an ostrich
4 a baby
5 an elephant
6 a cake

C
1 They're (given)
2 They're
3 It's
4 It's
5 They're
6 It's

D
1 I'm not (given)
2 She isn't
3 He's
4 They're
5 It isn't
6 We're

E
1 I am (given)
2 she isn't
3 they are
4 you/we are
5 it isn't
6 he isn't

F
1 They are my brothers. They are cool! (given)
2 She is my mum. She is nice.
3 He is my dad. He is tall.

Unit 4

Lesson 1
A
1 helicopter (given)
2 pupil
3 school
4 drawing

B
1 **sixteen** (given)
2 **fifteen**
3 se**ven**teen
4 **twelve**
5 **thirteen**
6 **eleven**

C
1 There are (given)
2 There are
3 There's
4 There's
5 There are
6 There's

D
1 There's (given)
2 There are
3 There are
4 There's
5 There's
6 There are

E
1 spid**er** (given)
2 tig**er**

Lesson 2
A
1 pen (given)
2 computer
3 book
4 board
5 lesson
6 notebook

B
1 computer (given)
2 notebook
3 board
4 pen
5 book

C
1 There aren't (given)
2 There isn't
3 There aren't
4 There isn't
5 There aren't

D
1 Is there, there is (given)
2 Are there, there aren't
3 Is there, there isn't
4 Are there, there are
5 Is there, there isn't
6 Are there, there are

E
There's (given)
Is there
There are
Are there

Lesson 3

A
1. apple (given)
2. desk
3. classroom
4. rubber
5. chair
6. teacher

B
1. √ (given)
2. X
3. √
4. X
5. X
6. X

C
1. a (given)
2. The
3. A
4. a
5. The

D
1. an (given)
2. The
3. a
4. A
5. the

E
1. Look! A pencil. The pencil is green. (given)
2. Look! An apple. The apple is red.
3. Look! A chair. The chair is brown.
4. Look! A rubber. The rubber is yellow.

Unit 5

Lesson 1
A
1. nose (given)
2. ear
3. eye
4. tail

B

K A N G A R O O
A K O A L A C A
N E S R W P C I
G Y E Y E O A L
A I O A T I O T
X W M E A R S U
R D K T I L E P
O E T E L O N G

1 ear (given)
2. eye
3. kangaroo
4. koala
5. long
6. nose
7. tail

C
1. It's got (given)
2. He's got
3. You've got
4. I've got
5. She's got

D
1. I've got (given)
2. He's got
3. It's got
4. You've got
5. She's got

E
Three green trees

Lesson 2
A

B
1. hair (given)
2. arm
3. finger
4. toe
5. leg
6. sad
7. wet

C
1. hair (given)
2. tails
3. legs
4. toes

D
1. You've got black hair. (given)
2. They've got long tails.
3. We've got two arms.
4. You've got brown eyes.

E
short (given
mum
tall
eyes

Lesson 3
A
1   THIN (given)
2   FISH
2   FAT
3   PARROT
3   PET
4   CAT

B
1   It's a pet. (given)
2   It's a fish.
3   It's a parrot.
4   It's thin.
5   It's a cat.
6   It's fat.

C
1   haven't (given)
2   hasn't
3   haven't
4   hasn't
5   haven't
6   haven't

D
1   haven't got (given)
2   haven't got
3   hasn't got
4   haven't got
5   haven't got
6   hasn't got

E
Pupils draw and colour accordingly.

Unit 6

Lesson 1
A
1   map (given)
2   flippers
3   mask
4   mobile phone
5   bag
6   beautiful

B
1   FLIPPERS (given)
2   BEAUTIFUL
3   MOBILEPHONE

3 ↓ MAP
4   BAG
5   MASK

C
1   Has (given)
2   Has
3   Have
4   Has
5   Have
6   Have

D
1   Have ... got, I have (given)
2   Have ... got, we haven't
3   Has ... got, he hasn't
4   Has ... got, she has
5   Have ... got, they haven't
6   Has ... got, he has

E
1   Yes, he has. (given)
2   No, she hasn't.
3   Yes, they have.
4   No, she hasn't.
5   Yes, they have.
6   No, we haven't.

Lesson 2
A
1   skirt (given)
2   shoes
3   clothes
4   dancer
5   socks
6   jacket
7   shirt

B
1   shirt (given)
2   jacket
3   skirt
4   bag
5   socks
6   shoes

C
1   boy's shirt (given)
2   Nick's bag
3   dancer's skirt
4   dog's ball

D
1   Jane's skirt is beautiful. (given)
2   The dancer's shoes are small.
3   The girl's birthday cake is fantastic.
4   The boy's shirt is white.
5   John's shoes are blue.

E
Pupils draw and colour accordingly.

Lesson 3
A

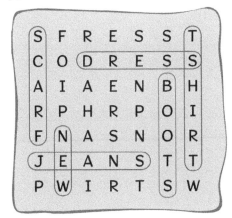

1 boots (given)
2 dress
3 jeans
4 new
5 scarf
6 T-shirt

B
Pupils draw and colour accordingly.

C
1 Their (given)
2 my
3 our
4 your
5 his
6 her

D
1 our (given)
2 Their
3 my
4 your

E
Pupils draw and colour accordingly.

Review 2 (Units 4-6)

A
1 teacher (given)
2 board
3 computer
4 chair
5 apple
6 ruler
7 rubber
8 book
9 mobile phone

10 pupil
11 notebook
12 pen
13 bag
14 desk

B
1 hair (given)
2 thin
3 shirt
4 jeans
5 shoes
6 fat
7 tail
8 legs
9 ears
10 beautiful

C
1 There's (given)
2 There aren't
3 Are there
4 There are
5 Is there
6 There isn't

D
1 Have ... got, have (given)
2 hasn't got
3 've got / have got
4 haven't got
5 Has ... got, hasn't
6 've got / have got

E
1 Our (given)
2 My
3 His
4 Their
5 Her
6 Its

F
1c Pete's mask is blue. (given)
2d Mum's parrot is red.
3a The cat's tail is long.
4b Sarah's dress is beautiful.

Unit 7

Lesson 1
A
1 jump (given)
2 look at
3 play volleyball
4 swim
5 run
6 sea

B
1 Look at (given)
2 sea
3 run
4 jump
5 swim
6 play volleyball

C
1 can't (given)
2 can't
3 can
4 can't
5 can
6 can

D
1 can (given)
2 can't
3 can
4 can
5 can't
6 can't

E
d**ance** (given)
stand
hands
right
can
j**um**p

Lesson 2
A
1 recorder (given)
2 piano
3 drums
4 music
5 guitar

B
1 GUITAR (given)
2 SING
3 PIANO
4 RECORDER
5 DRUMS
6 MUSIC

C
1 b (given)
2 d
3 a
4 f
5 c
6 e

D
Pupil's own answers

E
Pupil's own answers

Lesson 3
A
1a the guitar (given)
2b a bike
3c music
4d TV
5e a book

B
1 ride (given)
2 read
3 watch
4 listen to
5 sing
6 play

C
1 I'm reading (given)
2 She's dancing
3 You're listening
4 It's running
5 He's riding
6 They're singing

D
1 is watching (given)
2 'm playing
3 're singing
4 is looking at
5 's reading
6 'm riding

E
1 He's playing the drums. (given)
2 She's playing the guitar.
3 She's reading a book.
4 He's listening to music.
5 She's playing the piano.
6 She's singing.

Unit 8

Lesson 1
A
1 think (given)
2 tennis
3 basketball
4 win
5 baseball
6 football

B

1 baseball (given)
2 tennis
3 win
4 think
5 basketball
6 football

C
1 They're playing football. (given)
2 You're singing a song.
3 We're riding our bikes.
4 You're playing the piano.
5 They're playing basketball.
6 We're watching TV.

D
1 They're jumping (given)
2 We're playing
3 You're swimming
4 We're singing
5 They're listening
6 You're playing

E

They are playing basketball.

Lesson 2
A

B
1 stand (given)
2 sit
3 people
4 rollercoaster
5 town
6 old

C
1 'm (given)
2 aren't
3 isn't
4 aren't
5 aren't
6 isn't

D
1d (given) 2f 3a 4b 5e 6c

E
Rollercoasters (given)
Rollercoasters
up
Look at
down
Look at
fun
ha**nds**

Lesson 3
A
1 climb (given)
2 kick
3 dance
4 cook
5 rock

B
1 Mario's climbing a rock. (given)
2 Steve's dancing.
3 Jane's riding her bike.
4 Helen's making a cake.
5 Anne's climbing a tree.
6 Paul's kicking a ball.

C
1 Yes, they are. (given)
2 Yes, it is.
3 No, they aren't.
4 Yes, he is.
5 No, it isn't.
6 No, he isn't.

D
1b (given) 2d 3c 4a 5e

E
1 It's Tom. (given)
2 It's Anna.
3 It's Lisa.
4 It's Harry.
5 It's Penny.
6 It's Paula.

Unit 9

Lesson 1

A
1 **th**ea**t**re (given)
2 **c**i**ne**m**a
3 **mar**k**et**
4 **boa**t

B
1 MARKET
2 CINEMA
3 CITY
4 THEATRE
5 BOAT

C
1d (given) 2b 3a 4e 5c

D
1 What are you doing? (given)
2 What's she doing?
3 What are they doing?
4 What's it doing?
5 What's he doing?
6 What are you doing?

E
This (given)
thin

Lesson 2

A
1 sky (given)
2 dragon
3 colours
4 fireworks

B
1 Jump! (given)
2 Don't look!
3 Run!
4 Look!
5 Dance!
6 Kick!

C
1 New year (given)
2 dragon
3 fireworks
4 colours
5 sky

D
1d Play (given)
2f Don't cook
3c Sit
4b Climb
5e Don't swim
6a Don't play

E
Firework**s** (given) **sk**y
New **Y**ear
New **Y**ear

Lesson 3

A

B
1 park (given)
2 picnic
3 river
4 buy
5 shop

C
1f (given) 2b 3a 4d 5c 6e

D
1 Let's go (given)
2 Let's have
3 Let's buy
4 Let's look
5 Let's ride
6 Let's sit

E
Let'**s** d**a**n**ce**!

Review 3 (Units 7-9)

A

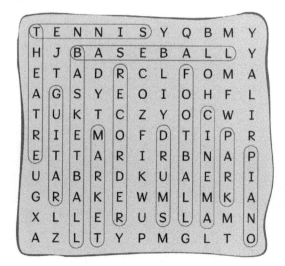

City
cinema (given)
market
park
theatre

Music
drums
guitar
piano
recorder

Sport
baseball
basketball
football
tennis

B
1 Let's read! (given)
2 Let's jump!
3 Let's play!
4 Let's dance!
5 Let's ride!
6 Let's sit!
7 Let's run!
8 Let's kick!

C
1 Are they running (given)
2 'm playing
3 isn't reading
4 Is he swimming
5 're listening

D
1 Can, Yes ... can, Can, it can't (given)
2 can't, can
3 can, can't
4 Can, Yes ... can, Can, No ... can't
5 can't, can
6 can, can't

E
1d given) 2a 3c 4b 5f 6e

F
Pupil's own answers. They should draw or glue a picture of themselves in the space provided.

Unit 10

Lesson 1
A
1 living room (given)
2 glass
3 man
4 bedroom
5 reporter
6 kitchen

B
1 kitchen (given)
2 living room
3 man
4 reporter
5 bedroom
6 glass

C

baby	babies
beach	beaches
bus	*buses*
child	children
foot	*feet*
fox	foxes
glass	*glasses*
man	men
tomato	*tomatoes*
woman	women

D
1 two men (given)
2 four mice
3 five glasses
4 two buses
5 four feet
6 three tomatoes

E
Pupils draw accordingly.

Lesson 2
A
1 butter (given)
2 flour
3 chocolate
4 milk
5 face

B
1 flour (given)
2 milk
3 butter
4 eggs
5 chocolate

C
1 any (given)
2 some
3 some
4 any
5 any
6 some

D
1 any (given)
2 some
3 some
4 any
5 some
6 any

E
mil**k** (given), **c**hocolate
Mil**k**, cake**s**

Lesson 3
A

1 basket (given)
2 sweets
3 potato
4 carrot
5 cheese
6 orange

B
1 sweets (given)
2 basket
3 carrot
4 cheese
5 orange
6 potato

C
1 behind (given)
2 on
3 in front of
4 under
5 in
6 next to

D
1 next to (given)
2 in
3 behind
4 in front of
5 under
6 on

E
Pupils draw accordingly.

Unit 11

Lesson 1
A
Monday
Tuesday
Wednesday
Thursday
Friday
Saturday
Sunday

B
1 Sunday (given)
2 Friday
3 Monday
4 Wednesday
5 Thursday
6 Saturday
7 Tuesday

C
1 rides (given)
2 watches
3 love
4 works
5 goes
6 plays

D
1 loves (given)
2 go
3 plays
4 swims
5 buy
6 sings

E
Monday (given)
Tuesday
Wednesday
Thursday
Friday
Saturday
Sunday

Lesson 2
A
1 **w**ear (given)
2 **b**reak**f**as**t**
3 **e**a**t**
4 **c**as**t**le
5 **g**e**t** u**p**
6 **s**no**w**

B

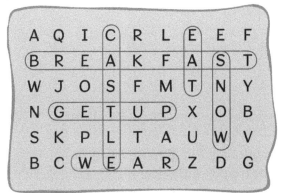

```
A  Q  I  C  R  L  E  E  F
B  R  E  A  K  F  A  S  T
W  J  O  S  F  M  T  N  Y
N  G  E  T  U  P  X  O  B
S  K  P  L  T  A  U  W  V
B  C  W  E  A  R  Z  D  G
```

1 wear (given)
2 castle
3 eat
4 get up
5 breakfast
6 snow

C

1a (given) 2c 3e 4b 5d 6f

D

1 You climb (given)
2 They play
3 We love
4 We read

E

love (given)
lessons
Sunday
picnic

Lesson 3
A
1 crisps (given)
2 maths
3 popcorn
4 scooter

B
1 maths (given)
2 popcorn
3 crisps
4 scooter
5 live
6 English

C
1 doesn't like (given)
2 doesn't ride
3 don't like
4 doesn't watch
5 doesn't play
6 don't drink

D
1 Mum doesn't drink milk. (given)
2 Jim doesn't play the drums.
3 Mark doesn't play basketball.
4 My brother doesn't eat crisps.
5 They don't swim in the sea.
6 Dad doesn't ride a bike.

E
1 popcorn (given), carrots
2 swimming, school

Unit 12

Lesson 1
A
1 island (given)
2 panda
3 sun
4 cave
5 moon
6 goat

B
1 DRAGONFLY (given)
2 CAVE
3 PANDA
4 MOON
5 SUN
6 ISLAND

C
1 No, it doesn't.
2 No, they don't.
3 Yes, they do.
4 No, we don't.
5 Yes, he does.
6 Yes, she does.

D Pupil's own answers

E
1 Yes, he does. (given)
2 Yes, he does.
3 Yes, she does.
4 No, she doesn't.
5 No, they don't.

Lesson 2
A
1 afternoon (given)
2 go to bed
3 laugh
4 night
5 morning
6 study

B
1 morning (given)
2 afternoon
3 study
4 go to bed
5 night
6 laugh

C
1e (given) 2d 3a 4c 5b

D
1 do (given)
2 does
3 do
4 does
5 do
6 does

E
Get up (given)
Eat
Run
bed
Go

Lesson 3
A
1 autumn (given)
2 hot
3 summer
4 cold
5 winter
6 spring

B

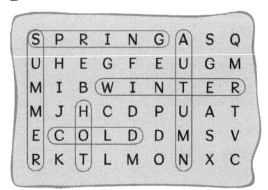

1 spring   (given)
2 winter
3 autumn
4 summer
5 cold
6 hot

C
1 What (given)
2 When
3 Who
4 Where

D
1c Who (given)
2a What
3e Where
4f When
5d Where
6b What

E
Where do you live? In China. (given)
Who is that man?   My dad.
When do you get up for school?   7 o'clock.
What is your favourite day?   Saturday.

Review 4 (Units 10-12)

A
Days
Monday (given)
Sunday
Thursday
Wednesday

Food
butter
chocolate
orange
potato

House
bedroom
castle
kitchen
living room

Seasons
autumn
spring
summer
winter

B
1 MORNING
2 PANDA (given)
3 CRISPS
4 AFTERNOON
5 BASKET

C
1 goes (given)
2 watch
3 doesn't swim
4 Do they live
5 doesn't like
6 Do we play

D

1 on (given)
2 in front of
3 next to
4 under
5 behind
6 in

E

1 What is your favourite day? (given)
2 I haven't got any popcorn.
3 Who is that girl?
4 Where is their school?
5 Have we got any carrots?
6 I've got some chocolate.

F Pupil's own answers

Wordsearches

Unit 1

1 baby (given)
2 brother
3 family
4 grandpa
5 sister
6 igloo
7 photo
8 dad
9 house
10 grandma
11 best friend
12 mum

Unit 2

1 ball (given)
2 short
3 lion
4 toy
5 present
6 giraffe
7 party
8 small
9 skateboard
10 tall
11 camera
12 teddy bear

Unit 3

1 animals (given)
2 bird
3 shark
4 penguin
5 rabbit

6 meerkat
7 flower
8 mountain
9 ostrich
10 whale
11 dolphin
12 snake

4 nose
5 finger
6 toe
7 tail
8 fat
9 thin
10 long
11 parrot
12 cat

Unit 4

1 board (given)
2 notebook
3 desk
4 ruler
5 teacher
6 computer
7 chair
8 classroom
9 lesson
10 rubber
11 school
12 pencil

Unit 5

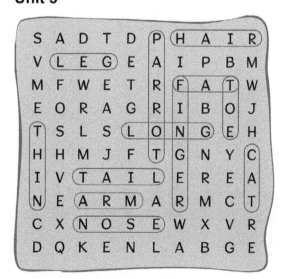

1 arm (given)
2 hair
3 leg

Unit 6

1 bag
2 clothes
3 shirt
4 boots
5 socks
6 scarf
7 jacket
8 jeans
9 dress
10 shoes
11 T-shirt
12 map

Unit 7

1 drums
2 recorder

3 piano
4 guitar
5 music
6 song
7 sing
8 run
9 jump
10 read
11 swim
12 watch

Unit 8

1 baseball (given)
2 football
3 basketball
4 tennis
5 kick
6 climb
7 win
8 rock
9 town
10 sit
11 dance
12 people

Unit 9

1 boat (given)
2 river

3 shop
4 cinema
5 theatre
6 fireworks
7 market
8 city
9 picnic
10 park
11 dragon
12 colours

Unit 10

1 basket (given)
2 glass
3 kitchen
4 cheese
5 carrot
6 chocolate
7 butter
8 potato
9 orange
10 sweets
11 milk
12 flour

Unit 11

1 castle (given)
2 snow
3 popcorn
4 crisps
5 maths
6 Monday
7 Tuesday
8 Wednesday
9 Thursday
10 Friday
11 Saturday
12 Sunday

Unit 12

1 afternoon (given)
2 morning
3 night
4 sun
5 moon
6 spring
7 summer
8 autumn
9 winter
10 hot
11 cold
12 goat

Progress Tests Key

Progress Test 1 (Units 1-3)

A
1 elephant
2 giraffe
3 insect
4 rabbit
5 whale
6 ball
7 computer game
8 skateboard
9 teddy bear
10 baby
11 brother
12 dad
13 grandma
14 mum
15 sister

B
1 Happy birthday!
2 house
3 fantastic
4 penguin
5 whale

C
1 is
2 isn't
3 Are
4 aren't
5 'm not

D
1 penguins
2 an
3 Dolphins
4 shark
5 monkeys

E
1 These
2 these
3 this
4 That
5 Those

Progress Test 2 (Units 4-6)

A
1 dancer
2 m**obi**le ph**one**
3 ja**cke**t
4 **k**an**ga**roo
5 p**arr**ot
6 sc**arf**
7 n**ote**bo**ok**
8 **ch**air
9 **tea**cher
10 **flippers**

B
1 tail
2 beautiful
3 map
4 shirt
5 pupils

C
1 Yes, there is.
2 Yes, there are.
3 No, there isn't. There's a koala.
4 No, there aren't.
There are two apples.

D
1 has got
2 hasn't got
3 have got
4 hasn't got
5 have got

E
1 The
2 His
3 Mum's
4 His
5 hasn't
6 Their

Progress Test 3 (Units 7-9)

A
1 drums
2 piano
3 recorder
4 basketball
5 football
6 tennis
7 cinema
8 market
9 theatre

B
1 sea
2 people
3 What a noise!
4 climbing
5 watch
6 sky

C
1 river
2 baseball
3 song
4 shop
5 colour

D
1 isn't listening
2 Are, riding
3 aren't having
4 is kicking
5 Are, swimming

E
1 Let's
2 sing
3 Play
4 Sit
5 is he

Progress Test 4 (Units 10-12)

A
1 cheese
2 maths
3 moon
4 sweets
5 castle

B
1 crisps
2 winter
3 season
4 Sunday
5 carrots

C
1 weekend
2 reporter
3 breakfast
4 morning
5 butter

D
1 children
2 any
3 When
4 some
5 Where

E
1 doesn't like
2 Do, eat
3 loves
4 doesn't
5 watches

Progress Test 1 🐾

Name: _____ Date: _____ Mark: /40

A Write.

baby	ball	brother	computer game	dad
elephant	giraffe	grandma	insect	lion	~~mum~~
rabbit	sister	skateboard	teddy bear	whale

Animals	Toys	Family
_____ lion _____	6 _____	10 _____
1 _____	7 _____	11 _____
2 _____	8 _____	12 _____
3 _____	9 _____	13 _____
4 _____		14 _____
5 _____		15 _____

/15

B Circle.

He's (tall)/ short.

1 Let's go! /
Happy birthday!

2 An igloo is a
lizard / house.

3 This party is
fantastic / hungry!

4 This is a penguin /
an ostrich.

5 A whale is big / small.

/10

C **Write.**

~~am~~   'm not   Are   aren't   is   isn't

I ____am____ a girl.

1   Dad _____ cool.

2   She's tall. She _____ short.

3   _____ they happy?

4   Are you hungry? No, we _____ .

5   Are you hungry? No, I _____ .

/5

D **Circle.**

It's (a)/ an flower.

1   Look! Five penguins / penguin.

2   What's that? It's an / a octopus.

3   Dolphin / Dolphins are great.

4   Oh no! It's a sharks / shark!

5   Are monkey / monkeys funny?

/5

E **Write this, that, these or those.**

____This____ is a flower.

1   _____ giraffes are tall.

2   What are _____?
    They're presents.

3   What's _____? It's a snake.

4   _____ is a big mountain.

5   _____ are big
    animals.

/5

Progress Test 2

Name: _____ Date: _____ Mark: ___ /40

A Look and write.

 p <u>u</u> p i <u>l</u>

1 d __ nc __ __

2  m __ __ ile ph __ __ __

3 j __ __ __ et

4 k __ __ g __ __ __ __ __

5 p __ __ r __ t

6  sc __ __ __ __

7 n __ __ __ b __ __ __ __

8 c __ __ __ r

9 t __ __ ch __ __

10 f __ i __ pe __ __

/10

B Circle.

There are fifteen (desks)/ pets in the classroom.

1 My cat has got a long finger / tail.
2 Those fish are sad / beautiful.
3 Jim's map / hair is in his bag.
4 My dad has got a new shirt / skirt.
5 Mark and John are new jeans / pupils.

/10

C **Look and write.**

Are there two birds? _No, there aren't. There is one bird._

1 Is there a helicopter? _____

2 Are there two cats? _____

3 Is there a kangaroo? _____

4 Are there three apples? _____

/4

D **Write have got, haven't got, has got or hasn't got.**

Oh no! I _____haven't got_____ my English book.

1 Fantastic! She _____ a new computer.

2 He's sad. He _____ any friends.

3 I _____ ten toes.

4 A snake _____ legs.

5 Cats _____ four legs.

/10

E **Circle.**

Have you got an apple? Yes, I (have)/ has.

1 Look. A dog. The / A dog is big!

2 I've got a brother. His / Our name is George.

3 This is Mum / Mum's mask.

4 Dad has got a new car. His / Its car is red.

5 Has he got a ruler? No, he has / hasn't.

6 They have got computers. Their / Your computers are great.

/6

Progress Test 3

Name: _____ Date: _____ Mark: ____ /40

A Write.

> basketball   cinema   drums   football   ~~guitar~~
> market   piano   recorder   tennis   theatre

Music	Sport	City
_____guitar_____		
1 _____	4 _____	7 _____
2 _____	5 _____	8 _____
3 _____	6 _____	9 _____

/9

B Circle.

I can play (volleyball) / fireworks.

1 Let's swim in the boat / sea.

2 There are lots of dragons / people on the rollercoaster.

3 She can't sing. What a noise! / Be careful!

4 We are climbing / dancing this rock.

5 Don't read / watch TV. Go to school!

6 There are fireworks in the river / sky.

/6

C Write.

baseball   colour   ~~picnic~~   river   shop   song

Let's have a ___picnic___ in the park.

1 There's a boat on the _____ .

2 We're playing _____ .

3 They're singing a _____ .

4 Can you buy toys in that _____?

5 My favourite _____ is purple.

/5

D Write.

~~am~~   'm not   Are   aren't   is   isn't

I ___am running___ (run) a girl.

1 Dad _____ (not listen) to music.

2 _____ they _____ (ride) bikes?

3 We _____ (not have) fun.

4 She _____ (kick) the ball.

5 _____ lots of people _____ (swim) in the sea?

/10

E Circle.

Let's (run)/ running.

1 Let / Let's play.

2 Don't singing / sing.

3 Play / Playing football with me.

4 Sit / Let's on that chair.

5 What he is / is he doing?

/10

Progress Test 4 🐾

Name: _____ Date: _____ Mark: [/40]

A Look and write.

scooter

1 _____

2 _____

3 _____

4 _____

5 _____

/10

B Circle.

We cook in the (kitchen) / living room.

1 I eat caves / crisps at the cinema.

2 It's cold in summer / winter.

3 Spring is a beautiful season / basket.

4 We don't go to school on Monday / Sunday.

5 My rabbit loves baskets / carrots.

/5

C Write.

breakfast   butter   chocolate   morning   reporter   weekend

There is a lot of ___chocolate___ in these cakes. Yummy!

1 We play football at the _____ .

2 Dad works every day. He's a _____.

3 I eat _____ every day at 7 o'clock.

4 Grandpa gets up at 6 o'clock in the _____ .

5 _____ is yellow or white.

/5

D **Circle.**

Where's the cat? It's in / (behind) the TV.

1 There are twelve child / children in the park.

2 Have you got some / any oranges?

3 When / What do you get up?

4 There are some / any apples in the kitchen.

5 Where / Who is my car?

/5

E **Circle.**

I ___wear___ (wear) boots in winter.

1 She _____ (not like) pandas.

2 _____ you _____ (eat) breakfast?

3 Grandma _____ (love) her pets!

4 Does your dog eat chocolate? No, it _____ .

5 Jane _____ (watch) TV on Saturday.

/10

F **Match.**

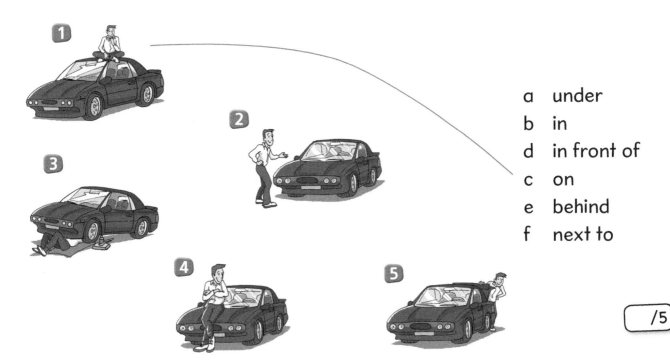

a under

b in

d in front of

c on

e behind

f next to

/5